CHILDREN OF THE 21ST CENTURY

From birth to nine months

Edited by Shirley Dex and Heather Joshi

First published in Great Britain in October 2005 by

The Policy Press
University of Bristol
Fourth Floor
Beacon House
Queen's Road
Bristol BS8 1QU
UK

Tel +44 (0)117 331 4054
Fax +44 (0)117 331 4093
e-mail tpp-info@bristol.ac.uk
www.policypress.org.uk

British Library Cataloguing in Publication Data
A catalogue record for this book is available from the British Library.

Library of Congress Cataloging-in-Publication Data
A catalog record for this book has been requested.

ISBN 1 86134 688 3 paperback

A hardcover version of this book is also available

Cover design by Qube Design Associates, Bristol.
Printed and bound in Great Britain by MPG Books, Bodmin.

Contents

List of figures

List of tables

List of boxes

Acknowledgements

We wish to acknowledge the funding of the Millennium Cohort Study by the Economic and Social Research Council and the consortium of government departments (led by the Office for National Statistics) including the Department for Education and Skills, Department for Work and Pensions, Department of Health, Office for National Statistics, Sure Start and the governments of Wales, Scotland and Northern Ireland. The International Centre for Child Studies has supplemented resources not least through the energy and expertise of Professor Neville Butler.

The Institute of Child Health also acknowledges funding from the International Centre for Child Studies, the Mercers' Company and the Child Health Research Appeal Trust which has contributed to carrying out analyses of the Millennium Cohort Study data.

We would like to acknowledge the mothers, fathers and other family members of the babies who form the Millennium Birth Cohort, and thank them for giving up time for the interviews.

Considerable thanks are due to Kelly Ward for her substantial contribution to collating, editing and checking much of the Millennium Cohort Study material contained in this book; also for her enthusiasm for the project, her work liaising and helping collaborators, and her patience through the many revisions.

A number of people have helped at different stages with commenting on the drafts, or organising the data and carrying out analyses that were first reported elsewhere but are cited in this volume. These include Charlie Owen, Julia Brannen, Peter Moss and Ann Mooney of the Thomas Coram Research Unit at the Institute of Education, and Nandika Velauthan, Catherine Law and Leslie Davidson of the Institute of Child Health, University College London.

The views expressed in this work are those of the authors and do not necessarily reflect the views of the Economic and Social Research Council or the Office for National Statistics. All errors and omissions remain those of the authors.

List of contributors

Name	Title	Institution
Suzanne Bartington	Research Assistant	Institute of Child Health, University College London
Mel Bartley	Professor of Medical Sociology	University College London
Helen Bedford	Lecturer	Institute of Child Health, University College London
Jonathan Bradshaw	Professor of Social Policy	Social Policy Research Unit, University of York
Neville Butler	Visiting Professor	Centre for Longitudinal Studies, Institute of Education, University of London
Lisa Calderwood	Research Officer	Centre for Longitudinal Studies, Institute of Education, University of London
Tim Cole	Professor of Medical Statistics	Institute of Child Health, University College London
Stephan Collishaw	Post-doctoral Researcher	Institute of Psychiatry, University of London
Shirley Dex	Professor of Longitudinal Social Research	Bedford Group, Institute of Education, University of London
Carol Dezateux	Professor of Paediatric Epidemiology	Institute of Child Health, University College London
Lucy Foster	Research Fellow	Institute of Child Health, University College London
Denise Hawkes	Research Officer	Centre for Longitudinal Studies, Institute of Education, University of London
Steven Hope	Research Officer	City University
Hiranthi Jayaweera	Researcher	National Perinatal Epidemiology Unit, University of Oxford
Heather Joshi	Professor of Economic and Developmental Demography	Centre for Longitudinal Studies, Institute of Education, University of London
Kathleen Kiernan	Professor of Social Policy and Demography	University of York

Name	Title	Institution
Alison Macfarlane	Professor of Perinatal Health	City University
Barbara Maughan	Reader in Developmental Psychopathology	Institute of Psychiatry, University of London
Emese Mayhew	Research Fellow	Social Policy Research Unit, University of York
Catherine Peckham	Professor of Paediatric Epidemiology	Institute of Child Health, University College London
Ian Plewis	Professor of Social Statistics	Centre for Longitudinal Studies, Institute of Education, University of London
Amanda Sacker	Principal Research Fellow	University College London
Lamiya Samad	Research Fellow	Institute of Child Health, University College London
Ingrid Schoon	Professor of Psychology	City University
Kate Smith	Research Fellow	Centre for Longitudinal Studies, Institute of Education, University of London
Rosemary Tate	Lecturer in Biostatistics	Institute of Child Health, University College London
Suzanne Walton	Honorary Research Fellow	Institute of Child Health, University College London
Kelly Ward	Research Officer	Centre for Longitudinal Studies, Institute of Education, University of London

ONE

Introduction

Shirley Dex, Heather Joshi, Kate Smith, Kelly Ward and Ian Plewis

The initiation of a new cohort study of approximately 18,800 UK babies born in the Millennium provides the opportunity to reflect on the circumstances of children in Britain at the start of a new century. Britain has become world-renowned for its tracking of large-scale and representative cohorts of babies from birth, through the rest of their lives, producing unrivalled data sources for longitudinal research in social sciences and health. This book focuses on the information collected in this new Millennium Cohort Study of these babies covering the period from pregnancy through to nine months old. However, it also offers a perspective from earlier generations in selected respects, to show how circumstances and experiences differ.

The book is a collection of chapters focusing on particular aspects of starting out on life in the 21st century; these include pregnancy experiences; birth experiences; child health; growth and development; parents' health; household structure; socioeconomic circumstances of parents; employment and education of mothers and fathers; childcare arrangements; household income and attitudes to parenting and employment.

Large-scale studies of this kind have already been found to be extremely valuable to policy makers and governments. They provide a window on children as they grow up. By drawing comparisons with earlier generations, it is possible to see how the new policies and frameworks are changing the life courses of new generations. These Millennium children were born and are spending their early years under a framework of government concern about child poverty. The Labour government that came to power in 1997 set out its aim to eliminate child poverty by 2020. Many new initiatives have been launched to this end. These cover encouragement to parents to enter and remain in paid work; better childcare provisions; more flexible employment; new legal frameworks about the care of children; a framework for considering the health of both adults and children; and attempts to tackle children's growing obesity. In many ways, the turn of the 21st century in the UK is a period of unprecedented policy interest and focus on children and family policy. Some might say it has gone too far, not least because the 2004 sittings of Parliament were voting on whether to allow families to smack their children.

One plank of addressing the child poverty target has been to encourage parents, and especially the growing group of lone mothers, into paid work. A large part of child poverty is seen as relating to the lack of employment income in households without paid work. Benefit payments and regulations have been gradually changed to try and make paid work pay. Also to meet this objective, the National Childcare Strategy has been aiming to provide good quality affordable childcare for children while their mothers are in employment. Other initiatives have encouraged employers to adopt more flexible working and parental leave arrangements to ease the balancing of work and family responsibilities for both mothers and fathers, on the assumption that this will not be a cost to employers, and may even lead to productivity improvements.

The Millennium Cohort Study has new data about these areas of policy. As well as child health indicators, there is information on parents' incomes and other indicators of child poverty; childcare arrangements and costs; and parents' access to flexible working arrangements. In addition, and because of far-sighted decisions about its sampling design, the Millennium Cohort Study contains valuable information about children of ethnic minorities in sufficient numbers for analysis; on children from disadvantaged and advantaged electoral wards; information directly from fathers; and sizeable samples from each of the four countries of the UK. These elements of the data provide valuable opportunities for analysis along the wide-ranging dimensions of this multidisciplinary survey.

The chapters of this book analyse some of the relationships relevant to a number of important cross-discipline questions, relevant to policy now and in the future:

1. How are babies developing under different household structures and parenting regimes?
2. How do babies develop where their father is involved with them, whether present or absent from the household, compared with babies whose fathers are not involved?
3. Are new century babies growing up in more insular privatised family units with less contact with other generations?
4. What proportion and which babies start out in poverty in the four countries at the turn of the 21st century?

5. How soon do mothers return to paid work after childbirth compared with earlier generations?
6. How many employed fathers and mothers have access to flexible working arrangements, and does taking these up make a difference to their childcare choices or to their feelings of work-life balance?
7. What proportion and which babies start out with good health across our four countries?
8. Are parents' health and circumstances related to the baby's health and development?
9. How do mothers' smoking and alcohol consumption affect birthweight and baby growth?
10. Is it an additional disadvantage to live in a poor neighbourhood?

The Millennium Cohort Study offers new data that can be used to address these and many other research questions. The questions are relevant to the scientific understandings of child development and central policy issues of our time. But these analyses also help to inform the consideration of service planning for the 21st century in health and social services; education and other public services; epidemiological analyses and forecasting; actuarial forecasts for pensions and life expectancy; four-country comparisons of inequalities and social exclusion; and national and four-country childcare strategies.

Why be interested in babies?

Clearly, parents have a variety of reasons for having children. The question for society is why should the public be interested in babies or children? Successive governments since the Second World War have adopted policies that are based on the assumption that the costs of babies and children should be shared by society and not left wholly for parents to bear. The main reasons for this are:

• Children are an investment in the future.
• The children of today are the labour force of tomorrow who will be called upon to generate the future pensions of the current adult labour force, and not just the pensions of their own parents.
• There has also been a strong redistributive objective. This is based on the belief that children from poorer families should not have to suffer the full extent of their parents' low incomes, especially if one of the contributory factors to families being poor is the fact of having children.

A report on social and economic aspects of maternity for the Royal Commission on Population in 1946 was influential in government thinking (RCOG, 1948). Inspired partly by concern about the declining birth rate evident over the 1930s and early 1940s, the report argued that government should offer greater subsidies towards the costs of childbearing as well as reviewing the state of maternity services at the dawn of the National Health Service. The alarm over the declining birth rate disappeared in the post-war years as a sustained baby boom emerged in the 1950s and 1960s. However, fertility started to decline from the 1960s onwards and by the late 1980s there was renewed concern about a 'demographic time-bomb' of population ageing and decline. In the latter decades of the 20th century, there was particular concern that rising women's employment might be leading to lower rates of childbearing. If there is a loss of earnings from stopping work to have children, and adverse effects on mothers' careers and pensions, more women might be expected to choose to avoid motherhood. Certainly, there has been an increase in the proportion of women in paid work,[1] but it is not clear how far employment opportunities have driven fertility decline or fertility decline has permitted the increase in employment (Joshi, 2002). Other factors like the rising cost of housing, increasing fragility of partnership, or the ideology of individualism are also possible explanations for delayed and declining fertility. However, the discussion and debate over the population size implications of fertility rates have been rather muted in the UK, especially compared with France. Some would also argue that the government support offered to UK families for children was also very meagre up to the late 1990s compared with many other European countries (Gornick and Meyers, 2003).

The method of funding pensions and caring for both children and older adults is illustrative of how intergenerational relationships are centrally important in our current economic support systems. Millennium babies are dependent for their care on today's parents and other adults. Taxes from the current adult labour force provide services used in maintaining the health and welfare of this new generation of babies as well as the retired. In future, these children will be the adult workers and taxpayers supporting their parents' generation through payment of their pensions as well as through informal care. Through these interlocking intergenerational relationships, we all, as a society, have a stake in children and their well-being. They are not merely a private matter for parents' individual choices; they are of importance to society and the economic well-being of successive generations.

The changing context of giving birth

Before we consider the findings from the Millennium Cohort Study babies, we need to set the scene in a general sense. Giving birth at the beginning of the 21st century is not the same as it was in earlier periods. Of course, much of the context has undergone far-reaching change, especially if we look back as far as the Second World War. The timing of childbearing has changed, the number of births, the partnership status of parents, as well as the context of the health services, possibilities of birth control, obstetric practices, pain control, hospital versus home births, antenatal classes, and so on. We are able to chart some of these changes partly because there were earlier cohort studies that surveyed mothers about their childbirth experiences, and partly through other sources of official statistics and one-off surveys. A selection of contextual factors is reviewed in this introductory chapter. More are considered in the process of introducing the experiences of Millennium mothers and babies.

Britain started what is now a unique tradition of birth cohort studies, following up babies for the rest of their lives. From the 1946 maternity survey, 5,362 babies were selected and are still being followed up, now in their late 50s. Further cohorts of a full week's births were initiated in 1958 and 1970 (see Box 1.1). The Millennium Cohort Study is therefore the fourth in this tradition but comes after a larger gap in time than intervened between earlier cohort studies.

Box 1.1 Brief details of the British birth cohort surveys

The National Survey of Health and Development (NSHD) is a prospective, longitudinal birth cohort study which surveyed some 13,000 mothers of legitimate singleton births in one week of March 1946, and then followed up a subset of 5,362 cases. Its aim was to map biological and social pathways to health and disease, from early life to ageing. The cohort was studied 21 times with the latest contact date in 1999 when respondents were 53 years old.

The National Child Development Study (NCDS) is a longitudinal multidisciplinary study which began in 1958, surveying 17,415 individuals in Great Britain who were all born in a particular week in March. To date, there have been seven contacts with all the birth cohort members to monitor their physical, educational, social and economic development: 1958; 1965 (NCDS1); 1969 (NCDS2); 1974 (NCDS3); 1981 (NCDS4); 1991 (NCDS5); and 1999/2000 (NCDS6). Other information about cohort members has been merged into the dataset at various ages (see www.cls.ioe.ac.uk).

The British Cohort Study (BCS70) is a longitudinal study of individuals living in Great Britain who were all born in a particular week in April 1970. Following the initial birth survey of 16,871 individuals in 1970, there have been five contacts with the full sample to gather information encompassing their physical, educational, social and economic development at ages 5, 10, 16, 26 and 29 in 1999/2000 (see www.cls.ioe.ac.uk).

Given the large cost of running such studies, especially when they have sample sizes of around 18,000 subjects to follow up, one might well ask why governments and research councils pay for this to take place. There are a number of reasons:

- Cohort studies, like other sources of longitudinal data, offer information that allows us to come as close as is possible to identifying causal mechanisms in individuals' behaviour.
- It is also possible to use cohort studies to conduct 'natural' experiments. It is sometimes possible to identify a control group of individuals who did not get exposed to a certain event or experience and, by comparing them with those who did get exposed, to identify more of the causal mechanisms at work that underpin, for example, social problems.
- By comparing cohorts, we can chart social change and start to untangle the reasons for any changes found. Changes can be due to individuals of the same age, but different cohorts, differing in their behaviour or attitudes (cohort effects); or they can be due to individuals in different cohorts facing different conditions in society when they are at the same age or stage of life (period effects). Age effects, developmental changes with age, can also vary across cohorts.
- The cohort studies show how histories of health, wealth, education, family and employment are interwoven for individuals, vary between them and affect outcomes and achievements later on in life.

The analyses to date of British cohort study data have generated a wealth of findings that have been very important to policy makers, findings that could not have been possible without these unique data resources (see review in Ferri et al, 2003, pp 15-27). The present volume can only present a cross-sectional snapshot of the Millennium Cohort, as there has only been one completed survey so far. As time goes by, the phenomena recorded here can be linked to later developments in the babies' lives. This study is dedicated to laying the foundation for such follow-up.

Number of births

The level of births in a year is often measured relative to the number of women of childbearing age in terms of the total fertility rate (TFR). TFR summarises the year's fertility rates by age, and counts the number of children a woman would have over the ages 15-45 if she experienced this year's rates over all those ages. The total fertility rate has been declining in the UK since 1964, when it was at a peak of 2.95 children per woman. It has been low (around 1.7) since 1977, but it reached an all-time low of 1.63 in 2001. The average number of live-born children for women who have in fact finished childbearing (cohort fertility rate) has been falling for cohorts of women born since the 1930s. Some of the fall in the TFR represents a delay in the onset of childbearing. Women born in the 1930s, who were in their late 20s in the 1960s, had the largest families with an average of 2.4 births per woman, the 1960s baby boom. Since then, the average has fallen to 2.0 births per woman for those born in 1960 (figures from www.gad.gov.uk/population/2002/uk/wukfert.xls). The proportion of women remaining childless is also rising. It roughly doubled from around 1 in 10 women born around 1940 to 1 in 5 of those born around 1960. Increased childlessness and smaller families arise partly through choice, but such choices are constrained by the opportunities available, pressure of opinion and by the biological limits to delaying childbirth. Factors thought to explain the fall in fertility include rising age at completing full-time education; changes in relationship patterns; later age at initiation of co-residential unions; women's greater propensity to have employment careers; and a general increase in lifestyle and standard of living aspirations. These considerations do not apply in a uniform way across all social groups. Bangladeshi and Pakistani families, for example, have larger families than whites, almost all born within marriage.

Britain has had the highest teenage birth rate in Western Europe, and these mothers are also much more likely than older mothers to have a birth outside marriage and to register the birth on their own. They are highly likely, also, to come from disadvantaged backgrounds and to have poor educational attainment.

Conceptual and theoretical concerns

This book's content draws on several conceptual frameworks and theoretical concerns from the social sciences. Babies, the cohort members who are the volume's focus, are born and grow up within a series of concentric circles: within their immediate family, within the wider family, within the local area, within a country, its institutions and policies, and so on. At the heart of this set of circles are a set of intergenerational relationships which need to be the subject of empirical and theoretical understanding (Figure 1.1). Child development and its context are areas of considerable societal interest, as already argued.

These concentric layers provide opportunities for analyses of the various levels of influence on the baby as it charts its pathway through life. Seeing the life of this child over time, in the context of many potential influences, is part of what has been called life-course analysis, elaborated by authors Elder (1978) and Hareven (1978).

Another concept of relevance, much discussed, is that of social capital or social infrastructure which is relevant to the baby's starting point, and its continued life course. Social capital has come to mean many different things.

Figure 1.1: The child in the wider context

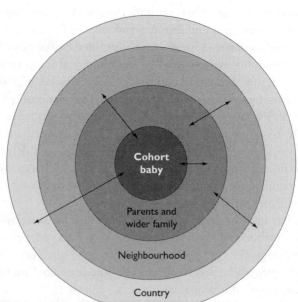

The notion of individuals having and generating capital is one which has gained in popularity in academic and policy discourses in the 1980s and 1990s. Economists were probably the first to coin the term *human capital* to mean investment in individuals through education, training and work experience with a view to recouping future labour market rewards of this investment (Schultz, 1961; Becker, 1975). *Cultural capital* was introduced into the discourse largely by French sociologist, Bourdieu; this included education, and was argued to be instrumental in reproducing social inequalities in society, either from its presence or its absence (Bourdieu and Passeron, 1977). Bourdieu and other sociologists and political scientists also introduced the notion of *social capital* to describe the social relationships, networks and community strength in certain spatial areas, including the existence of reciprocity, good neighbourliness and trust (Coleman, 1988; Putnam, 1999). Social capital has been argued, by these writers, to be important in the building of individuals' human capital. Further notions of *identity capital* as social esteem and purpose in life and *intellectual capital* have also been suggested.

Amid the growing plethora of terminology and concepts, a helpful framework for placing and linking them together has been offered by Schuller et al (2004). This work provides a coherent conceptual framework as the background for empirical work using longitudinal data to examine the development and effects of learning on individuals' lifetime experiences. It makes a triangle of relationships between three forms of capital at the apexes: human capital, social capital and identity capital. Sen's elaboration of another concept, *capability*, is used to extend this framework of capitals. *Capabilities* are the 'various combinations of functionings (beings and doings) that the person can achieve' (Sen, 1992, p 39)[2] Capabilities are the capacity and freedom that allow individuals to achieve well-being and make choices. Schuller et al (2004) elaborated a set of capabilities as attributes that are the building blocks of their three 'capitals' and appear within the triangle. We need to consider how this framework is relevant to our focus here on Millennium babies and on the related areas of policy.

Clearly babies, at the start of life, enter the world, in addition to their genetic endowments, with parental nurturing capabilities. From the baby's perspective, these parental capabilities form part of their initial stock of social and parental capital. A Millennium baby will have levels of capital stock from their parents' financial circumstances and wealth, from their parents' human capital as education and knowledge, from their parents' and wider family's social and relationship capital, and from the neighbourhood's social capital and infrastructure of services. Because, in the first instance, we are focusing on a baby's start in life, almost at a point in time, parents' capabilities and capital all appear as capital to the baby. Parents' capabilities for caring for the baby are also likely to be related to their own levels, at the outset, of human, social and identity capital. In this volume, we consider parental human capital to include their education, socioeconomic status and health, alongside their earning potential and wealth. For social capital, we have information about the wider family and the characteristics of their residential neighbourhoods.

At any one point in time – for example, at the first sweep of a cohort study – this can appear to be a fairly static picture, even though the focus is on intergenerational relationships which must be lived out over time. It is important to remember, therefore, that parents can develop more capabilities over time and these can feed into their parenting of the Millennium baby. Also, the baby will develop capabilities and higher levels of functioning as it grows, which can interact with parents' capabilities. This interaction can produce higher capital levels for the baby but also for its parents. Thus, a complex and dynamic set of interactions map out a framework for understanding the intergenerational relationships which underpin a process of child to adult development. It is the start of this process that we are viewing in this volume when the Millennium babies are 9-10 months old. Clearly, there is a long way to go from here.

Governments have been recognising the crucial importance of understanding these intergenerational and intragenerational relationships and transmission processes. If there are transmission mechanisms from parents to children, or neighbourhoods to children, and especially if they have unwelcome outcomes, then it is important to understand them in order to consider whether and how best to intervene. This assumes, of course, that there is a political will to alter the outcomes.

The life courses of these babies and their parents are all played out against a large canvas of late or post-capitalist economic relationships and associated demographic changes. This is a canvas where many women are employed and fertility, as described already, has declined to below replacement levels. These trends may have put at risk the implicit intergenerational commitments to care for each other at the beginning and end of life. The welfare states of advanced industrialised countries, financed from the public purse, are discussing how to fill gaps in private care, but it is not yet clear whether a sustainable equilibrium is attainable.

Each generation passes on to the next some of the wealth and knowledge it has accumulated. In turn, each generation is provided for by succeeding ones. The transfers take different forms at different stages of the life course. Some of the transfers take place within a legal framework – for example, some inheritance of wealth. Other social obligations, for both younger and older generations, are unwritten and can be widely understood, or open to misunderstanding. In the UK, the state in general and the Welfare State in particular, have grown to have a role in regulating some of these transfers and acting as a buffer when they break down. The state has also made large investments in education to improve the human capital of successive generations, and some families are able to accumulate the benefits of this investment. The private monetary and non-monetary transfers (as well as genetic endowments) that take place within families and across generations, alongside public support, will be part of the landscape through which these UK cohort children make their way in life.

In the face of changes in patterns of employment, family stability and educational achievement, particularly of women, the welfare support for children and grandparents from both their families and the Welfare State have come under pressure. Some commentators have suggested that, as families become smaller and more fluid, society has become atomised, individuals looking out only for themselves. But is this the case? Clearly, there are class and ethnic differences that mediate and influence the lifetime outcomes of individuals and families. Is the social fabric disintegrating, reconfiguring, or fundamentally unchanged, bearing in mind the different experiences across class and ethnic boundaries? Certainly, the system of private welfare and support across family generations can no longer be taken for granted, although the strains may be worse in some class and ethnic identity groups than others. Neither is the public Welfare State able to fill all the gaps. There are important questions to ask and answer, not least about what policy should be in this new era. Should it be helping to underpin a private welfare system in a way that is affordable? What can be left to reciprocal relationships or the market and what needs state intervention, given the changing times? Is current policy serving to undermine private welfare, either intentionally or unintentionally? What are the outcomes of state investments as compared with intergenerational transfers?

Additional questions are raised by the new era – for example, whether the social fabric, as represented by intergenerational transfers, is disintegrating in the face of increasing individualisation and flexibility, and new family structures. Is family care withering, and by so doing contributing to a crisis of care? Does the workplace, and new employment practices and patterns, weaken family relations? How far does economic change depend on these relations to support employed carers in coping with flexible employment? Are relations and transfers between families reconfiguring, through processes of negotiation, to adapt to new conditions? How do changes affect women's and men's roles in intergenerational transfers? Are women engaging more in material transfers, men more in care? How do transfers contribute to processes of inequality and exclusion, and are these processes changing? Who are the winners, who the losers? Relationships across the generations are in need of an extensive analysis and review. We are only at the start of this new agenda with much to be done. However, these analyses of new Millennium babies provide one small piece of a very large 3D jigsaw of intergenerational relationships.

The policy context in 2000-01

This book is largely focused on policy. The relevant areas of practical policy touched by this new survey of babies are numerous and wide-ranging. They include policies about children, families and parents, employment and parenting, issues of equality in the labour market between fathers and mothers, regulations of the benefit system and the legal framework of children's and parents' rights and responsibilities, as elaborated under The 1989 Children Act (England and Wales).

A book of this kind cannot provide a comprehensive analysis of all these relevant policies. However, it is important to remember that they exist as a backcloth to this volume, even if, in many cases, the details are beyond its scope.

Government support for childbearing and childrearing

Government support for childbearing and childrearing comes through a number of specific channels, each with its own history. Support for the birth process comes through the National Health Service in the form of free healthcare, antenatal care and delivery for the mother and baby, including follow-up vaccinations and checkups and treatment for eyes and teeth as well as for any health problems that arise.

Box 1.2 UK provisions available for families with children – 2000/01

- **Child Benefit.** As of April 2001, the Child Benefit rate for the first child in a family amounted to £15.50 per week plus £10.35 for every additional child. This allowance is payable until the child(ren) leaves school between the ages of 16 and 19.
- **Maternity leave and pay conditions.** Entitlements of mothers to return to their employers after childbirth was introduced in 1973 and has also been subject to regular update and extension in duration, period of paid leave and the range of mothers covered and eligible for benefit.

  In 2001, pregnant women were entitled to 18 weeks' ordinary maternity leave; regardless of the length of their service to employers (this has since been increased to 26 weeks in 2003). Statutory Maternity Pay is paid at a rate of 90% of a woman's average weekly earnings or £75, whichever is the greater, for the first 6 weeks. After this time, a standard rate is applicable of £75.

  Women who have completed at least one year of service with their employers are also entitled to additional maternity leave, which starts at the end of their ordinary maternity leave and ends 29 weeks after the birth of their child.

  Women who are not entitled to Statutory Maternity Pay may be entitled to Maternity Allowance. This entitles the woman to a maximum of £75 per week or, if her earnings are at least £30 per week, 90% of her earnings but no more than £75. This is payable for 18 weeks. (This provision changed again in 2003.)

  During pregnancy, women are entitled to time off for antenatal care and also have a two-week compulsory maternity leave period (four weeks for women who work in factories).
- **Working Families Tax Credit.** Replacing Family Credit in 1999, this credit is available to working families who are responsible for at least one dependent child under 16 (or under 19 if still in full-time education). This is payable to one- and two-parent families. Eligibility rests on the applicant or their partner being over the age of 16, working at least 16 hours per week, regardless of whether they are employed or self-employed and providing they have no more than £8,000 in savings. A childcare tax credit element is calculated under this benefit. A maximum amount of £100 per week is paid for one child and a maximum of £150 per week for two or more children. The benefit is usually paid directly to the person who is mainly responsible for caring for the child (www.taxcredits.inlandrevenue.gov.uk). This system changed in 2003.

- **Income support.** Intended to help people on low incomes, aged 16 upwards who are working less than 16 hours per week (partners can work up to 24 hours) and who are not available for employment (otherwise they would claim Jobseekers' Allowance). The main recipients are pensioners, lone parents and those who experience long- or short-term sickness or are disabled. In 2001, the average number of claimants in the UK was 3.9 million. On average, claimants without dependants received £52.20 (single) to £81.95 (couples) per week, depending on age, in 2001. Claimants with dependants received on average £101.53 (for single parents) and £123.43 (for couples), depending on the ages of the claimant and the dependants. Claimants with dependent children received weekly amounts of approximately £26.60 per child under the age of 16 and £31.75 per child aged 16–18 in full-time education. Many of these claimants were also eligible for Housing Benefit which can make substantial additions to the amount received. Child Benefit would also be in addition to this benefit.

- **National Childcare Strategy.** Launched in 1998, the National Childcare Strategy proposed to provide accessible, affordable and quality childcare for all children aged up to 14 years old. This strategy includes aims that will integrate children's early education and childcare through better support for parents and informal childcarers and a new training programme for formal childcarers. This strategy has also introduced a new childcare tax credit for working families (outlined earlier). It aims to increase the number of formal childcare places available and, in particular in 2001, offer every 4-year-old a free nursery education place. Sure Start aims to achieve better outcomes for children, parents and communities by improving the health and emotional development of children, increasing the availability of childcare and supporting parents' employment aspirations (www.surestart.gov.uk). The programme takes different forms in England, Wales, Scotland and Northern Ireland.

- **Child Poverty.** In 2001, the government set about initiating and reviewing their policy targets to reduce and eradicate the high levels of child poverty found in the UK. Their long-term goal has been to cut child poverty in half by 2010 and to eradicate it by 2020. The first step of this target has been to reduce the number of children in low-income households by at least a quarter by 2004–05. To achieve these targets, their aim involves ensuring decent family incomes, with work for those who can and support for those who cannot; supporting parents in their parenting role; delivering high quality public services to break cycles of deprivation; and harnessing the power and expertise of the voluntary and community sectors (HM Treasury, 2004). The government's child poverty reviews have resulted in a number of Public Service Agreement targets which will all contribute to their long-term goal by, for example, improving public services for all; making work possible; and providing financial security and social inclusion in order to break cycles of deprivation (see DWP, 2003).

There is help from the government with the costs of having children (Box 1.2). In 1945, Family Allowance was introduced to provide an allowance for any second or further children born. This allowance was replaced in 1977 with Child Benefit which was an allowance for every child.

Maternity grants and allowances, and paid leave from employment for maternity, have been available for eligible mothers since 1948. Payments have varied in size, in real as opposed to nominal value and in eligibility conditions. Each of these government contributions to childbearing and childrearing has its own history which, in many cases, can be extensive and far too detailed to cover in this volume. For example, the history of maternity benefits up to 1985 was covered in Brown and Small (1985). This volume concentrates on describing the main provisions that were available to mothers, and their amounts and eligibility at the turn of the 21st century (see Box 1.2).

The Millennium Cohort Study data

This large-scale survey of 18,819 of the new century's babies, and the 18,553 families who are bringing them up, made its first contact in 2001-02 when the babies were aged nine months. The first survey recorded the circumstances of pregnancy and birth, as well as those of the all-important early months of life, and the social and economic background of the family into which the children have been born. These baseline data reveal the diversity of starting points from which these children of the new century are setting out. Full details about the survey – its origins, objectives, sampling, content, fieldwork, agency and funding – are contained in the survey's documentation (Natcen, 2004; Plewis et al, 2004; Shepherd et al, 2004).

As mentioned earlier, the design of the Millennium Cohort Study broke new ground in a number of ways: it contains sufficient samples of families in the UK countries, in disadvantaged areas and in minority ethnic groups to allow separate country, area and minority ethnic analyses.

These design elements of the Millennium compared with earlier cohort surveys are reflections of changing behaviour and a changed policy environment. Minority ethnic differences and fathers' views are important areas of policy in the new millennium. They were not central in 1958 or 1970. Earlier surveys of childbirth, including the earlier cohort studies, have mainly interviewed mothers. Interestingly, the NHS provided data collection free of charge for the first contact at two previous cohort studies in 1958 and 1970.

The institution of Child Benefit provided a new way to draw the sample. Children with sample birth dates eligible for the survey were taken from the Child Benefit register if they were living in one of 398 electoral wards sampled from the whole of the UK when they were 9 months old. This sampling strategy meant that, apart from a few excluded by DWP as 'sensitive cases', children who were not eligible for Child Benefit or for whom the benefit was not claimed were not eligible for the survey. We believe this applied to about 3% of births nationally, most of whom were involved in very recent and possibly transient international migration. The survey also, by definition, did not include births where the child had died before 9 months, another small minority of around 0.6%.

The sample for the first sweep included babies born between 1 September 2000 and 31 August 2001 in England and Wales, who form an academic year cohort. In Scotland and Northern Ireland, the start date of the birthdays was delayed to 23 November 2000 in order to avoid an overlap with an infant feeding survey being carried out in September and October (see Hamlyn et al, 2002). In the event, the sampled cohort was extended to 59 weeks of births in these countries to make up for a shortfall in numbers, which became apparent during fieldwork, as birth rates dropped below the level anticipated. The last eligible birth date in Scotland and Northern Ireland was 11 January 2002. There was no such attempt to replace 'unborn' 2000-01 babies in England and Wales, so the overall achieved sample fell some 1,000 below its original target. This reflects the changed conditions of the low-fertility environment of this survey, compared to earlier birth cohort surveys.

The first sweep of data collection covered a range of topics as listed in Table 1.1 with the two or one parent(s) resident in the household. Parents were asked to provide this information partly face-to-face with the interviewer who entered it into a computer using computer-assisted interviewing (CAPI) and partly by entering their answers confidentially by self-completion into a computer. Seventy-five per cent of main interviews took place while the baby was aged 9 months, 19% at 10 months, with 3% at 8 months and 3% taking place late, at 11 months.

Table 1.1 Summary of MCS sweep 1 survey elements

Respondent	Mode	Summary of content
Mother/main	Interview	Household module Module A: Non-resident parents Module C: Pregnancy, labour and delivery Module D: Baby's health and development Module E: Childcare Module F: Grandparents and friends Module G: Parent's health
	Self-completion	Module H: • Baby's temperament & behaviour • Relationship with partner • Previous relationships • Domestic tasks • Previous pregnancies • Mental health • Attitudes to relationships, parenting, work, etc
	Interview	Module J: Employment and Education Module K: Housing and local area Module L: Interests and time with baby
Father/partner	Interview	Module B: Father's involvement with baby Module C: Pregnancy, labour and delivery (where applicable) Module F: Grandparents and friends Module G: Parent's health
	Self-completion	Module H: • Baby's temperament & behaviour • Relationship with partner • Previous relationships • Previous children • Mental health • Attitudes to marriage, parenting, work, etc
	Interview	Module J: Employment and education Module L: Interests and time with baby

An introductory leaflet, the advance letter and the thank-you letter were translated into the most common non-English languages spoken in the 19 selected wards of high minority ethnic populations. The languages appropriate for translation were Bengali, Gujerati, Kurdish, Punjabi, Somali, Turkish and Urdu. The first leaflet had already been translated into Welsh. Some interviews were carried out in verbal translation in these and other languages by relatives or friends. In certain circumstances, where no-one was available to translate into English, translator interviewers were provided. Other languages encountered in non-trivial numbers included Arabic, Hindi and Tamil. Main interviews were carried out in a non-English language in 226 cases (1%), of which one main respondent interview was in Welsh. A further 547 (3%) were done in a mix of English and another language, of which three were in Welsh. For partners, the corresponding figures were 306 (2%) interviews in a non-English language, of which one was in Welsh, and 94 (1%) in a mix of English and another language, of which two were in Welsh.

Achieved sample

Parents interviewed were distributed over the four countries of the UK (Table 1.2).

In the vast majority of cases, the natural mother did the main interview. The exceptions were 2 adoptive mothers, 2 foster mothers, 18 lone fathers, 2 natural fathers where the natural mothers answered the partner interview, 1 natural father who also gave a proxy partner interview for the natural mother, and 5 maternal grandmothers.

In the case of the collection of information directly from partners, 13,192 of the total 13,441 were natural fathers of the cohort baby, 1 a foster father, 32 step fathers and 2 adoptive fathers. Proxy information was obtained about 215 natural fathers who were not available to have an interview. Four mothers also gave the information requested about partners because the fathers in these cases were either the only natural parent or the main carer of the child in the household and therefore gave the information for the main interview. One mother was relegated to the partner interview as she was incapacitated. Information was also obtained from 13 partners of the natural mother, one paternal grandfather and one partner of a maternal grandmother. Contained in the 18,553 families were:

- 246 sets of twins and 10 sets of triplets;
- 3,194 parents who were living without a resident partner, of which:
  - 3,173 were lone mothers and 3 were lone grandmothers, and
  - 18 were lone fathers.

Table 1.2: MCS unweighted achieved sample sizes by country

Country	Number of sample 'wards'*	Target sample boosted++	Achieved responses**			
			Children	Families interviewed	Partners	Lone parents
England	200	13146	11695	11533	8485	1853
Wales	73	3000	2799	2761	1933	590
Scotland	62	2500	2370	2336	1727	375
N. Ireland	63	2000	1955	1923	1296	376
Total UK	398	20646	18819	18553	13441	3194

Notes: * Counting 'super wards' as a single unit. ** All productive contacts.

++ Target sample included booster samples to Scotland and Northern Ireland to allow for sufficient sample sizes for country analyses to be undertaken.

The achieved overall response rate was 72%. An in-scope response rate is also calculated. It has a different denominator from the achieved overall rate. The denominator for the in-scope response rate includes only the cases issued to the fieldwork agency after initial filtering through the Department for Work and Pensions, and it also omits those cases which became ineligible because the families had moved out of the sample areas before the interviewer had contacted them. The in-scope response rate, therefore, measures interviewers' successes at finding their targets. The overall in-scope response rate was 82%. Response rates varied by the areas in which families lived. They were highest in areas of relative advantage and lowest in areas of high minority ethnic population. Those families living in (non-ethnic) other disadvantaged areas had response rates lying between the high rates of non-disadvantaged areas and the lowest rates for families living in areas of high minority ethnic population. Response in Northern Ireland was also relatively low. Further details about response, and the characteristics of the non-respondents, can be found in Plewis et al (2004).

Box 1.3 Areas used in sample design

Three types of area were used in the sample design:

1. The *'minority ethnic'* stratum: children living in wards which, in the 1991 Census of Population, had at least 30% of their total population falling into the two categories 'Black' or 'Asian'.
2. The *'other disadvantaged'* stratum: children living in wards, other than those falling into stratum (1), which fell into the upper quartile (ie the poorest 25% of wards) of the ward-based Child Poverty Index (CPI) for England and Wales. The cut-off for the upper quartile was 38.4%. Almost all minority ethnic wards could also have been classified as disadvantaged by this definition.
3. The *'non-disadvantaged'* stratum: children living in wards, other than those falling into stratum (1) or (2), which were not in the top quartile of the CPI.

In the tables and text, these areas are referred to by shorthand labels as follows: 'Non-disadvantaged', 'Minority ethnic' and 'Other disadvantaged'.

Children of minority ethnic groups

Babies from cohort mothers of minority ethnic identities did not just live in wards with high minority ethnic populations, but in wards of all three types. Of the non-white babies in this sample, 64.8% lived in the wards of high minority ethnic population in England, 24.6% lived in other UK disadvantaged wards and 10.7% lived in non-disadvantaged wards across the UK. There were of course some babies of minority ethnic origin in the smaller UK countries, although in low numbers and insufficient for separate analysis; however, they were included in the total UK sample for some of the analyses in this book. Of the babies who lived in wards of high minority ethnic population, 82.6% were non-white, 17.4% were white babies. Of babies living in other disadvantaged areas, 16.5% were non-white and 7% of babies living in non-disadvantaged areas were also non-white.

First-born children[3]

Of the UK babies, 42.5% were the first born in the family, the lowest being in Northern Ireland (39.4%) and the highest in Scotland (45.2%). First-born children in the family were least frequent in wards with high minority ethnic populations (35.9%) and most likely in other disadvantaged wards (43.5%). The breakdown by ethnic identity showed that the cohort child was the first born in only 23.6% of Bangladeshi families, reflecting their propensity to have more children than average (Table 1.3). The proportion of first-born children was also well below the average in Pakistani (29.9%) and Black African (29.0%) families, but above average in the white (43.3%) and the other minority ethnic identity category (46.7%). This means that at least half the cohort children already had at least one older sibling, more than two thirds in the case of Pakistani, Bangladeshi and Black African families.

Plan of this book

Important new opportunities are provided by the data. The full extent of the possibilities for analysis go far beyond the findings presented in this volume which are necessarily selective and driven mainly by what we have found to be interesting and policy relevant at this stage of our analyses. However, we present a selection of findings. These are important in themselves, as well as being a taster for the type of analyses that are possible which others will hopefully be stimulated to take up,

Table 1.3: First-born cohort children in the family by mother's ethnic identity, UK

	Ethnic group (%)								
Whether cohort child was first-born	White	Mixed	Indian	Pakistani	Bangladeshi	Black Caribbean	Black African	Other	UK total %
First-born	43.3	40.7	40.6	29.9	23.6	38.5	29.0	46.7	42.5
Not first-born	56.7	59.3	59.4	70.1	76.4	61.5	71.0	53.3	57.5
Total	100.0	100.0	100.0	100.0	100.0	100.0	100.0	100.0	100.0
Unweighted sample size	15420	186	456	848	351	256	369	354	18240

Base: All UK MCS natural mothers when cohort baby 9-10 months old. Sample size excludes those with missing data. Percentages weighted.

especially when the data have been enriched by the future sweeps planned to turn this into a longitudinal survey.

We present our material according to the chronological sequence of the lives it portrays. These babies started out in life in a certain context – the initial conditions into which they were born and over which they have no control. Chapter Two offers a number of dimensions of the babies' origins: the structure of their household – including parents, siblings, grandparents and ethnic origins; their birthplace; the languages spoken in the home; parental health – including height and weight, smoking and alcohol consumption; and the housing and neighbourhoods that these children grow up in. In modern terminology, these are also aspects of social and health capital. Chapter Three offers insights into the financial capital of babies' origins and, in particular, the extent to which they started out life in poverty. We follow by considering the pregnancy and birth process (Chapter Four), and the variations in infant health (Chapter Five) and psychosocial development (Chapter Six). Parenting is the subject of Chapter Seven with a focus on parents' responses to their new baby and their experiences, attitudes and division of labour in the early months. Chapter Eight considers the extent of parents' involvement in paid work and the childcare arrangements of couples and lone parents who engage in the labour market.

While these chapters mostly focus on a substantive area of babies' lives, there are many cross–cutting links incorporated at each stage. The data offer this potential to explore links between babies' origins and early outcomes, and parents' behaviour and resources with babies' health measures. Many analyses have sought to capitalise on the potential for rich cross–disciplinary analyses, which of course are more lifelike, and policy relevant.

In the analyses presented in this book, the authors have tried to capture and report on the unique strengths of the Millennium Cohort Study data. Since the design provides sample sizes sufficient to allow for examination of the four UK countries and their differences, these become an interesting element of this new cohort. Devolution and UK country differences were not topics high on the agenda when the earlier 1958 and 1970 cohorts were planned – another social change. This means we do not have earlier sources of comparison on country differences to tell how circumstances in the smaller UK countries have been changing. Nonetheless, it is interesting to see here the extent to which children of the new century born in separate UK countries have different or similar experiences at the outset of their lives. UK countries are allowed to vary in their educational provision and health services. We might expect, therefore, that these will be the areas where most differences will be evident although, in the case of educational experiences, these will only become apparent in later sweeps of the cohort when the children are older. However, there is no long history of analysing UK country differences and it is relatively early days in charting separate country paths. In this sense, the Millennium Cohort Study provides an early benchmark. Clearly, important questions will need to be raised and followed up where significant differences arise in access to public services.

The over-representation of wards with high minority ethnic populations is another dimension in which the Millennium Cohort survey findings can offer unique insights. Certain things are known about babies from different minority ethnic groups in comparison with babies of white ethnic identity, as reviewed in Chapters Two, Four and Five. However, there are many gaps in knowledge about minority ethnic experiences for children which this survey will help to fill.

The fact that the sample was clustered and designed around residential ward areas with known characteristics offers another opportunity for analysis. Questions are often raised about whether it is individuals' characteristics that are responsible for their experiences and behaviour, or whether, in the case of people who live in disadvantaged areas, the area and its lack of opportunities, its culture or barriers determine or deepen individuals' disadvantages. The design of the Millennium Cohort Study was such that it is possible to do analyses that partly identify how far the area people live in is likely to be responsible for their experiences and behaviour in comparison to their characteristics and preferences. A rigorous example of such analysis is provided in Chapter Two.

Our conclusions are brought together with their policy implications in Chapter Nine. There are, of course, many unanswered questions, alongside our valuable insights. We hope these will spur other researchers to take the work on from here, as well as creating an interested audience for the next contacts with these babies at ages 3, 5 and 7.

Box 1.4 Reporting of sample sizes and weights

In all the tables included, the usual practice is to report weighted percentages and unweighted sample sizes, unless otherwise stated. It was normal practice to weight analyses by the country or UK weights, as appropriate. In multivariate analyses, weights were generally not applied when variables were included to capture the design elements in the data but were weighted if these variables were not included. All multivariate analyses and significance tests have included adjustments to standard errors from the cluster sampling design. Unit non-response weights have *not* been used in these analyses.

Notes

[1] The economic activity rate – 73% in the UK in 2001 for women of working age – is roughly twice what it was in 1951 (Joshi et al, 1985).

[2] Functionings are the performance elements of how well we achieve in adult life.

[3] The cohort baby will not have been the first-born in all families. The cohort baby may have older siblings, including siblings who do not currently live in the home.

TWO

Children's origins

*Mel Bartley, Lisa Calderwood, Hiranthi Jayaweera,
Ian Plewis and Kelly Ward*

When babies are born, they enter the world with a certain endowment. Some characteristics are inherited; others come from the particular environment into which the child arrives. There are relationships with the immediate family, parents and others living in the home, finances and housing, the wider kin network, the neighbourhood, the local and national economy and the social framework provided by national and devolved government. In this chapter, we set out to review these circumstances of birth for babies born at the start of the 21st century. These are the initial conditions of life for this new generation. Of course, in future we will be able to see how the generation progressed from the different starting points represented here, and how easy or difficult it is for children to benefit or escape from their earliest origins.

In this chapter, we consider first the family into which the baby was born – in particular, parents and their relationship, siblings and wider kin. We then examine the ethnic identities and religion of parents, and their own languages and national and cultural heritages. Parents' health is another important element of the 'endowment set' for cohort babies which may affect the extent to which parents can provide effective care for the baby. Finally, we describe the housing conditions and neighbourhood context in which these families live. The financial aspects of children's origins, broadly defined, are considered in Chapter 3.

Household structure

Of considerable importance to a new baby is the type of household they enter. As reviewed in the Introduction to this volume (Chapter 1), dramatic changes have occurred to the demography of the family brought about by changing relationships between men and women leading to a diversity of family types.

Parents in the household

In 1971, 92% of families with dependent children were married or cohabiting couple families. By 1994, this proportion had reached its lowest point – 77% – and by 1996 it had recovered to 80% of such families (Dex, 1999, Table 2). The proportion of families headed by a lone parent increased over the same period from less than 8% to approximately one fifth. The Millennium Cohort Study (MCS) families are distinguished from families at large in that they had a new baby around the Millennium. They are part of the subset of families who have very young children. It is perhaps not surprising therefore to see that Millennium Cohort families were more likely to be in a two-resident parent household (84.3%)[1] than all UK families, and therefore less likely at 15.7% than all UK families around the year 2000 to be lone-parent families. At the point that a baby is born, couples who were the parents of the baby were likely to be together. The risks of splitting up grow as the baby grows older.

Among the families without two resident parents, there was a very small proportion where one parent had died (0.1% of all families). Other one-parent families either had the other parent absent and uninvolved (5.4% of all families), the other parent absent but involved (8.4% of all families), or resident part of the time (1.8%).[2] This way of classifying mainly the non-resident partner's role in the family is unique to the Millennium Cohort Study. It takes the classification of families beyond the simple one or two-parent dichotomy by noting the absent father's relationships with his child. This finer breakdown allows, as can be seen in Chapter 7, an examination of whether this involvement is associated with other characteristics of the family, and whether it makes any difference to the financial circumstances of the family. In due course, as the cohort child grows up, it will also be possible to examine whether the partial involvement of the child's father has any further effects on the outcomes for the child in later life (Chapters 3 and 7). Such refinements offer a better foundation for policy making about fathers' rights than has been possible with earlier data.

The vast majority of Millennium babies were living with both their natural parents at 9 months. Approximately 86% of families contained both natural parents (when part-time resident natural fathers are included). In about a quarter of families the baby's parents were living together without being married. The most common arrangement, accounting for 6 in 10 families, was the 'traditional' married couple. In the one in seven cases with only one parent living with the baby, almost all the lone parents were the baby's natural mother. Other family types were extremely rare – under 100 families in total. There were a handful of families in which the baby's main carers were foster/adoptive parents or maternal grandparents.

The overall pattern of family types varied little by country (Figure 2.1). There were slightly higher proportions of lone-mother families in Wales and Northern Ireland compared with England, although the difference was extremely small and on the borders of statistical significance. The only notable country difference was that a much higher proportion of families in Northern Ireland contained two natural parents who were married – nearly 7 in 10 compared with 6 in 10 in the other UK countries. Wales had the lowest percentage (57.1%) of families containing two natural married parents, and Northern Ireland had the lowest percentage (14.9%) of families who were cohabiting natural parents.

Family circumstances were strongly related to mother's age (Figure 2.2). Half of teenage mothers and just under a third of mothers aged 20-24 at interview were not living with the baby's father. About 3 in 10 mothers in their early 20s were married and living with the baby's father, and 4 in 10 were living together without being married. Teenage mothers were very unlikely to be married to the baby's father

Figure 2.1: MCS family types by country

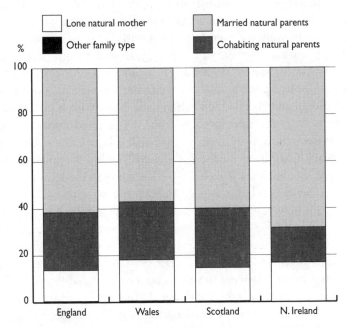

Base: All UK MCS main respondents when cohort baby was 9-10 months old. Weighted percentages.

Figure 2.2: Family type by mother's age

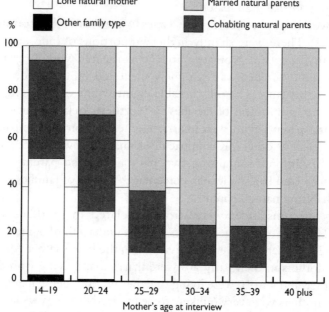

Base: All UK MCS main respondents when cohort baby was 9-10 months old. Weighted percentages.

(1 in 20), although a substantial proportion (4 in 10) were living together without being married. The majority of mothers in all the other age groups were married and living with the baby's father.

Family circumstances were also strongly related to ethnic group (Figure 2.3). Almost half of Black Caribbean and 4 in 10 Black African babies were not living with their natural father. In contrast, almost all Indian, Pakistani and Bangladeshi babies were living with both natural parents who were married to each other. Unmarried cohabitation was almost non-existent in these South Asian ethnic groups. Of UK families, Black Caribbean mothers in the MCS were the most likely never to have been legally married (56.6%). Some in this group were clearly in cohabiting relationships, which accounts for the difference in proportions between the never married group and the lone parent group. Nearly half (46.0%) of all mothers in the mixed ethnic group were also 'never married', as were around a third of white (33.0%) and Black African (30.3%) mothers. In contrast, only a very small proportion of South Asian mothers were in this category (2.9%, 1.5% and 1.0% in the case of Indian, Pakistani and Bangladeshi mothers, respectively). These inter-ethnic marital patterns, particularly differences between Black Caribbean, white and South Asian mothers, corroborate other

Figure 2.3: Family type by baby's ethnic identity

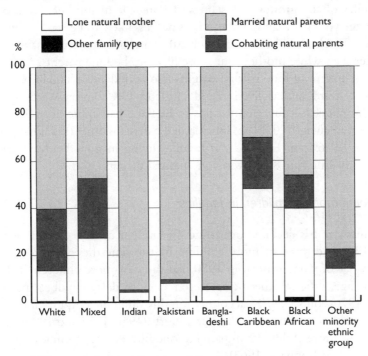

Base: All UK MCS main respondents when cohort baby was 9-10 months old. Weighted percentages.

recent evidence of trends over the past decade (Modood et al, 1997). Other survey evidence also suggests the importance of controlling for age in looking at marital patterns as there is evidence that Black Caribbean women get married as they get older (Berthoud, 2001b; Lindley et al, 2004). If we look at marital status by age at interview in the MCS, we find that 79.2% of Black Caribbean mothers in their 20s were never married, compared with 46.2% of all mothers.

The prevalence of lone parenthood appears highest among the black mothers, particularly Black Caribbean mothers, of whom nearly half were living as lone parents (Table A2.1, row 5). Nearly a third of the mothers with mixed ethnic origins were also lone parents. Cohabiting was most evident in mothers of white, mixed and Black African ethnic identities. Over a quarter of white and mixed mothers were living as part of non-married couples. These diverse ethnic patterns fit in with the findings of other surveys (see Labour Force Survey data in Lindley et al, 2004). Data from birth registration show that under 3% of births in England and Wales to mothers born in South Asian countries occurred outside marriage (Collingwood Bakeo, 2004).

Although mother's age is related to ethnicity, these ethnic group differences do not seem to be explained by differences in the age profiles of the groups. Pakistani and Bangladeshi mothers were on average younger than white mothers but less likely to be lone parents, while Black Caribbean and Black African mothers were on average older than white mothers but more likely to be lone parents.

The extent of lone natural parents also varied considerably by the type of ward families lived in and a little by UK country. Wards with high minority ethnic populations in England had approximately the same percentage (20.3%) of lone natural parents as other disadvantaged wards (21.6%) in England. Of families living in non-disadvantaged wards in England, 8.4% were lone natural parents.

Total number of children in families[3]

Family size has declined over time. Twenty per cent of women born in 1946 had three or more children by the time they were 31. But only 7% of women born in 1970 had three or more children at the same age, although the increased tendency to delay childbearing by the 1970 cohort partly accounts for this difference. Approximately one third of women in the earlier cohorts (1946, 1958 and 1970) had three or more children compared to one fifth of women in the MCS (Butler and Bonham, 1963).

In the MCS, family size so far has varied from 1 to 10 children in the household, including both the cohort child and their siblings. In 42% of families, the cohort baby was the only child (so far). Just over one third of families (36.3%) had two children, 14.8% three children and 6.8% of families had four or more children.

Family size varied by country. Northern Ireland had a notably larger proportion than other countries (29.0%) with three or more children, whereas in the other three countries the proportion of families with three or more children was around 20%. The proportion of families in Northern Ireland with four or more children (11.1%) was about twice the proportion elsewhere. A much higher proportion of children living in wards with high minority ethnic populations had large families (16.2% had four or more children). Pakistani, Bangladeshi and Black African mothers had the greatest number of children already. Bangladeshi mothers, the youngest at first birth, also had the highest proportion with three or more previous children (47.3%).

Siblings

The Millennium baby had at least one brother or sister (who was almost always older than them!) in 57.9% of families. Lone-mother families and families in which the parents were living together without being married were slightly less likely to contain a sibling (around 50%), and families with married parents were slightly more likely to include one sibling (62%).

Bangladeshi mothers, followed by Pakistani and Black Africans, had larger numbers of live births. Nearly half of all Bangladeshi mothers had three or more children at the time of interview, compared to one fifth of both white and Indian mothers. An analysis of Labour Force Survey data for a similar time period shows that Bangladeshi women, followed by Pakistani women, were the most likely among all ethnic groups to have more than two children (Lindley et al, 2004, p 31).

Half siblings

Across the UK families, 9.3% contained a half brother or sister to the cohort child living in the same home. Wales had the highest proportion at 11.3%, and Northern Ireland the lowest at 5.6%.

The Millennium baby was much less likely to have a half brother or sister if their parents were married (5.3%), compared with lone-parent families (15.3%) and cohabiting families (16.1%).

Parents' ages at interview

Of all cohort mothers, 51.2% were in their 30s at the interview. The figure for fathers was 60.3%. For mothers where the cohort child was the first born, the proportion in their 30s was 40.6%, and for fathers the proportion was 54.6% (Table A2.2). Age of mother at current and first birth is examined in more detail in Chapter 4, since it overlaps with many dimensions of disadvantage and relative advantage.

The context of changing age of motherhood can be seen from earlier birth cohort studies. Ninety-two per cent of women born in 1946 had their first baby by the age of 30, compared to 66% of those born in 1958 and 50% born in 1970 (Ferri et al, 2003).

Lone parents

Lone-parent families constituted 13.8% of families in the survey. These living arrangements varied in frequency across country, but more so across different types of ward. They were far more evident among families living in other disadvantaged areas, with the highest percentage among the families in Northern Ireland (Figure 2.4).

Grandparents in household[4]

About 6% of the Millennium babies lived with one or more of their grandparents as well as their parent(s). However, among Indian, Pakistani and Bangladeshi families, this proportion was much higher – between a quarter and one third (Figure 2.5). It was also more common for Asian families to live with the father's parent(s) rather than the mother's parent(s), whereas in all other ethnic groups living with maternal grandparent(s) was more common.

Having grandparents alive

In early adult life, over 80% of the population have three or more generations of their family alive (Dench and Ogg, 2002). By the age of 50, three fifths of the British population still have a living parent and just over a third are grandparents (Grundy et al, 1999). It is therefore unsurprising that a very large majority of the Millennium Cohort parents themselves had parents who were alive. Perhaps reflecting women's greater life expectancy and earlier age at parenthood, the proportion of mothers and fathers with a living mother was higher than the proportion with a living father. On average, 93% of cohort mothers[5] had their own mothers alive and 83% had a father alive. Of the 73% of families where the mother also had a partner who responded

Figure 2.4: MCS lone parent families by type of ward and country

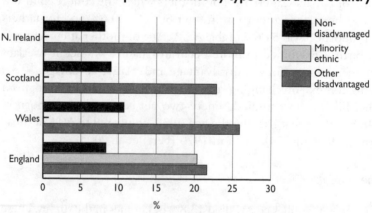

Base: All UK MCS main respondents when cohort baby was 9-10 months old. Unweighted percentages.

Figure 2.5: Grandparents in household by baby's ethnic identity

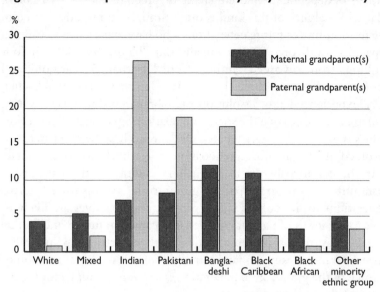

Base: All UK MCS main respondents when cohort baby was 9-10 months old. Weighted percentages.

to the survey[6], slightly fewer of these partners had living parents, but again more had a mother alive (90%) than a father (79%).

There were differences between ethnic groups. Families from all the minority ethnic groups were less likely to have grandparents alive compared to white families, as found by Berthoud (2003). The higher percentage of live grandmothers than live grandfathers was similar across all minority ethnic families, the gap being wider in the case of minority ethnic families than white families. In the case of Bangladeshi families, 90% of cohort mothers had their mother alive – only a little below average – but only 64% had their father alive. Similarly for Bangladeshi partners, 84% had their mother alive but only 57% had their father alive. Black families were the least likely to have a grandmother alive, either maternal (85%) or paternal (78%). It was not the case that minority ethnic babies' parents were older and less likely to have their own parents alive for this reason. The explanation is likely to be, at least in part, higher mortality in the countries of origin, but it could also be related to age gaps between parents.

Separation and divorce in grandparent generation

In the UK, changes in partnerships have led to a growth in the numbers experiencing marital dissolution (Scott, 1997), with reportedly 149,000 parents of dependent children having divorced in 2002 (ONS, 2004). Marital instability of this kind is often thought to reproduce itself in the relationships of future generations who have experienced a parental separation or divorce (Diekmann and Engelhardt, 1999). One in four children from divorced families were less than 5 years old, and approximately two in three children were less than 10 years old, when they experienced the dissolution of their parents' marriage (ONS, 2004b). This means that the social and relationship capital of the cohort babies is potentially lower where grandparents have been separated or divorced, if one or more grandparent is less likely to be in contact with the cohort baby (or its parents). In addition, if this partnership instability in the grandparent generation is transmitted across generations to the cohort baby's parents, cohort babies are likely to have lower levels of parental relationship capital in future, and, in due course, may themselves experience further partnership instability through transmission of a family tradition. In this sense, separation or divorce in the grandparent generation is a potential risk factor for the cohort baby in the future.

Divorce and separation often lead to reduced standards of living – in particular, lower household income and changes in accommodation for both the parent and the child. For the children at the centre of these dissolved relationships, further impacts are often found in terms of lower levels of education, leaving home prematurely, assuming adult roles at younger ages, lower paid and lower status occupations, and experiencing early partnerships as well as increased chances of partnership dissolution. Furthermore, research also indicates that children who have experienced parental separation have lower satisfaction with adult life, a decreased frequency of contact and exchange with their parents and a considerably weaker relationship with the parent who left the family home. Children are likely to remain with their mothers after a marital or partnership dissolution. Therefore, reduced contact with fathers is common for such children (Kiernan, 1997, 2004a; Allen and Bourke-Dowling, 1998; Diekmann and Engelhardt, 1999; Amato and Sobolewski, 2001; Braun, 2001).

Data collected on the Millennium babies' grandparents refer only to the cohort parents' own biological parents.[7] This section considers, using the limited data collected to date, ways in which partnership formations and dissolutions among the grandparent and parent generations of the cohort babies may be linked and contribute to risk factors in future for the cohort babies. Studies suggest such impacts on children can potentially alter the economic and educational circumstances, as well as future partnership formations, of these cohort babies (see Ermisch, 1991; Joshi et al, 1999; Kiernan, 1997; Hobcraft, 1998; Tallman et al, 2001). Clearly, the full effects will only become apparent in future sweeps of the survey.

Of cohort mothers in the MCS, 29.5% had experienced a parental separation or divorce prior to the Sweep 1 interview contact. The figure for fathers was 23.7%. Of all cohort parents, the frequency of those experiencing a parental partnership dissolution varied by country and ward type. Those mothers least likely to have experienced a parental partnership dissolution were living in non-disadvantaged areas of Northern Ireland (15.1% of cohort mothers) or in wards with high minority ethnic populations in England (15.3% of mothers). However, if we examine mothers in couples only, 11.6% of those living in wards with high minority ethnic populations have the lowest experience of their own parents splitting up, beating Northern Ireland's couple mothers (13.9%) with the same experience. The same low figures for experiencing one's parents having split up can be noted among cohort fathers – 9.2% of cohort fathers living in wards with high minority ethnic populations and 13.5% of those living in non-disadvantaged areas of Northern Ireland again being the lowest rates of this experience. These figures are likely to be related to ethnic group and religious adherence. Minority ethnic families are known to be more religious and uphold traditional family values more than the white majority. Also, over four out of five families in Northern Ireland identified themselves with the two main catholic or protestant communities, whereas more than half of parents in the rest of the UK claimed to have no religion. Those cohort parents least likely to have experienced their own parents' partnership dissolution lived in wards with high minority ethnic populations (Figure 2.6), many of whom, but not all, were from minority ethnic groups.

Cohort parents, either mothers or fathers, least likely to have experienced their own parents splitting up were either of Indian (3.2% for mothers and 3.1% for fathers who had experienced parental separation), Pakistani (5.0% for mothers and 4.6% for fathers) or Bangladeshi (2.9% for mothers and 1.6% for fathers) minority ethnic identity. Overall, cohort mothers who were most likely to have experienced a parental separation or divorce were of mixed (51.1%) or Black Caribbean (53%) ethnic identity (Figure 2.7).

Cohort parents who indicated that their religion was Hindu, Muslim/Islam or Sikh[8] had the smallest frequencies of experiencing their own parents' separation or divorce – only 1.5% of cohort mothers and 1.4% of cohort fathers of Hindu, Muslim or Sikh cohort parents had a history of the separation or divorce of their own parents. If we assume

Figure 2.6: Percentages of cohort mothers and cohort fathers who experienced a parental partnership dissolution by country and type of ward

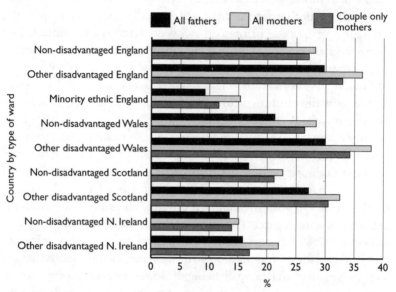

Base: All UK MCS mothers and fathers when cohort baby was 9-10 months old. Unweighted percentages.

Figure 2.7: Percentages of cohort mothers and fathers who experienced a parental partnership dissolution by ethnic identity

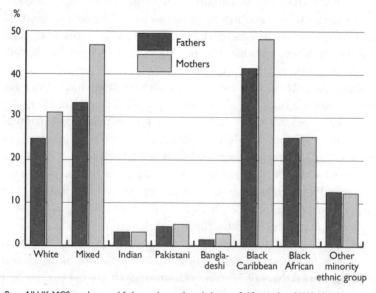

Base: All UK MCS mothers and fathers when cohort baby was 9-10 months old. Weighted percentages.

that cohort grandparents were likely to share the religious beliefs reported by their offspring, this would reflect the pro-marriage values embedded in these cultures making it less likely that partnerships will dissolve. Cohort parents of 'no religion' were the most likely to have experienced the breakdown of their own parents' partnerships.

Age at separation

Where cohort parents' own parents had split up, cohort mothers were most likely to have been under 7 years old when it occurred (44.6%), or between 8 and 16 years (37%), leaving 18.4% having this experience at 17 years or over. For cohort fathers with an experience of their own parent's separation or divorce, 39.3% were under 7 years old, 38.9% were aged 8-16 and 21.8% were 17 years old or more when it happened. As others have noted, this highlights the likelihood of women experiencing a parental separation or divorce in early childhood rather than in adulthood (Kiernan, 2004a). Men, on the other hand, seem to experience parental partnership breakdowns equally in childhood and teenage years, rather than adulthood. This contrast remained even when lone mothers were removed from the analysis, as both couple mothers (41.3%) and fathers (38.3%) were more likely to experience a parental partnership dissolution in childhood compared with adulthood (21.7% of mothers and 22.4% of fathers).

There was a link between the age at which the baby's parents experienced their own parents splitting up, on the one hand, and the educational qualifications they achieved and their NS-SEC, on the other. Cohort mothers who had experienced a parental separation or divorce prior to the age of 7 were nearly twice as likely (18.9%) as those who experienced this separation aged 17 plus (9.3%) to have no educational qualifications. Cohort parents who had experienced the separation or divorce at 17 years plus were more likely to have NVQ levels 4 or 5, and to occupy management or professional occupations, compared to those who had experienced parental partnership breakdowns before the age of 7 (Table 2.1).

Becoming a parent early

Research suggests that children from separated or divorced families are often more likely to commence sexual relations, partnership formation and partnership dissolution earlier than others (Kiernan, 1997).

Nearly one fifth of cohort mothers whose parents had separated or

Table 2.1: Qualifications and current economic circumstances of the cohort parents by cohort parents' ages when cohort grandparents separated/divorced

Cohort parents' socioeconomic circumstances	Cohort parents' ages when they experienced separation or divorce of their own parents (%)			
	Up to 7 years old	8 to 16 years old	17 plus years old	Total
Cohort mothers				
No qualifications	18.9	15.4	9.3	15.7
NVQ levels 4 & 5	19.2	26.2	38.1	25.6
Management/professional occupation	20.7	24.3	37.8	25.6
Semi routine/routine occupation	53.4	46.2	33.2	46.6
Below 60% median income*	42.2	34.6	24.1	35.7
Maximum unweighted sample size	2341	1939	965	5245
Cohort fathers				
No qualifications	15.6	12.3	10.9	13.2
NVQ levels 4 & 5	24.3	30.1	36.0	29.3
Management/professional occupation	31.6	38.4	42.6	36.8
Semi routine/routine occupation	32.0	27.3	22.7	28.1
Below 60% median income*	27.2	20.0	15.9	21.9
Maximum unweighted sample size	1170	1160	649	2979

Base: All UK MCS mothers and fathers who had experienced a parental separation or divorce by time cohort baby was 9-10 months old. Weighted percentages.

* Based on equivalised income not including housing benefits.

divorced had a child by the age of 18 years old compared with only 7.5% of cohort mothers whose parents had never separated or divorced. Also, 44.9% of cohort mothers whose parents had not separated entered motherhood when they were over 27 years compared with 28.9% of cohort mothers who had experienced a parental partnership dissolution. Children of younger cohort mothers, aged up to 19 years old, were more likely to have half or step siblings in their home (22.2%) compared with families where the cohort mothers postponed childbearing until after the age of 27 years (12.8%). Further analysis on the advantages and disadvantages of teenage childbearing is included in Chapter 4.

A multivariate logistic regression analysis of cohort mothers becoming a parent by age 19 was undertaken, examining whether the past marital breakdown of the cohort mother's own parents was a significant determinant of becoming a mother at this young age (Table A2.3). The results showed that having had an experience of one's own parents separating in childhood was associated with double the likelihood of becoming a young mother oneself after controlling for ethnic identity, religion as stated at the interview and the survey design factors of UK country and type of ward the mother lived in.[9] Living in Wales, living in one of the other disadvantaged areas or an area of high minority ethnic populations were all associated with a higher likelihood of becoming a mother under 19 years old. Identifying oneself as minority ethnic was generally insignificant, except in the case of Indian and Black African mothers who had a lower likelihood than white mothers and those from other minority ethnic groups of being a young mother. Mothers saying they had a religion were all less likely to be a young mother than the women who identified themselves as being of no religion. In this way, our findings support earlier studies that suggested partnership breakdown in one generation transmits a higher likelihood of teenage motherhood to the next generation.

This early evidence from the parents of the Millennium babies supports earlier research findings that instability in marital relationships and partnerships in the grandparent generation may have consequences in the cohort parents' generation and eventually be a risk factor for a subset of Millennium Cohort babies.

The role of grandparents in supporting the cohort families currently is explored in Chapter 3, and their association with child development in Chapter 6.

Country of birth[10]

Among the minority ethnic mothers in England, Bangladeshi mothers were the most likely to be immigrants, with over 90% born outside the UK. Around three quarters of Black African mothers, and around 60% of Pakistani mothers were also born outside the UK. In contrast, 80% of Black Caribbean mothers were born in the UK (Figure 2.8). These differences in birthplace reflect differences in migration timescales and patterns among the different ethnic groups (Peach, 1996). They will also be potentially important in a child's development and the extent to which children are inducted and socialised into the mother's birthplace as opposed to host UK culture and language. However, such integration is also likely to depend on the length of time parents have lived in the UK.

English fluency

The ability to communicate in English has major implications for access to and use of a range of services and the ability to induct one's children into the language of the host country. Evidence exists about the disadvantaging effects of a lack of English fluency among minority

Figure 2.8: Mothers born in the UK in different ethnic groups

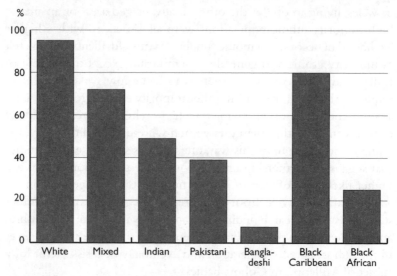

Base: All MCS natural mothers living in England where linkage was successfully carried out to birth registration information. Weighted percentages.

Figure 2.9: Languages spoken at home

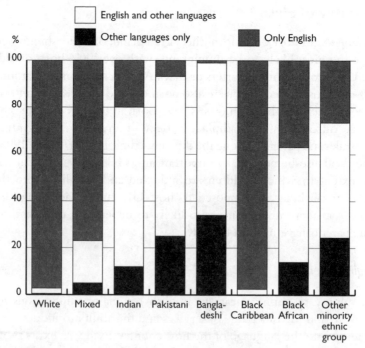

Base: All MCS main respondents living in England only. Weighted percentages.

ethnic groups in relation to their access to maternity and child health services (D'Souza et al, 2002). Variations in fluency in English derive from the varied origins and migration histories of different ethnic groups. The majority of MCS mothers, originating in non-UK countries where English is not the main language, lived in households where English was spoken to some extent. The proportions of mothers living in households in which English and another language were both spoken ranged from nearly half (49%) among Black African mothers to over two thirds (69%) among Pakistani mothers. Speaking English was very high among Black Caribbean and mixed ethnic groups. Virtually all the Caribbean mothers spoke English only but only 37% of Black African, 20% of Indian, 10% of Pakistani and less than 1% of Bangladeshi families did so. At the other end of the spectrum, around a quarter of Pakistani mothers and a third of Bangladeshi mothers were in households where there was no English spoken at all (Table A2.1 row 8). Further examination of these groups shows that the vast majority of these mothers were born outside the UK.

These findings are broadly in line with other surveys of mothers at a similar life cycle stage. The Infant Feeding Survey of Asian families found that English was the main language spoken at home for 20% of Indian mothers, but only for 3% of Bangladeshi and 9% of Pakistani mothers. Wide differences in mothers' understanding of English were also evident in the Infant Feeding Survey between Indian mothers, on the one hand, and Bangladeshi and Pakistani mothers on the other: only 2% of Indian mothers in that survey did not understand English at all, compared to 9% of Pakistani and 16% of Bangladeshi mothers (Thomas and Avery, 1997, p 142).

Indian and Black African mothers in the MCS were examples where there appeared to be an association between fluency in English and the area in which they lived. Both Indian and Black African mothers who lived in households where no English was spoken at all were more likely to be in wards with high minority ethnic populations or in other disadvantaged wards. In comparison, non-English speaking Pakistanis were largely distributed across all the ward types, and Bangladeshis who were not fluent in English were more likely to live in other disadvantaged areas than in areas of high minority ethnic density.

Parental health

Considerable changes have been taking place in individuals' health and this is the context against which we can view the health of Millennium parents. Earlier cohorts have been involved in mapping some of these health changes (Ferri et al, 2003). People who were born in 1946 and their parents faced a far higher risk of dying from infectious diseases than people born in 1958 and 1970. In 1946, antibiotics were rare, whereas nowadays they are part of everyday life.

Some diseases have become more prevalent over time. For example, the number of people who said they had asthma when they were in their 30s increased from 3% of men and women born in 1946 to 8% of men and 10% of women born in 1958. This rose again to 13% of men and 14% of women born in 1970. Among parents of Millennium babies, 18% of mothers and 12% of fathers suffered from asthma.[11]

Depression and anxiety have also increased across successive cohorts. Twenty per cent of women born in 1970 said they suffered from depression or anxiety when they were in their 30s, compared to only 12% of women born in 1958. The proportion of men in their 30s saying they had depression or anxiety doubled to 14% of those born in 1970 compared to 7% of those born in 1958. Among Millennium Cohort parents, 13% of mothers could be classified as depressed.[12] Using more subjective indicators of depression raises these figures substantially (Dex and Joshi, 2004b). In Chapter 6, maternal distress was found to be related to delayed development of the child.

The health of the parents of the Millennium Cohort was investigated in the study for a number of reasons. The main reason is that the health of parents forms part of the child's closest environment from the day they are born, if not before. It takes quite a lot of physical resilience to conceive a pregnancy, follow it successfully to term and produce a healthy baby. According to some estimates, as many as 30% of conceptions result in natural miscarriage. Women of reproductive age, in particular, are relatively young and at an age when the most common serious diseases are extremely rare. However, although few parents of these new century children had serious long-term diseases, a rather large number reported to the survey that they felt their health was generally not good, or even poor. These low levels of general health and vitality may have implications for the children that are as important as the inheritance of serious disease. Another reason to record parents' health is that, in the future, investigators may wish to undertake studies of the genetics of diseases that afflict the children themselves. For example, there is some indication that asthma, and problems with being overweight, may to some extent find their origins in genetic tendencies passed from parent to child.

Height and weight of parents

Height and weight are part of a child's genetic endowment from their parents. Weight is more affected by environment than height and can change right across the whole of the life course, long after growth has stopped. Weight, obesity and the associated health implications are now topics of public concern. These measures are also the most objective biological features relevant to health. However, in the MCS data, parents reported these measures themselves and no attempt was made by interviewers to verify their answers.

The earlier cohort studies show how many more people are unhealthily overweight than they used to be. Twelve per cent of men and 11% of women born in 1970 were obese by the time they reached their 20s. Only 5% of men and 7% of women born in 1946 were vastly overweight at the same age (Ferri et al, 2003). However, obesity increased among people born in 1946 as they got older and may follow a similar trend in the later cohorts. At the time of the first interview (2001) of the Millennium Cohort parents, 43.9% of fathers were overweight and a further 13.3% were obese. Among Millennium Cohort mothers before pregnancy, 19.7% were overweight and a further 8.9% were obese.

There are many ways in which the health of the MCS babies' parents is related to their own social position and origins. One of the most basic aspects of the biological resources available to adults is reflected in their height. Height is partly genetically determined. However, in the past 100 years, the average height of the British population, to take one example, has increased by around 3.5cm. Earlier cohorts map this increase. For men in their 30s, their average height was 175cm if they were born in 1946, 177cm if born in 1958 and 179cm if born in 1970. For women in their 30s, the average height if born in 1946 was 162cm, 163cm if born in 1958 and 164cm if born in 1970. Such a change could not be due to genetic factors – it is far too rapid. This means that height in adulthood is also a reflection of processes taking place during the periods of childhood and adolescence when growth can take place (Baxter Jones et al, 1999). After the age of around 21, the ends of the bones in the human body seal, and at that moment final adult height is fixed. However, we know that both nutrition and emotional well-being in childhood and adolescence can influence growth (Skuse et al, 1994; Gunnell et al, 1996; Montgomery et al,

1997; Smith et al, 2000), and for this reason height may be regarded as a 'record' of earlier life (Gunnell et al, 1999). Differences in height between ethnic groups, therefore, may be in part due to genetic differences, but also reflect the different experiences of migration, and the discrimination and disadvantage that may go along with these experiences.

Mothers' height

The height of the cohort mothers did, as expected, vary according to their own ethnic group. The tallest mothers were those of Black African and Black Caribbean origin, closely followed by mothers of mixed ethnic identity, and then white mothers. Bangladeshi mothers were the shortest, and in this respect Bangladeshi mothers and fathers resembled each other. Height differences by UK country were again rather small, English mothers once again being the tallest and Northern Irish the shortest. Social class is also related to height of mothers. There was a difference in height of around 2.5cm between mothers whose own occupations involved the least advantaged versus the most advantaged employment conditions.

Mothers' weight

Mothers' weight varied with social class, in a different way from height. Mothers in lower supervisory and technical occupations are around 4kg heavier on average than those in higher professional and management jobs, and 3kg heavier than those in routine occupations.

Fathers' height

The tallest fathers were white men; Black (Caribbean and other) were the next tallest followed by fathers of mixed origin; Bangladeshi fathers were the shortest. Comparisons by country showed that fathers in Northern Ireland were the shortest and those in England the tallest, although the differences were rather small. What we can see is a difference of some 3cm, or about 1.5 inches, between the average height of fathers in jobs with the least favourable and those with the most favourable employment conditions. Fathers in the most advantageous employment conditions (NS-SEC 1) were on average some 2.5cm taller than those in the most routine occupations (NS-SEC 7).

Fathers' weight

Fathers' weight was rather lower in NS–SEC 6 and 7, the routine and semi-routine occupations, than among the self employed or fathers with contracts of employment in higher or lower professional and managerial work (NS–SEC 1 and 2).

Body mass index

Some researchers have put forward the idea that one reason why some populations grow overweight is that their height is 'fixed' in young adulthood, so that, if the availability of food improves greatly later in life, some people become too heavy for their height (Jackson et al, 1996; Law, 1996; Eriksson et al, 1999). If children and young people always had access to plenty of food during the period of life when they were growing, they would have been taller and therefore more able to 'carry' greater weight. Indeed, when we examine the risk of being overweight in Millennium mothers, we can see that the reason why certain groups are 'fatter' is not so much that they weigh more, but that they weigh more for their height. This relationship is captured most commonly in the measure called 'body mass index' (BMI). The BMI is the ratio of a person's kilogram weight to their metres of height squared.

Mothers in the least advantageous employment conditions, the routine socioeconomic category, weighed somewhat more (around 3.5kg) than those in the most privileged circumstances with higher level management or professional socioeconomic occupations. However, the average BMI of mothers in routine occupations was lower than that of those with lower professional or managerial work.

BMI can also be grouped into categories. Mothers in the social classes with least advantaged employment conditions were considerably more likely to be underweight, and to be seriously overweight. Mothers in semi-routine and routine occupations, for example, had approximately the same risk of being seriously overweight as they did of being underweight.

Mothers from Bangladeshi, Pakistani and Indian ethnic origins were most likely to be underweight (Table 2.2). Mothers from Black African and white ethnic groups were least likely to be underweight. Mothers of Indian and other ethnic origin were mostly likely to fall within the normal range of BMI. Mothers of Black Caribbean or Black African origin had the highest rates of obesity and severe obesity.

It is well known that BMI in men is not related to socioeconomic

Table 2.2 Mother's weight category by mother's ethnic group

Mothers' ethnic origin	Mothers' weight category						
	Less than 18.5 - underweight	18.5 to 25 - normal	Over 25-30 - overweight	Over 30-35 - obese	Over 35 - morbidly obese	Total %	Unweighted sample size
White	3.5	58.7	24.9	9.6	3.4	100	14552
Mixed	3.8	57.7	25.6	8.3	4.5	100	169
Indian	5.8	62.5	23.4	7.1	1.3	100	421
Pakistani	6.1	50.7	29.0	10.4	3.8	100	730
Bangladeshi	9.1	51.2	30.6	8.3	0.8	100	263
Black Caribbean	4.5	41.9	30.2	15.6	7.8	100	234
Black African	2.6	35.9	36.9	17.9	6.7	100	269
Other (Chinese, other Asian)	6.2	63.0	19.9	7.2	3.6	100	328
All UK	3.7	58.1	25.1	9.6	3.5	100	16966

Base: All UK MCS mothers who had provided information on their present height and weight when the cohort child was 9-10 months old. Weighted percentages.

Figure 2.10: Mothers and fathers whose BMI indicates they are overweight* according to their socioeconomic status

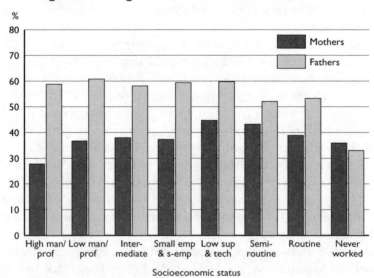

Socioeconomic status

Base: All UK MCS mothers and fathers when cohort baby was 9-10 months old.
Weighted percentages.
BMI relationship by mothers' NS-SEC indicated an F statistic of 7.5749 and $p = 0.000$
rejecting the null hypothesis that mothers' BMI will be the same for each NS-SEC category.
BMI relationship by fathers' NS-SEC indicated an F statistic of 6.0994 and $p = 0.000$, rejecting
the null hypothesis that fathers' BMI will be the same for each NS-SEC category.
* Overweight category is based on BMI > 25 which includes the obese and morbidly obese categories.

group in a linear manner and Millennium Cohort fathers were no exception in this respect. Fathers in intermediate socioeconomic groups and the lower supervisor and technical category had, on average, higher weight-for-height than men in either higher managerial or semi-routine and routine socioeconomic groups. There were large differences in the BMI of fathers in the most and least advantaged socioeconomic classes (Figure 2.10).

Smoking

Smoking is important because it directly affects the health of parents and their children. The relationship of smoking and birthweight of the baby is explored in Chapter 5. Here we can note that over 70% of mothers and mother figures were not smoking at the time of the interview when their cohort baby was approximately 9 months old. Most of these mothers (52%) had never smoked, and 20% were ex-smokers. Approximately the same proportions of fathers as mothers reported they had never smoked (52%), although mothers were more likely than fathers (12.5%) to have given up smoking. Where they did smoke, mothers were likely to smoke less than fathers, especially less likely to be smoking 15 or more cigarettes per day (11.1% of fathers but only 5.3% of mothers). There were large differences in smoking behaviour by socioeconomic classification. Only 8% of mothers and under 18% of fathers classified in the higher professional or managerial socioeconomic category were smoking at the time of interview. This contrasts with approximately half of all those classified in semi-routine or routine socioeconomic categories, traditionally thought of as the least secure and least autonomous employment conditions. The percentages of those who had smoked but who had given up also displayed striking variation by socioeconomic classification with 44.3% of those in higher managerial or professional occupations having given up smoking compared with 15-16% of those classified as semi-routine or routine.

Parents are nowadays warned of the dangers of smoking in the same room as babies and young children. Figure 2.11 shows that, as with smoking overall, there are large social class differences in the proportion of mothers who reported that somebody did smoke in the same room as the Millennium baby.

There is a very strong relationship of social class to the likelihood that someone smokes in the baby's room, varying from around 2% of those in higher managerial or professional occupations to 24% of those in the routine occupations and 22% of those who have never

Figure 2.11: Percentage of mothers who smoked in baby's room by their socioeconomic status

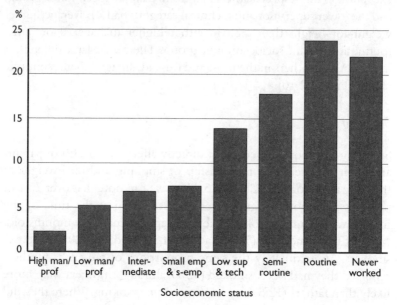

Base: All UK MCS mothers when the cohort baby was 9-10 months old. Weighted percentages.

worked. These sorts of relationships were also evident in earlier cohorts. Studies of the 1970 cohort of men found that better-educated people were less likely to smoke; 47% of men born in 1970 who had no qualifications were smokers compared to just 20% of men who had a university or similar qualification (Ferri et al, 2003). Studies of people born in 1958 showed that children of women who smoked during pregnancy were at greater risk of becoming obese and of developing type 2 diabetes.

Approximately one quarter of mothers of mixed ethic origin and one fifth of white and Black Caribbean mothers smoked during pregnancy in comparison with less than 4% of mothers of one of the Asian minority ethnic groups. These patterns are broadly in line with those reported in other recent national surveys of smoking in pregnancy (Health Education Authority, 1999). Most mothers who smoked in pregnancy smoked relatively few cigarettes. (See Chapter 5 for further details about the association of maternal smoking and child health, and Chapter 6 for an investigation of its effect among other factors on delays in the child's development milestones.)

Alcohol consumption

The earlier 1958 and 1970 cohort studies have charted societal changes in women's and men's consumption of alcohol (Ferri et al, 2003). The number of women who drink alcohol in Britain nearly doubled in the last decade of the 20th century. The women who are drinking most are those in top jobs with the highest qualifications. Women are drinking more as they get older. Men, on the other hand, have been found to be drinking less as they get older. Against this background of increasing alcohol consumption of women, it is interesting to see how parents of young children were behaving.

There is some debate over the relationship of alcohol consumption to health. Whereas some experts judge that moderate consumption may be beneficial to health, not all agree. And it is certain that excessive alcohol consumption in the parents will adversely affect the health and development of their children. As we can see, relatively few of the mothers in the most advantaged social classes were non-drinkers (Figure 2.12). Drinking every day or almost every day was far more common for mothers in NS-SEC 1 occupations than in any other social group. Very few mothers in semi-routine or routine occupations drank alcohol five to seven times per week.

Figure 2.12: Mothers' current alcohol consumption by socioeconomic status

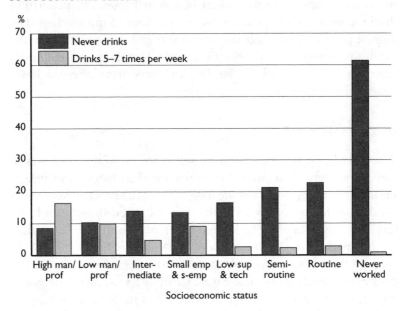

Base: All UK MCS mothers when the cohort baby was 9-10 months old. Weighted percentages.

Figure 2.13: Fathers' current alcohol consumption by socioeconomic status

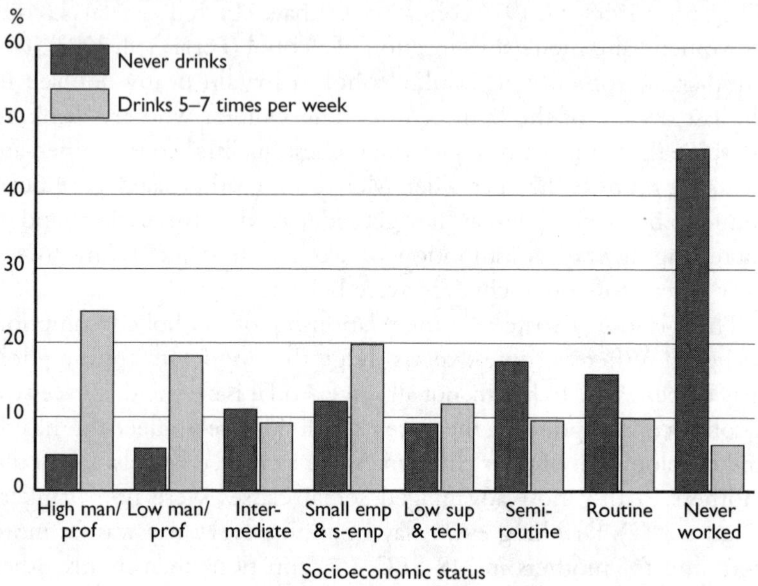

Base: All UK MCS fathers interviewed when cohort baby was 9-10 months old. Weighted percentages.

Figure 2.13 shows the relationship of socioeconomic circumstances to drinking patterns in the fathers of cohort babies. The patterns of drinking were rather similar in fathers to those of the mothers. The highest proportion of daily drinkers was found among fathers in the most advantaged socioeconomic groups. However, self-employed fathers were more likely to be daily drinkers than fathers in lower managerial or intermediate occupations.

Longstanding illness

There is a long tradition of using self-reported health measures in surveys. Clearly, these are more subjective than height and weight measures, but they do give some indication of the prevalence of major conditions among parents. Parents who indicated they had a long-term illness were asked what it was. These replies were coded according to the International Classification of Diseases (WHO, 1992b). In addition, parents were asked whether they had ever suffered from certain diseases indicated on a list. There were relatively few Millennium parents who said they had 'ever suffered' from any of the significant illnesses on the list, and of these the great majority did not tell the interviewer that they were still experiencing this condition as a 'longstanding health problem' at the time of the interview.

Serious conditions were rare in the parents of Millennium babies. However, having some form of long-term illness that is severe enough to limit activities was not uncommon. Approximately 21% of mothers reported some kind of long-term health problem and of these 43% reported that the illness limited them in some way. The most commonly cited diagnoses were asthma (4.4% of mothers), back pain (2.9%) and depression (1.6%). However, it was not possible to code 9% of the answers due to insufficient information. Many more respondents reported that they had at some time suffered from these illnesses.

Just under 16% of fathers reported a long-term illness of which 41% limited their activity to some extent. The most frequently reported illnesses were again asthma (3.2% of fathers) and back pain (2.2%). Depression was lower among fathers (0.4%) and unclassified illnesses were also lower (7.6%). For both mothers and fathers, the prevalence of limiting longstanding illness was clearly related to socioeconomic classification whereas longstanding illnesses that were not limiting activities was not clearly related to socioeconomic classification.

We might expect that the prevalence of long-term illness might vary by ethnic origin and age of parents. These expectations were upheld, especially among fathers. After using a statistical model to take account of age differences between mothers of different ethnicity, differences in long-term illness between ethnic groups were relatively small. Compared with white mothers, mothers who were of mixed or Indian origin were 1.25 times as likely to have a long-term illness; Pakistani and Bangladeshi were 1.6 times as likely as white mothers to have a long-term illness, and other mothers had approximately the same chance as white mothers of having a long-term illness. Compared with white fathers, Black fathers were over 2.5 times as likely and Indian fathers were over twice as likely to have a long-term illness.

General self-rated health

Perhaps the most useful measure of health and vitality when considering the health of parents as a factor in children's development is how the adults themselves feel. There is not total agreement among researchers as to the validity of this kind of measure, as it appears rather a vague question and does not refer to specific conditions. However, as we have seen, parents are on the whole at a healthy time of life, and few have specific serious conditions. Research has also shown that a question on how people feel generally about their health is a good predictor of more serious health problems in the future.

Approximately 15% of mothers and fathers reported 'fair' or 'poor' self-rated health. This is in fact a lower proportion than the 20-21% reporting that they had a longstanding illness. In fact, many parents' long-term illnesses, as we have seen, were not regarded by them as placing limitations on their daily activities, and, when this was the case, were quite likely to regard their health at least as 'good', despite the presence of the long-term condition.

Very few mothers with no long-term illness regarded their health as 'poor'. Of those who did have a long-term condition but not one they regarded as limiting their daily activities, under 4% reported 'poor' health. This is in contrast to over 17% who had a limiting long-term illness. Over 70% of mothers with non-limiting longstanding illness regarded their health as excellent or good.

The government's objectives in respect of the reduction in health inequalities in the early 21st century have been focusing on differences between more or less affluent residential areas (DH, 1998). As we consider that self-rated health is an important factor in the child's environment, parents' general health may be regarded as part of the explanation for area differences in children's health and development. In order to equalise the life chances of children, therefore, a better understanding of parental health inequality will be helpful. In seeking to examine how self-rated health is related to other characteristics of mothers and fathers and their areas of residence, and subsequently to their children, a series of multivariate analyses were carried out to explain mothers and fathers reporting themselves as having poor health. We sought to examine how far differences in health between more or less disadvantaged areas (after allowing for the different ages at which people have children in different types of area) can be understood in terms of recognised risk factors, both material risk factors (socioeconomic classification, household income and ethnic identity) and, separately, behavioural risk factors (smoking, weight and alcohol consumption).

As expected, before controlling for other things, mothers and fathers living in disadvantaged areas were more likely to report fair or poor health. Mothers of all minority ethnic identities were more likely to have less good health than white women. Being in a less advantaged socioeconomic group and having a lower household income were also associated with a higher risk of ill health (Table 2.3). After adding in controls, individuals' own ethnic identity, socioeconomic group and income explained quite a lot of the excess ill health in the other

Table 2.3: Relationships of material risk factors on mothers' and fathers' self-rated poor health

Variable	Mothers		Fathers	
	Adjusted for age only	Model	Adjusted for age only	Model
Area type				
Non-disadvantaged	I	I	I	I
Minority ethnic	1.72*	0.99	1.56*	0.89
Other disadvantaged	1.51*	1.15*	1.43*	1.05
Ethnic group				
White	I	I	I	I
Mixed	1.29	1.21	1.53	1.13
Indian	1.49*	1.53**	1.12	1.09
Pakistani & Bangladeshi	1.74*	1.51**	1.676*	1.15
Black	1.83*	1.48**	0.91	0.72*
Other	1.66*	1.91**	1.32	0.93
NS-SEC				
High professional/managerial	I	I	I	I
Low professional/managerial	1.18	0.96	1.27*	1.08
Intermediate	1.36*	1.00	1.58*	1.12
Self-employed	1.44	1.02	2.02*	1.41**
Low supervisory & technical	2.31*	1.66**	2.01*	1.33**
Semi routine	2.48*	1.45**	2.90*	1.66**
Routine	2.70*	1.51**	2.96*	1.58**
Annual household income				
£0-£3100	I	I	I	I
£3100-£10400	1.01	0.92	1.75*	1.98**
£10400-£20800	0.72	0.78	0.89	1.04
£20800-£31200	0.42*	0.52**	0.54*	0.72
£31200-£52000	0.29*	0.41**	0.45*	0.64
£52000+	0.30*	0.42**	0.35*	0.56*
Unweighted N		15118		11668

Base: All UK MCS mothers/fathers when cohort baby was 9-10 months old.

Note: Model columns report unweighted results as both country and ward dummies were used in regressions (country dummies not reported in table). Standard errors were adjusted for clustered sampling. Fathers' household income is based on reported couple income only. Mothers' household income reports a combined lone income and couple income value.

* indicates significant at p = 0.05 level and ** indicates significant at p = 0.01 level.

disadvantaged areas, and all of the differences between non-disadvantaged areas and areas of high minority ethnic population. The contributions of ethnic identity, socioeconomic circumstances and household income to explaining poor health remained significant independently of each other. The analysis indicated that differences in health between mothers living in these different types of local area could be reduced by improving income and employment conditions in areas of high minority ethnic population and other disadvantaged areas. However, women of minority ethnic identity experienced poorer health regardless of the area they lived in, their socioeconomic circumstances or their household income level.

There was also a high importance of some health behaviours for explaining mothers' general health. Notably, mothers' smoking, alcohol consumption and BMI scores were all significantly correlated with their general self-rated health (Table 2.4). Mothers smoking more than 15 cigarettes per day had nearly three times the risk of only fair or poor general health; those with a very high BMI of over 35 had almost twice the risk to their general health. Being underweight was also a health risk – almost double the risk compared with those of normal weight and 30% more than those who were moderately

Table 2.4: Relationships of behaviour risk factors on mothers' and fathers' self-rated poor health

Variable	Mothers		Fathers	
	Adjusted for age only	Model	Adjusted for age only	Model
Area type				
Non-disadvantaged	1	1	1	1
Minority ethnic	1.72*	1.39**	1.47*	1.17
Other disadvantaged	1.51*	1.28**	1.36*	1.24**
Smoking history				
Never smoked	1	1	1	1
Ex smoker	1.17*	1.26	1.12	1.76
<5/day	1.44*	1.46**	1.95*	1.75**
5-10/day	1.89*	1.80**	2.38*	2.11**
11-15/day	2.48*	2.16**	2.72*	2.21**
15+	3.15*	2.86**	4.14*	3.36**
Alcohol				
Every day	1	1	1	1
5-6x/week	0.87	0.84	0.68*	0.75*
3-4x/week	0.9	0.90	0.79*	0.77*
1-2x/week	1.06	0.94	0.71*	0.66**
1-2x/month	1.47*	1.19	1.11	0.96
<1x/month	1.73*	1.43*	1.44*	1.22
Never	2.23*	1.86**	1.51*	1.33*
BMI				
<18.5 underweight	1	1	1	1
18.5-25 normal	0.54*	0.67**	0.32*	0.43**
26-30 overweight	0.72*	0.81*	0.32*	0.48**
31-35 obese	1.07	1.26*	0.54*	0.86
>35 morbidly obese	1.68*	1.93**	0.9	1.32
Unweighted N		16573		11939

Base: All UK MCS mothers/fathers when cohort baby was 9-10 months old.

Note: Model columns report unweighted results as both country and ward dummies were used in regressions (country dummies not reported in table). Standard errors were adjusted for clustered sampling.

* indicates significant at p = 0.05 level and ** indicates significant at p = 0.01 level.

overweight. Very low alcohol consumption also appeared to be associated with less good general health. However, even after including all these factors, the additional risk of poorer general health to mothers living in areas of high minority ethnic population and other disadvantaged areas, while slightly reduced, remained significantly higher than that for mothers living in non-disadvantaged areas. Changing these particular health behaviours would reduce health disadvantage in mothers in the less advantaged areas to a small extent but not eliminate it.

For fathers, as for mothers, there was a significant additional risk of ill health for individuals living in disadvantaged areas after controlling for other things, but not for those living in areas of high minority ethnic populations and only in the case of risk behaviours (Table 2.4). There were also similarly higher risks of poorer health in fathers in less advantaged socioeconomic categories, and with low household income. There were in fact few statistically significant differences according to ethnic identity; fathers of Pakistani or Bangladeshi identity were significantly more likely to suffer poor health than white fathers. Once ethnic identity, socioeconomic classification and household income were taken into account, there was no significant difference in health between fathers living in other disadvantaged areas and those living in non-disadvantaged areas or areas of high minority ethnic population.

Smoking was even more strongly associated with general health in fathers than it was in mothers. There was also a similar health advantage in moderate drinking. Being underweight or morbidly obese were also a disadvantage for fathers' health. Being a non-smoker, moderate drinking and body mass at or near to the normal level were independently associated with lower health risk. These behavioural factors more or less completely accounted for the tendency of fathers living in either areas of high minority ethnic population or other disadvantaged areas to experience poorer health than those living in non-disadvantaged areas.

Housing

Housing tenure

Rates of home ownership were fairly similar across the four UK countries. Approximately two thirds of families owned their housing either outright or through a mortgage. There were greater variations by country in the extent to which families were renting from a Housing

Association, privately or from local authorities. Ownership rates were highest in non-disadvantaged wards and lowest in wards high in minority ethnic populations. Country differences became more pronounced after controlling for type of ward.

The extent of owner occupation varied across the ethnic identity groups (Figure 2.14, in relation to England only). It was highest among Indian and white families where two thirds of families owned their accommodation (outright or by mortgage). Owning the housing was lowest among Black African, Black Caribbean and Bangladeshi families. Other research evidence indicates that there is a relatively high level of owner occupied housing among Pakistani families, but it is of poor quality housing (Chahal, 2000). Black families, and particularly Africans, were the most likely to live in housing that was rented from the local authority or from a Housing Association. In the case of Black Caribbean mothers, they were less likely to be living in local authority housing than in Housing Association owned homes, but the pattern was reversed for Black African families. More families in the Asian origin groups compared to other groups were likely to live with their parents or rent free.

Figure 2.14: Mothers' housing tenure

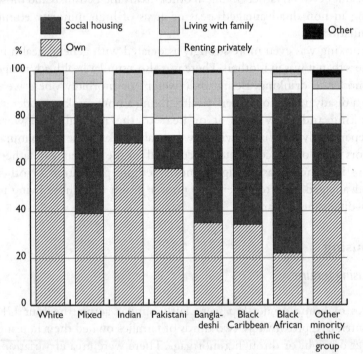

Base: All MCS mothers in England when cohort child was 9-10 months old. Weighted percentages.

Qualitative evidence from local studies has shown that it is not uncommon among some Bangladeshi and Pakistani families to have shared living arrangements with siblings. There is also a pattern of living rent free in sibling owned housing (Jayaweera, 2003). The MCS families have small percentages who were living with their extended family, and this arrangement was practised more commonly by Pakistani, Bangladeshi and Indian families.

Housing conditions

One quarter of families lived in accommodation with four rooms or fewer. Approximately one third had five rooms.[13] A further fifth had six rooms and a fifth had more than six rooms. There were large variations in house size by country with Scotland having the highest proportion with only four or fewer rooms in their accommodation. Northern Ireland families had the largest proportion with seven or more rooms. Country differences remained after also controlling for the type of ward.

Across the UK, 86.5% of main respondents said they had access to a garden for their sole use and a further 3.6% had a shared garden. Access to a garden was highest in Wales and lowest in England and Scotland.

Central heating was also widespread. Over 90% of the UK sample had central heating, with small variations by country but larger variations by type of ward. Central heating was least evident in the housing of wards with high minority ethnic populations where 16.6% did not have central heating.

Damp or condensation was reported in 13.1% of UK families' housing, but a much lower proportion in Northern Ireland, despite their higher rainfall. Housing stock in advantaged wards reported the lowest levels of damp or condensation (10.9% of families); wards high in minority ethnic populations reported the highest levels of damp or condensation (20.0% of families). Country differences became more pronounced after controlling for type of ward.

There was considerable variation in experiences of damp between families from different ethnic identities. Indian mothers (7.6%), followed by white mothers (13%), had the lowest rates of damp in their housing. Pakistani mothers (16%) and 'other' ethnic groups (17%) suffered from slightly more damp in their housing with much larger percentages of mixed (25%), Bangladeshi (25%), Black Caribbean (23%) and Black African (23%) families reporting that there was damp in their homes.

These differences may be related to differences in housing tenure between groups.

Local area

Dissatisfaction with their neighbourhood was higher among Black Caribbean mothers and mothers of mixed ethnic identity than among mothers identifying themselves with other ethnic groups (Figure 2.15). Mothers of white or mixed ethnic identity who were dissatisfied with their area were more likely to live in wards with high minority ethnic populations. Black Caribbean mothers who were dissatisfied tended to live in other disadvantaged areas rather than in wards with high minority ethnic populations.

Women who became mothers under the age of 19 were twice as likely as the average to be dissatisfied with their area.

Neighbourhood infrastructure

Neighbourhoods can be an important feature of the child's social and physical context. As well as varying in housing stock, social class profiles, family structure and extent of poverty, they are often the routes through

Figure 2.15: Dissatisfaction with area: mothers (in England) by ethnic identity and area type

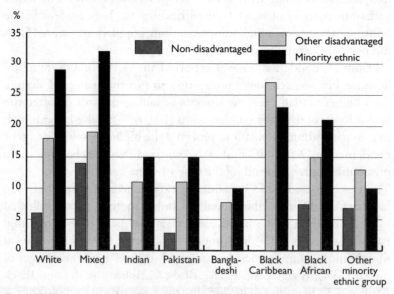

Base: All MCS natural mothers in England when cohort baby was 9-10 months old.
Unweighted percentages.

which local government is organised and, in particular, public services are provided. Non-disadvantaged wards, viewed through the eyes of these parents, tended to have lower levels of noisy neighbours, vandalism, rubbish, racist insults and pollution compared to wards with high minority ethnic population and other disadvantaged wards (Table 2.5). However, public transport was mostly thought to be worse in non-disadvantaged and better in other disadvantaged areas. The level of car ownership across ward areas was clearly inversely related to the perceptions about the adequacy of public transport.

We examined two potential components of the social capital of neighbourhoods in which these families live: the time spent at current addresses, and families' feelings of satisfaction with the area. 'Time at current address' is one characteristic of families that could be an indicator of residential stability for them and, in terms of its area mean, for the area they live in (albeit one that is based only on families with young children). In turn, we might hypothesise that more stable areas, with higher mean durations of time at current address, have a greater stock of social capital that will benefit the children and families growing up in them – for example, better relationships, greater commitment to and pride in the area. We might also suppose that residential stability is associated with the level of poverty in an area: poorer areas with lower rates of owner occupation could be less stable, although professional workers who are well off are also known to be highly mobile. Similarly, we might expect levels of neighbourhood satisfaction to be linked to the amount of poverty in the area. Children growing up in neighbourhoods perceived to be satisfactory on average are likely to have some advantages over their peers growing up in neighbourhoods that are seen as less desirable places to bring up children in.

Our interest here is to try to break down how much of the difference between the residential stability and satisfaction with the area of MCS families is due to their individual characteristics and how much can be explained by their location in particular areas, the latter known as 'neighbourhood influences'. A recurring difficulty in analyses of neighbourhood influences is that what appear as differences between areas can in fact reflect differences in the characteristics of the individuals living in those areas – composition effects. So, for example, we find that levels of satisfaction with the neighbourhood vary across areas, but we also know that we are measuring individuals' perceptions of their neighbourhood and these perceptions can vary according to the other characteristics of those individuals. Within an area, cohort parents with an older child as well as the cohort baby might report lower levels of satisfaction because play facilities for older children are

Table 2.5: Perceptions of neighbourhoods by country and type of ward

Country by type of ward	Per cent who said this was fairly or very common in their neighbourhood								Maximum unweighted sample size for both categories (N)
	Noisy neighbours	Rubbish and litter	Vandalism	Racist insults	Poor public transport	Easy access to food shops*	Pollution		
England									
Non-disadvantaged	10.2	18.7	12.0	2.0	29.8	14.8	16.5		4610
Other disadvantaged	23.8	44.7	33.8	10.1	24.0	13.6	30.4		4511
Minority ethnic	24.4	50.7	27.6	12.6	23.7	9.7	42.9		2371
Wales									
Non-disadvantaged	9.7	16.4	8.9	1.1	28.1	17.1	15.6		831
Other disadvantaged	21.0	37.1	27.7	4.6	29.1	16.7	18.2		1927
Scotland									
Non-disadvantaged	7.7	14.5	10.7	1.4	32.5	18.5	8.8		1142
Other disadvantaged	20.9	35.1	29.5	6.3	21.0	13.4	21.1		1187
Northern Ireland									
Non-disadvantaged	4.3	8.2	5.4	0.7	39.9	23.5	7.2		720
Other disadvantaged	12.7	27.6	23.0	5.1	34.3	20.3	16.7		1192
Total unweighted sample size									18491

Base: All UK MCS main respondents when cohort child was 9-10 months old. Unweighted percentages.

Figures do not add to 100% as only describes those who indicated very common or fairly common responses.

* Figures in this column (easy access to food shops) relate to those who indicated not very common or not at all common responses.

vandalised. This might not influence the perceptions of a parent with just one very young child. Consequently, when we seek to understand differences between areas, we also need to establish whether these differences can be explained by the characteristics of the families living in those areas. The method of disentangling these separate effects is through statistical models known as multilevel models (see Plewis, 2003, for a brief introduction).

Time at current address

'Time at current address' was obtained simply by subtracting the month the main respondent moved into their current address from the month at interview. The distribution is very skewed toward short durations. A substantial proportion (13%) of main respondents in the sample had moved to their current address in the previous nine months (since the birth of the cohort child), and a further 16% had moved in the previous 18 months (since conception of the cohort child). On the other hand, over 7% of the main respondents had lived at their current address for at least 10 years and 1.3% for at least 20 years. The UK weighted median time spent at the current address was 35 months, the weighted mean was 48 months.

Compared with main respondents in the non-disadvantaged wards in England, those living in wards with high minority ethnic populations in England and, especially, those living anywhere in Northern Ireland had been at their current addresses somewhat longer on average. Those living in other disadvantaged wards in England and Wales (but not in Scotland) had been at their current address for a little less time. The variability between wards was statistically significant (p < 0.001) but small.[14] Families had spent marginally less time at their current address in poorer wards.[15]

Area satisfaction scores

Main respondents (mainly mothers) gave their views about their local area, defined as an area 'within a mile or 20 minutes' walk from here'. Responses to five specific questions – about noisy neighbours, rubbish and litter, vandalism, racist insults and pollution, each on a four-point scale – were combined to form a neighbourhood satisfaction scale, varying from zero (very dissatisfied) to 15 (entirely satisfied).[16] The distribution was moderately skewed to the right, indicating quite a high level of overall satisfaction; the UK weighted median satisfaction score for main respondents was 12. These neighbourhood satisfaction scores followed the same pattern, being higher among families in non-disadvantaged than other disadvantaged wards (Table 2.6).

Satisfaction tended to be lower for families in England, especially in the wards with high minority ethnic populations, and highest in Northern Ireland. The variability in satisfaction between wards was much more substantial than it was for time at current address. The intra-ward satisfaction score correlation was 0.15 (p < 0.001). Moreover, 26% of the intra-ward variance was explained by the Child Poverty Index (CPI) for the area. Mean satisfaction with the area declined as poverty increased, such that a 10% increase in the CPI led to nearly a fifth of a standard deviation unit decline in satisfaction.

We can also analyse the neighbourhood satisfaction and duration of residence jointly in a bivariate multilevel model in order to estimate the correlations between the two variables at both the ward and individual levels. Individuals' satisfaction with their neighbourhood appeared to be unrelated to how long they had lived at this address. However, at the ward level, there was a substantial correlation (0.63) between mean satisfaction with the area and the mean length of time lived there. In other words, as the mean length of time at the current

Table 2.6: Neighbourhood satisfaction score (mean and standard deviation) by ward and country

	Neighbourhood satisfaction score	
Country by type of ward	Individuals' mean score across those wards	Ward range*
England		
Non-disadvantaged	11.8 (2.6)	9.4-14.3
Other disadvantaged	9.8 (3.4)	6.7-12.4
Minority ethnic	9.2 (3.2)	6.3-10.9
Total	11.0 (3.2)	–
Wales		
Non-disadvantaged	12.2 (2.6)	9.5-14.9
Other disadvantaged	10.7 (3.2)	7.0-14.6
Total	11.6 (3.0)	–
Scotland		
Non-disadvantaged	12.7 (2.5)	9.6-14.8
Other disadvantaged	10.6 (3.4)	6.5-13.7
Total	11.9 (3.1)	–
Northern Ireland		
Non-disadvantaged	13.2 (2.1)	11.6-14.6
Other disadvantaged	11.5 (3.2)	7.9-14.6
Total	12.4 (2.8)	–

Base: All UK MCS main respondents when cohort baby was 9-10 months old. Standard deviation in parentheses.

*Ward range is range of mean individuals' score per ward.

address increased, so did the mean satisfaction with the area, and this relationship held even after allowing for the effects of CPI on both variables. This may signify that cohort parents tended to be more dissatisfied in areas with larger mobility of the local population.

Conclusions

This chapter has reviewed components of Millennium babies' origins at the start of their lives. These components of social capital have encompassed the relationship capital embedded in their parents and wider families; cultural capital embedded in ethnic communities, religion and language acquisition; elements of housing and neighbourhood capital; and the health capital of parents. This review has confirmed that Millennium babies are starting out in life with considerable variations in their social and other capitals, a picture of substantial inequalities and instabilities between families and, by derivation, these cohort babies. Many of the lines of division between advantaged and disadvantaged family circumstances corresponded with neighbourhood boundaries, the areas built into the design of this survey, but not all. There are also many overlaps of advantage and disadvantage with socioeconomic classifications based on occupations. However, minority ethnic status, especially in the case of South Asian ethnic minorities, crosses these lines of disadvantage.

In terms of circles of influence surrounding the babies, the variations in the immediate family capital of parents' partnership relationships showed that babies are offered different degrees of stability at the start of life. While the vast majority of babies were living with their natural parents, there was more variation in whether the cohort baby was joining their parents' first or a later family. Earlier instability in grandparents' partnerships showed signs of being linked to teenage motherhood in the cohort parents' generation. Further analysis and more data are needed to establish whether a robust intergenerational transmission mechanism of partnership instability can be identified.

South Asian minority ethnic families stood out as having higher rates of marriage and partnership stability across generations. They also had the highest rates of grandparents living with the family. South Asian minority ethnic cultures were offering their babies a start in life high in relationship capital and partnership stability, through their marriage, family values, wider kin relationships and their religions. This is despite such families often living in otherwise disadvantaged areas. Although the country differences were far smaller than differences between ethnic groups, families in Northern Ireland stood out from those in the other UK countries on family stability, religious adherence and residential stability. However, while South Asian minority ethnic families incorporated grandparents into their family relationships to a greater extent than other UK families, the grandparents were also less likely to be alive and probably less likely to be present in the UK. Babies from Pakistani and Bangladeshi families were also growing up with lower levels of host country cultural capital in the form of English language capability, experience of living in the UK, and lower quality housing and neighbourhood environments. Future sweeps of the MCS will allow us to see how far the higher levels of relationship capital in these communities help to compensate children's development for the lower levels of other forms of social and neighbourhood capital they face.

Wider kin relationships were clearly active and important to the majority of Millennium babies. In this sense, the majority of babies were well endowed. Wider family capital was lower because of the absence of some relationships where partnership breakdown had occurred in the grandparent generation, and especially on the cohort father's side of the family and where the breakdown occurred early in the parent's life.

Country differences across the devolved UK administrations tended to be small, especially in comparison with other differences. However, Wales stood out in having slightly higher rates of lone-parent families, shorter times at current address and more mobility in the ward, and the highest access to a garden. Families in Northern Ireland lived in the largest houses and had the best housing conditions, but perceived they had the lowest amounts of public transport. Public transport was perceived as being more abundant in disadvantaged than in non-disadvantaged areas, especially in Scotland, although not in Wales.

Health inequalities between parents were clearly related to well-known socioeconomic status divisions. Being over or underweight, smoking and self-rated health problems were all lower among parents in professional and managerial occupations and higher among parents in routine and semi-routine occupations. Parents of South Asian minority ethnic identity had lower general health capital. These lines of division coincide with disadvantaged and relatively advantaged area boundaries. However, our initial analyses suggested that the concentration of poorer health in poorer neighbourhoods could be accounted for by the characteristics of the families, their ethnic identity, socioeconomic circumstances and household income. By contrast, variations in satisfaction with the neighbourhood are not entirely explained by the characteristics of individual families, which reinforces the case for looking at the wider circles surrounding the cohort child's family.

Table A2.1: Selected demographic characteristics of MCS mothers by mother's ethnic group

Characteristics	Ethnic group								
	White	Mixed	Indian	Pakistani	Bangladeshi	Black Caribbean	Black African	Other ethnic groups*	All UK total
1) % who were teenage mothers at birth of first baby (whether cohort baby or not)	17.5	25.8	5.5	15.2	25.8	23.5	11.3	7.8	17.2
2) % whose cohort baby is first born	43.6	41.4	41.1	30.3	23.7	39.1	29.0	46.8	42.8
3) Median/mean age at birth of cohort baby	29/29.0	27/27.9	28/28.8	26/26.6	25/26.4	30/29.9	31/31.0	30/30.1	29/28.9
4) % who have had 3 or more live births	20.5	27.2	21.2	39.2	46.9	28.2	38.9	17.3	21.5
5) % living as lone parents	13.4	29.3	3.9	7.0	5.0	46.8	38.3	10.2	13.8
6) % in households with 3 or more other siblings of cohort baby	5.9	7.8	2.9	18.4	27.2	11.5	13.5	8.6	6.6
7) % of households with at least one Grandparent	4.7	8.4	30.0	25.4	28.6	11.1	4.3	7.2	6.2
8) % with no English spoken at home	0.5	5.1	11.9	24.8	34.1	0.2	13.8	24.2	2.3
Maximum unweighted sample size (N) **	15545	191	480	893	371	264	379	382	18505

For each row, the null hypotheses that there is no variation by ethnic identity was rejected at p values < 0.001

*A heterogeneous category comprised of mothers of all other ethnicities.

** Unweighted sample of natural mothers before missing cases on particular variables were dropped

Base: All UK MCS mothers when cohort baby was 9-10 months old. Weighted percentages

Table A2.2: Parents' ages by country when cohort child is first-born or later child

| | Country (%) | | | | | | | | All UK total (%) | |
| | England | | Wales | | Scotland | | N Ireland | | | |
Age at interview (years)	First child	All parents	First child	All parents	First child	All parents	First child	All parents	First child	All parents
Mothers'										
14 to 19	9.6	4.5	15.0	7.0	11.0	5.4	10.5	4.5	10.1	4.8
20 to 29	47.2	40.4	51.3	43.5	45.7	39.0	55.6	40.9	47.6	40.5
30 to 39	41.4	51.5	32.2	46.3	41.7	51.3	32.0	51.0	40.6	51.2
40 +	1.7	3.5	1.5	3.1	1.6	4.2	1.8	3.7	1.7	3.5
Total	100.0	100.0	100.0	100.0	100.0	100.0	100.0	100.0	100.0	100.0
Unweighted sample size	4785	11513	1183	2753	1057	2334	752	1922	7777	18525
Fathers'										
16 to 19	1.4	0.7	1.9	1.0	2.3	1.0	2.1	0.8	1.5	0.7
20 to 29	34.4	25.9	38.5	27.6	34.3	26.2	39.7	25.9	34.8	26.1
30 to 39	54.9	60.3	51.3	60.6	55.0	60.2	49.5	59.2	54.6	60.3
40 +	9.3	13.1	8.3	10.9	8.3	12.5	8.8	14.1	9.1	12.9
Total	100.0	100.0	100.0	100.0	100.0	100.0	100.0	100.0	100.0	100.0
Unweighted sample size	3979	9676	857	2169	850	1961	546	1548	6232	15834

Base: All UK MCS mothers/fathers when cohort baby was 9-10 months old. Weighted percentages.

Information provided by main respondents in household grid questions.

Table A2.3: Odds ratios for odds of being a teenage mother

Characteristics	Birth before 19 years old
Cohort mother's experience of parental separation	
None	1.00
Experienced by age 7	2.82***
Experienced between ages 8 and 16	2.27***
Experienced from age 17 onwards	0.92NS
Cohort mother's ethnicity	
White	1.00
Mixed	1.32NS
Indian	0.23***
Pakistani	0.79NS
Bangladeshi	1.12NS
Black Caribbean	1.08NS
Black African	0.58**
Other	0.59*
Cohort mother's religion	
None	1.00
Christian/no denomination	0.58***
Catholic	0.62***
Protestant	0.43***
Hindu/Muslim/Sikh	0.52***
Other religion	0.38***
Country	
England	1.00
Wales	1.23**
Scotland	1.11NS
Northern Ireland	1.18NS
Type of ward	
Non-disadvantaged	1.00
Other disadvantaged	2.56***
Minority ethnic	3.31***
Unweighted sample size	18424

Dependent variable = 1 where MCS mother had a teenage birth by the age of 19, zero otherwise.

Base: All UK MCS mothers when cohort baby was 9-10 months old. $p < 0.001$***, $p < 0.01$**, $p < 0.05$*, NS = Not Significant.

Standard errors corrected for cluster sample design.

Notes

[1] This percentage does not include households which had a part-time resident partner (1.8% of all families) or households where the relationship of the natural mother's partner to the cohort child was only declared as 'other non-relative' rather than, for example, 'step-parents' (0.1% of all families).

[2] 'Uninvolved' is defined as being non-resident in the household and 'never' seeing the cohort child. 'Involved' is defined for absent parents as seeing the cohort child, however infrequently.

[3] Total children here includes biological, half, adoptive, foster and step siblings of the cohort child.

[4] The social origins of the grandparents were not collected in sweep 1 of the MCS survey but will be collected in sweep 2.

[5] In two cases this was an adoptive mother and in one case a foster mother, rather than the natural mother.

[6] The term 'partner' is used throughout this chapter. In all but four cases this was a male partner, mostly the baby's father.

[7] Separation and divorce is generally a long drawn out process and one which can entail forms of conflict within the family home (for instance, increased or prolonged arguments) (Green Paper, 2004; Braun, 2001). The cohort baby's grandparents may also, in the period after the separation, have formed new partnerships. Families change over time with new partners (and their children) entering (and leaving) the relationship. Children who have experienced these types of altering parental status may also experience multiple parental partnership dissolutions (Amato and Sobolewski, 2001).

[8] These were grouped together as one category for the purposes of comparative analysis with the other types of religions.

[9] While economic circumstances may also be influential, we do not have measures of past economic circumstances to control for, and current economic circumstances may be the outcome of this process.

[10] At the time of writing, this linkage was only completed for the England sample. It is intended to complete this exercise for all the countries in this sample.

[11] MCS parents are not strictly a comparable group to earlier birth cohorts in their 30s.

[12] This is based on the 9-point Malaise scale using a cut off of four and above.

[13] The definition of 'room' excluded bathrooms, toilets, halls and garages.

[14] Only 1.5% of the total variance was between ward variance (in other words, the intra-ward correlation was 0.015).

[15] A statistically significant ($p < 0.01$) but small proportion (3.5%) of the between ward variance was explained by the Child Poverty Index.

[16] Responses to two other specific questions – about public transport and easy access to shops – were not included in the scale as they did not correlate with the other five items.

THREE

Socioeconomic origins of parents and child poverty

Jonathan Bradshaw, Emese Mayhew, Shirley Dex, Heather Joshi and Kelly Ward

Probably one of the single most important elements of a child's origins that affect their development and subsequent life chances is the family's economic circumstances. Clearly, these circumstances rest on a number of interlocking characteristics: their economic activity status; the socioeconomic classification of any employment; their qualification levels; the number of resident parents; and their health. These elements combine to identify whether families live in poverty or in plenty. Since 1997, the government has made the reduction of child poverty a central policy target. These Millennium Cohort children are directly in line to be the target for this set of policies. This first sweep gives us a measure of children living in poverty at the start of their lives. Future sweeps will show whether those who start out in poverty continue to live in this state, and to what extent their parents manage to escape poverty. In this chapter, therefore, we review parents' socioeconomic circumstances at nine months in order to see the starting out point for these children.

In Britain, socioeconomic differentials in birth outcomes are wide and appear to be growing. Babies born to families in social classes IV and V have higher infant mortality and morbidity rates, and lower birthweights, than babies born to families in social classes I and II (ONS, 2003). Class differentials in infant mortality, after narrowing up to 1998, have since then been growing (DWP, 2003). Poverty-related health inequalities in early years have been found to affect children's physical and intellectual development in the long term (Gregg et al, 1999; Bradshaw, 2001).

The first sweep of the Millennium Cohort Survey (MCS) offers the opportunity for a new and more up-to-date investigation of the relationship between poverty and childbirth. This chapter sets out to:

- describe an important set of the socioeconomic circumstances of Millennium babies at the start of their lives;
- derive measures of poverty and social exclusion from the range of questions asked in the survey;
- estimate the proportion of babies born to women who were poor during their pregnancy and/or childbirth – including an estimate of those who were born to women receiving Income Support (IS); and
- estimate the role of employment in keeping families out of poverty.

Other associations of living in poverty are considered in Chapter 4.

Children born into economically disadvantaged families are more likely to live in poorer, urban housing conditions with high rates of traffic and air pollution (Acheson, 1998). They are more likely to be affected by food poverty (Lobstein, 1991; Dobson et al, 1994; Dowler and Calvert, 1995), lower rates of breastfeeding (Beresford, 2002) and higher rates of parental smoking (Searle, 2002). Health inequality at birth is partly attributable to the relatively poor health status and living environment of mothers from low-income households. Children born in lower socioeconomic groups also have a higher chance of having parents with self-perceived poor health and acute, chronic illness (Acheson, 1998; Gordon et al, 1999). Groups particularly vulnerable to health disadvantage are lone and teenage mothers and their children (Shouls et al, 1999).

Poverty at birth has both immediate and long-term effects on adults and children. In 2002, babies of fathers in semi-routine occupations had infant mortality rates over two and a half times higher than those of babies whose fathers were in higher professional occupations – rates of 7.5 and 2.7 per thousand, respectively (ONS, 2003).

Poor people consume more tobacco and alcohol (DEFRA, 2002) leading in childbirth to reduced birthweight, premature labour and developmental delays. In the long term, reduced growth in the uterus – attributed among others to poor nutrition and exposure to harmful substances – is associated with increased rates of death from cardiovascular disease in adult life, and higher levels of its major risk factors such as hypertension, raised levels of cholesterol and impaired glucose tolerance (Campbell et al, 1996; Acheson, 1998).

The adverse effects of poverty on child well-being are measurable from a very early age – in fact, from conception onwards – and put children from poor families at a disadvantage in physical, intellectual and emotional development, which follows them into adulthood (Gregg et al, 1999; Bradshaw, 2001). In other words, as government documents have pointed out: 'Today's poverty can translate into tomorrow's poor outcomes' (DWP, 2003a). The first year of life is crucial (Harker and Kendall, 2003).

Plan of this chapter

This chapter first reviews the socioeconomic human capital of parents of Millennium Cohort babies and then considers families' financial resources. The extent of families living in poverty at the start of the cohort child's life is measured and the family characteristics associated with living in poverty are described. Measuring poverty involves discussing how to assess it using income and relative poverty measures available in the data. The chapter also includes an examination of how families feel their financial circumstances changed over the time of having this birth. Finally, we consider the contribution to family resources and relationships of wider kin, in the form of grandparents who are part of babies' social, relationship and financial capitals at the start of their lives.

Socioeconomic classification

The NS-SEC measure of occupational class is a broad measure of the parents' economic welfare. It is based on their present occupation (in the case of both mothers and fathers who have ever worked) or their previous occupation (where mothers and fathers were not employed at the interview but had been employed previously). Those who have never been employed cannot be classified but are given an unclassified status and are included in the distribution. Clearly, those who have never had a job are likely to be less well off in economic terms than those who have a current occupation. Mothers and fathers of cohort children can each be given their own NS-SEC classification, according to their own status and past experience.

It can be seen that the occupational distribution of Pakistani and Bangladeshi mothers is highly skewed towards the lower half of the occupational structure, made up of having never worked or having worked in semi-routine and routine jobs (Figure 3.1). White, Indian and Black Caribbean mothers were the most likely to be in managerial and professional jobs, closely followed by mothers of mixed ethnic identity.

The age profile of mothers varied across NS-SEC categories. Approximately one half of mothers under 18 at the time of birth were in routine and manual occupations, and two-fifths did not state an

Figure 3.1: Mother's NS-SEC by ethnic group

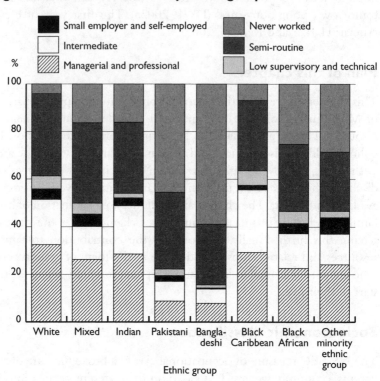

Base: All UK MCS main respondent mothers when cohort baby was 9-10 months old. Weighted percentages.

occupation. In contrast, well over two fifths of mothers in their 30s and 40s were in managerial and professional occupations. For mothers having their first birth in the cohort, the peak age at first birth was just over 30 for mothers in managerial occupations. It was under 20 for mothers in routine and manual occupations, and even younger for mothers who gave no occupation. Clearly, there are higher opportunity costs of career breaks for those in the top NS-SEC categories of managerial and professional occupations. This has been one of the factors encouraging delays in childbirth and family formation among this group in comparison with those in the lower NS-SEC categories.

These patterns are congruent with partners' socioeconomic classifications (Figure 3.2) for those families with a resident father who gave the information. As other evidence also suggests (Modood et al, 1997), more partners in all ethnic groups were generally in managerial, professional or intermediate occupations compared to the mothers. Bangladeshi and Pakistani fathers were more likely to be at the lower end of the occupational structure in semi-routine and routine

Figure 3.2: Father's NS-SEC by ethnic group

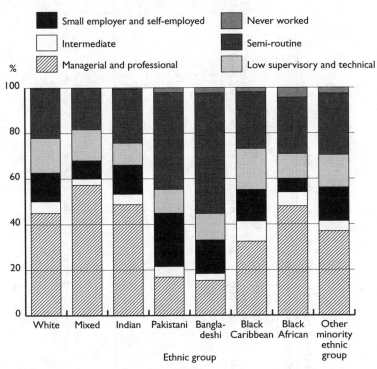

Base: All UK MCS main respondent fathers when cohort baby was 9-10 months old.
Weighted percentages.

jobs, while fathers in the mixed ethnic group were the most likely to be in managerial and professional jobs, followed by Indian, Black African and white fathers.

In comparing couples, there is, not unexpectedly, an association between the socioeconomic classification of mothers and partners (Table 3.1). It is highest among managerial and professional groups where 67.1% of couple mothers with this classification also had partners with the same classification. Mothers who were small employers or self employed had partners who had this classification in 28.9% of cases. Among mothers who were in or had been in semi-routine or routine occupations, 38.3% of their partners had the same classification.

Education capital is also important to families. It is part of individuals' own human capital, but it is also a component of their social capital (Figure 3.3) and important for obtaining jobs in the labour market, as a contributor to household income, and for access to jobs and longer-term job security. Fathers had slightly higher levels of qualifications than mothers: 38% of fathers and 33% of mothers had qualifications

Table 3.1: Socioeconomic classifications of mothers and their resident partners compared

Resident partner's NS-SEC	Cohort mother's NS-SEC (%)						All UK total (%)
	Managerial and professional	Intermediate	Small employer and self-employed	Low supervisory and technical	Semi-routine and routine	Never worked	
Managerial & professional	67.1	46.9	42.2	31.7	22.8	11.6	44.5
Intermediate	4.0	7.5	5.5	3.9	5.4	4.2	5.2
Small employer & self-employed	10.6	12.8	28.9	13.4	12.6	16.9	12.9
Low supervisory & technical	9.2	16.0	12.9	22.3	20.6	13.2	14.9
Semi-routine and routine	9.1	16.6	10.5	28.6	38.3	47.0	22.0
Never worked	0.0	0.2	0.0	0.1	0.3	7.1	0.5
Total %	100	100	100	100	100	100	100
Unweighted sample size	4104	2361	504	667	4080	982	12698

Base: All UK MCS main respondent mothers with resident partners (who may be the natural, step, adoptive or foster father of the cohort baby). Table also includes small number of partners who were not declared as 'step-parent' to the cohort child (n = 13). Weighted percentages.

Figure 3.3: NVQ levels among cohort parents

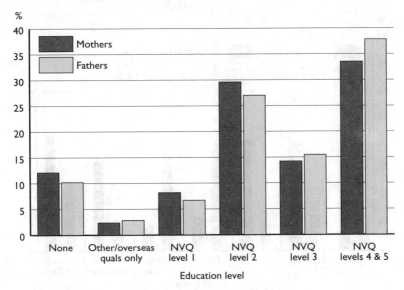

Base: All UK MCS mothers/fathers when cohort baby was 9-10 months old.
Weighted percentages.

equivalent to NVQ levels 4 or 5 (degree level or postgraduate). These levels of educational qualifications among MCS parents closely resemble those of the members of the 1970 cohort aged 30 in 2003 (Ferri et al, 2003). This is reassuring rather than surprising, since many MCS parents could have been members of the British Cohort Study, born around 1970.

Levels of education among mothers and fathers varied considerably by ethnic identity of parents (Figure 3.4). Mothers and fathers of Pakistani and Bangladeshi origin were least likely, by far, than other mothers and fathers to have any (UK) qualifications, and had relatively low levels of the highest NVQ level 4 or 5 qualifications (degree level or postgraduate). Mothers of Indian and Black African identity had the highest proportions with NVQ level 4 or 5. Fathers in these same ethnic groups, as well as fathers of mixed ethnic identity, were also those with the highest proportions of NVQ levels 4 or 5. Clearly, these forms of human capital among mothers and fathers of Millennium babies varied considerably by ethnic identity. Pakistani and Bangladeshi families stand out as being more disadvantaged in terms of these forms of human capital than other families, although there were fewer differences between other families.

A range of other educational and socioeconomic characteristics of MCS mothers by ethnic identity are displayed in Table A3.1.

Figure 3.4: NVQ levels by ethnic identity of cohort parents

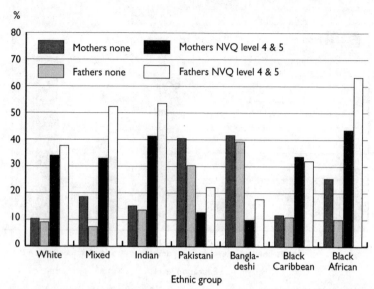

Base: All UK MCS mothers/fathers when cohort baby was 9-10 months old. Weighted percentages. 'Other' ethnic group classification is omitted here.

Poverty

Children who live in poverty are a central policy concern at the outset of the 21st century, with clear targets set by the government for reducing child poverty.

Official measures of poverty

The Government's report on tackling and monitoring poverty and social exclusion, *Opportunity for all* (OFA) (DWP, 2003a), contained three low-income indicators relating to children:

- A relative low-income indicator – the proportions of each group that fall below thresholds of contemporary mean or median income.
- An 'absolute' low-income indicator – the proportions of each group that fall below fixed thresholds of 1996-97 mean and median income, updated in real terms each year.
- A persistent low-income indicator – the proportion of each group experiencing low-income for three out of four years.

The government set a Public Service Agreement target of making substantial progress towards eradicating child poverty by reducing the number of children in low-income households by at least a quarter by 2004, from a 1998-99 baseline. For this, they used a relative low-income indicator, defined as children living below 60% of median income. The most commonly used official poverty measure is based on the one used in *Households below average income* (HBAI), which is an annual statistical report published by the Department for Work and Pensions (DWP, 2000-01, 2003b). This is a relative measure of poverty: it measures the proportion of children living in households with an equivalent income below 60% of the contemporary median household income. The equivalent income is calculated using the McClements equivalence scale, which is then measured both before and after housing costs.[1] Its purpose is to allow for variations in the size and composition of households, in recognition that the same level of income to households of varying size leads to varying standards of living.

A new measure of child poverty was announced by Ministers in December 2003; *Measuring child poverty*, published by the Department for Work and Pensions, consists of three tiers – namely, updated versions of the relative and absolute measures, and a new *material deprivation and relative low income combined* – to provide a wider measure of people's living standards. Child poverty will be judged to be falling in future when all three indicators are moving in the right direction.

MCS poverty measures

The design of the MCS data gives it several notable advantages over other datasets which make it suitable for the investigation of poverty at birth as well as poverty at large. The overrepresentation of ethnic minorities, residents living in areas of relatively high levels of deprivation and the residents of the three smaller countries of the UK (namely, Wales, Scotland and Northern Ireland) mean that it is possible to examine poverty for subgroups that are often difficult to analyse in other nationally representative datasets.

A number of MCS questions were available for use in measuring poverty on four dimensions:

1. **Lack of assets.** The measure used here follows the principle of measuring poverty as a lack of (socially perceived) necessities (Gordon et al, 1999). However, the MCS data offered a partial measure of assets and necessities. Respondents were asked about the availability of a number of appliances in the household. There

were no questions on activities and there are no data on the reasons why certain items are not present in a household (for example, whether they were not affordable or not wanted). Instead, the number of assets in 'working order' is recorded. Moreover, as can be seen in Table 3.2, not all the assets included in the MCS questionnaire are considered as 'necessities' by most of the population (as measured by the Poverty and Social Exclusion Survey [PSE] 1999). Hence, this poverty measure is more of an indicator of a *relative lack of assets* than a measurement of necessity deprivation. After exploring the proportion lacking the items, we decided to include, as potentially poor, those lacking three or more items; 27.3% of households fell into this category.

2. **Low income.** This is the conventional relative poverty measure, defining income poverty as having a net equivalent household income below 60% of the national median. For the calculation of equivalent income, we used the McClements equivalence scale, also used by the government in its annual publication of HBAI. We did not take account of the detailed child weights in the McClements scale, partly on the grounds that it gives a very small weight of 0.09 for a baby. Instead, we assigned to children under 16 in the household an average child weight of 0.23.

   The MCS questionnaire used separate income bands for lone parents and for couples.[2] Equivalent household income was constructed by assigning the mean of the income band to the household.[3] The equivalence scale was applied to mean household income for each family type in order to create one aggregate income

Table 3.2: Percentage lacking items in MCS and degree of necessity of item as in Poverty and Social Exclusion Survey

Consumer durables	% of the population considering the item a necessity in the PSE	% lacking this item in the MCS
Fridge	89	1.0
Freezer	68	3.1
Washing machine	76	2.3
Microwave oven	23	7.8
Dishwasher	7	63.5
Home computer	11	42.0
Video recorder	19	5.8
Tumble dryer	20	34.9
Car	38	14.6
Telephone	71	2.9

Base: All UK MCS main respondents when cohort baby was 9-10 months old. Weighted percentages.

variable. This is a *before* housing costs measure since MCS does not contain information on housing costs.

In 2000-01, the median income for a childless couple in official surveys was £293 per week before housing costs (DWP, 2000-01). The proportion of MCS households with equivalent income below 60% of this median income was 27.5% covering 30% of children living in MCS families. This percentage for MCS children is somewhat higher than the national estimate of 21% of children living in poverty in HBAI in approximately the same year (DWP, 2000-01). This discrepancy may be because the MCS families were not representative of all families with children, being a sample with a newborn child. It could also be caused by different methods of collecting income data and different response biases in the two surveys.

3. **Subjective poverty.** Respondents' own assessment of their poverty status was recorded. The question used here was: 'How well would you say you (and your partner) are managing financially these days?' The answers given are presented in Table 3.3. We defined 'subjectively poor' as those who were finding it quite difficult or very difficult to manage – 10.2% of all families.

4. **Receiving means-tested benefits.** Another useful indicator of living on a low family income was being in receipt of state benefits. Information was available on the receipt of Income Support, Jobseekers' Allowance (JSA), Housing Benefit, Working Families Tax Credit (WFTC) and Disability Living Allowance (DLA). With the exceptions of contributory JSA and DLA, the other benefits are all based on a means test of household income. The overlap in receipt of these benefits is substantial in some cases (Table 3.4). Being poor was defined as 'being in receipt of Income Support, or Jobseekers' Allowance if they were also receiving Housing Benefit

Table 3.3: Subjective poverty in MCS

How well mothers (and their partners) are financially managing	Percentages* of MCS families	Unweighted sample size
Living comfortably	26.3	4302
Doing all right	37.1	6946
Just about getting by	26.4	5206
Finding it quite difficult	7.7	1533
Finding it very difficult	2.5	508

Base: All UK MCS main respondent mothers when cohort baby was 9-10 months old.

* Weighted percentages.

Table 3.4: Overlap between means-tested benefits (row percentages and number of cases)

	Income support		Housing benefit		JSA		WFTC		Council tax benefit	
	%	N*	%	N*	%	N*	%	N*	%	N*
Income support	–	–	65.3	1,879	1.4	40	1.0	28	60.3	1,735
Housing benefit	75.6	1,879	–	–	10.9	270	10.6	263	85.3	2,121
Jobseeker's Allowance	8.0	40	53.8	270	–		10.1	51	52.7	265
WFTC	0.9	28	8.2	263	1.6	51	–	–	7.1	227
Council tax benefit	75.2	1,735	91.9	2,121	11.5	265	9.8	227	–	–

Base: All UK MCS main respondent mothers when cohort baby was 9-10 months old. Weighted percentages.

* Unweighted sample sizes.

or Council Tax Benefit (CTB), or WFTC if they were also receiving Housing Benefit or CTB'. Those with Housing Benefit/CTB were more likely to be receiving income-tested JSA rather than contributory JSA, and to be towards the bottom of the distribution of those receiving WFTC. This definition of poverty identified 19.8% of MCS families.[4]

Sensitivity analysis of the four poverty measures

None of the four measures of poverty is, by itself, entirely satisfactory. They vary considerably in the extent of poverty they identify (Table 3.5).

Lacking three or more assets could be a lifestyle choice. The income data are not very precise. People may or may not feel poor due to 'false consciousness' or because they are living with well-off parents. There may be confusions in the reported benefits received.

Though the asset poor and the low-income poor account for the same proportion of families, they do not account for anything like all the same individuals, just over half in each (Table 3.6). Overlap is

Table 3.5: Percentage of main respondent mothers defined as poor on these four poverty measures

Poverty measure	Percentage households poor	Unweighted sample size
Asset poor	27.3	18507
Low-income poor	27.5	16942
Subjectively poor	10.2	18495
Receiving means-tested benefits	19.8	17473

Base: All UK MCS main respondent mothers when cohort baby was 9-10 months old. Weighted percentages.

largest between those receiving means-tested benefits and those who are low-income poor, which is to be expected since the latter is the prerequisite of the former. The relative lack of overlap between asset poverty, subjective poverty and the other poverty measures can be explained partly by the deficiencies of the data these measures are based on and partly by the subjective nature of these measures. 'Subjective poverty' is a highly individual experience and can be coloured by people's own perceptions and expectations of the world. The measure of 'asset poverty' is based on a limited number of household goods, not necessarily giving a true picture of material deprivation.[5]

Thus a number of alternative measures were constructed and compared. One measure used the technique of overlaps analysis (Bradshaw and Finch, 2003). Fifty per cent of families were poor on at least one of the domains, 24% on two domains, 6% on three, but only 1% were poor on them all.

In order to explain patterns of interaction between the measures, we examined the permutations of the overlapping measure. We decided to use a cumulative approach to increase the sensitivity of our final poverty measure by defining as 'poor' all those who were poor on at least two measures – 23.7%. This is roughly the same percentage defined as poor by the government in HBAI which is a purely income measure.

By country, the extent of poverty varied only slightly. Wales had a higher percentage of MCS families in poverty at 27.1% compared to England (23.5%), Scotland (23.1%) and Northern Ireland (23.2%).

The MCS combined measure is less robust than the official measure used in HBAI partly because MCS collected household income in bands thus making it impossible to know the precise income of individual households. It will also vary from official statistics in that MCS overrepresents families with young children (containing at least

Table 3.6: Overlap between the different measurements of poverty (row percentages)

	Asset poor	Low-income poor	Subjectively poor	Receiving means-tested benefits	Unweighted maximum sample sizes
Asset poor	–	56.1	17.5	44.9	18507
Low-income poor	55.0	–	20.5	59.8	16942
Subjectively poor	46.9	54.6	–	39.4	18495
Receiving means-tested benefits	65.5	86.2	21.5	–	17473

Base: All UK MCS main respondent mothers when cohort baby was 9-10 months old. Weighted percentages.

one baby), and was not intended to be representative of the population of all families with children. In the analysis, we also carried out estimations based on single measures of poverty based on household income and the receipt of means-tested benefits to test out the sensitivity of the findings in comparison with analysing the combined measure.

Characteristics of poor mothers

The odds of being a poor mother on the combined measure were calculated using multivariate logistic regression analyses (Table 3.7). Model 1 shows the results from the multivariate logistic model of being poor, entering all but current employment of this range of factors together. Employment is excluded at this stage as it might be viewed as an outcome, like poverty itself, of the other disadvantaging characteristics. Similarly, the lack of employment can increase the chance of poverty if a person cannot then afford transport to go to interviews or even to work. Lone motherhood was the strongest predictor of a mother being in poverty. Being a lone mother still increased the odds of experiencing poverty by 22 times, when the other factors were controlled. Not being gainfully employed during pregnancy increased the odds of poverty by nearly four times compared with mothers who had paid work. Mothers who had been employed in pregnancy were largely entitled to maternity benefits – and were more likely to have started earning again. The odds of being in poverty according to mothers' highest educational qualifications showed an orderly progression. The least risk of poverty was associated with the highest level of education (NVQ level 5, postgraduate).

Everything else being equal, cohabiting mothers were 2.6 times more likely to be living in poverty than married parents. Having several children in the household significantly increased the risk of being poor, especially for large families containing three or more children. This is partly because more children, other things being equal, reduce equivalent income, but also because they reduce the chances of the mother being currently employed (Hawkes et al, 2004).

Before the range of controls were added, mothers from all minority ethnic groups, except Indian mothers, were more likely to be poor than white mothers. Controlling for other characteristics (Model 1) reduced the sizes of the odds of being in poverty attached to mixed, Pakistani/Bangladeshi and Black minority ethnic families. Factors which helped change poverty risk attaching to ethnic identity per se included their larger family size, lower levels of qualifications, lack of

Table 3.7: The relationship of socioeconomic factors to the odds of being a poor mother using the combined measure of poverty

	All natural mothers		Couple mothers	Lone mothers
	Model 1	Model 2	Model 3	Model 4
Parents' marital status		–	–	–
Married natural parents	1.00	–	–	–
Cohabiting natural parents	2.60***	–	–	–
Lone natural mother	21.84***	–	–	–
Mother's highest qualification				
None on the list shown	1.00	1.00	1.00	1.00
NVQ Level 1	0.71***	0.84NS	0.88NS	0.65NS
NVQ Level 2	0.45***	0.57***	0.62***	0.40***
NVQ Level 3	0.39***	0.50***	0.51***	0.45***
NVQ Level 4	0.23***	0.32***	0.34***	0.27***
NVQ Level 5	0.15***	0.18***	0.22***	0.06***
Employment during pregnancy				
No	1.00	1.00	1.00	1.00
Yes	0.27***	0.83**	0.84*	0.74NS
Mother's age at birth				
14 to 19	1.00	1.00	1.00	1.00
20 to 29	0.38***	0.48***	0.36***	0.89NS
30 to 39	0.20***	0.28***	0.20***	0.64NS
40 plus	0.24***	0.32***	0.26***	0.45NS
Mother's ethnicity				
White	1.00	1.00	1.00	1.00
Mixed	2.87***	2.30***	2.33**	2.22NS
Indian	0.89NS	1.22NS	1.24NS	1.62NS
Pakistani or Bangladeshi	1.85***	2.70***	2.76***	1.29NS
Black or Black British	2.47***	2.96***	3.58***	1.81*
Other	1.60***	2.05***	2.04***	2.56NS
Number of siblings of baby				
Only child	1.00	1.00	1.00	1.00
1 sibling	1.34***	1.52***	1.50***	1.61**
2 siblings	1.89***	1.99***	1.92***	3.13***
3+ siblings	3.05***	2.65***	2.77***	1.63NS
Country				
England	1.00	1.00	1.00	1.00
Wales	1.01NS	0.96NS	0.93NS	1.08NS
Scotland	1.18NS	1.25*	1.26*	1.16NS
Northern Ireland	0.94NS	0.97NS	1.08NS	0.76NS
Type of ward				
Non-disadvantaged	1.00	1.00	1.00	1.00
Other disadvantaged	1.85***	1.75***	1.93***	1.09NS
Minority ethnic	2.51***	2.06***	2.25***	1.24NS
Combined marital and employment status				
Married, both employed	–	1.00	1.00	–
Married, one earner	–	4.07***	4.08***	–
Married, zero earners	–	60.79***	61.19***	–
Cohabiting, both employed	–	2.09***	2.00***	–
Cohabiting, one earner	–	10.44***	10.10***	–
Cohabiting, zero earners	–	208.76***	203.29***	–
Lone, earner	–	10.69***	–	1.00
Lone, not employed	–	355.45***	–	32.01***
Unweighted sample size	17873	17828	14766	3062
F statistic	161.59	166.68	109.44	42.00
Chi square	0.000	0.000	0.000	0.000

Dependant variable = 1 where mothers were identified as poor on at least 2 measures: Asset poor, Low-income poor, Subjective poor or Means-tested benefits poor, zero otherwise.

Base: All UK MCS natural mothers. $p < 0.001$***, $p < 0.01$**, $p < 0.05$* NS = Not Significant. Standard errors adjusted for cluster sample design.

employment in pregnancy and residence in disadvantaged neighbourhoods and areas of high minority ethnic populations.

Model 2 introduced information on current employment, a proximate cause of poverty. The impact of not earning in a lone-parent family was to raise the odds of poverty by 33 fold, all else equal. The relative impact on the odds of being in poverty of having no earner rather than two earners in couple families was, perhaps, logically greater: all else equal, it was a 61-fold increase in the odds of poverty for a married couple and a 100-fold increase for a cohabiting couple. The significance of the employment status and the other background factors tells us that, even if we know how many earners there are in a family, there are further factors which determine whether they are poor. Nevertheless, it is worth noting that mothers who were not earning were much more likely to be in poverty. Approximately one quarter (26.6%) of mothers who had a partner but were not employed were likely to be in poverty compared with 29% of mothers who were lone parents and employed. Only 4% of mothers who had a partner and were employed were likely to be living in poverty compared with 94% of mothers who were lone parents with no paid work.[6]

When the sample was split into couple and lone mothers and separate estimates calculated (Models 3 and 4), there was little difference between the results of couple mothers and all mothers. However, a large number of coefficients for the lone mother sample (Model 4) were insignificant. We expect this was because lone mothers' characteristics show far less variation than do couple mothers' characteristics.

In a further step, we estimated two sets of models based on two of the components of the combined poverty measure – the means-tested benefit measure and the low-income measure, as presented in Table A3.2.[7] There were relatively few differences in the significance of the characteristics associated with being poor across all these groups as far as all mothers and couple mothers were concerned. As before, lone mothers' estimates had many insignificant results. The log odds of being in poverty as a result of not being employed for the sample of all mothers were far lower in the low-income measure of poverty model. In this low-income poverty model, compared with a married couple where both were employed, the one-earner married mother had four times and the no-earner married mother 39 times the chance of being in poverty. Compared with a two-earner married mother, the lone earner had seven times and the no-earner lone mother 137 times the chance of being in poverty. Among lone mothers in this model, compared with having employment, the lone mother without earnings was 20 times as likely to be in poverty.

Babies born to mothers on Income Support

Box 3.1 Income Support (IS)

If a young lone mother (aged 18-24) became pregnant with her first baby on IS in 2000-01, until 11 weeks before the due date she would be in receipt of JSA and expected to look for work. After that time, she would move on to IS (£41.35 per week for a single person in 2000-01). She would be eligible for Housing Benefit and CTB as well as receiving various other benefits. After the birth, she would receive a higher rate of IS as well as Child Benefit. Since 2003, she would also qualify for Child Tax Credit.

Of particular concern in policy discussions has been the proportion of (young) mothers becoming pregnant and bearing children on IS (Maternity Alliance, 2002). Particular anxiety has been expressed about first-time mothers dependent on IS because the level of that benefit has not increased in real terms since the end of the 1970s. The MCS is not a perfect sample for estimating the size of this group because this survey collected information on benefit status at nine months after the birth, rather than at childbirth or conception. But it is the best available data. Sixteen per cent of all mothers, were on IS when the baby was 9-10 months old, and being in receipt of IS was strongly associated with family type (Table 3.8). Only 6.1% of mothers who lived with the father of their child received IS. On the other hand, 74.3% of lone mothers received IS, which means that 10% of all MCS babies lived with lone mothers who were on IS. Only 35% of lone mothers on IS at the time of the interview had a paid job when they were pregnant. This suggests that two thirds of lone mothers may also have been on IS before and during their pregnancy. Over two thirds of all lone mothers where the cohort baby was the first born (68.6%) were on IS.

Changes in financial circumstances

Research reviews have shown that day-to-day costs associated with a new baby have serious implications for family finances, particularly among low-income families (Henderson and Garcia, 2000; Jayaweera and Garcia, 2000). The arrival of a child is one of the events triggering transitions into poverty (Jenkins and Rigg, 2001). Although the MCS questions did not provide information about the extent of poverty

Table 3.8: Families receiving Income Support by type of family

Family type	Proportion receiving IS		% of all mothers with first-born babies on IS		% of all mothers with later babies on IS	
	%	N*	%	N*	%	N*
Two natural parents	6.1	15296	4.8	6032	6.9	9063
Lone mothers	74.3	3172	68.6	1536	80.5	1567
All family types	15.6	18548	15.4	7632	15.7	10650

Base: All UK MCS main respondent mothers. Weighted percentages.

* all N values are unweighted sample sizes.

before childbirth, these families were asked to assess changes in their circumstances.

Two fifths of families said they were worse off (40.4%) than one year ago. Another two fifths (40.6%) said their position was about the same, and one fifth (19.0%) said that their financial position had improved. Families where the mother had stopped working because of childbirth were most likely to be feeling financially worse off (54%), although 44% of families where the mother had stayed employed also felt worse off, in this case due largely to childcare costs and reduced earnings. Families having their first baby were particularly likely to report being worse off financially. Families who felt financially better off were either those where the partner's earnings had increased or those younger un-partnered mothers without jobs who were receiving increased benefits from having had the child. This may account for the fact that there is relatively little difference in reported life satisfaction between mothers who said they were financially better off, the same, or worse off.

Among mothers where the cohort child was the first born, 79.7% of those who were in financial difficulties indicated that their financial situation was worse compared to a year ago. Of mothers who were in financial difficulties, those most likely to indicate that their situation had not changed over the last year were mothers whose cohort baby was not the first born (79.6%).

Most mothers who indicated it was difficult to manage felt that they were worse off than they were a year ago (85% of mixed, 70% of white, 65% of Indian, 71% of Black Caribbean and 65% of Black African mothers). The proportions reporting this among Bangladeshi and Pakistani mothers were smaller (49% and 51%, respectively) than for other mothers. Around two fifths of Bangladeshi and Pakistani mothers felt that their situation had remained the same over the past year. They were also least likely to have been employed at either point.

Savings

The financial adjustment to the arrival of the cohort baby could also have involved the running down of savings. One third (34%) had no savings before or after the baby was born. Of the rest, 37% reported that savings had been partly, mostly or all used up (completely for 9.9%). The proportion using up some or all savings was greater where the mother had been employed and not returned to a job after the birth (65%) than where the mother had a job after the baby (40.9%). However, using up some or all savings was also the experience of 45.3% of mothers who were out of employment at both points. It is also noteworthy that 6% of all mothers said their savings had increased.

Have those who said they were not worse off in fact been running down their savings to maintain their living standards? This was the case for a minority (25%) of those who said they were better off and 31% of those who said they were about the same. Running down savings was most common among those who felt worse off, 50% altogether, and they were twice as likely as the others to have run down their savings completely.

Wider family capital and relationships as resources

Talk about more atomised and individualised western societies can often give the impression that wider kin networks and relationships are no longer important. However, the importance of kin relationships has been identified in a number of studies. They are clearly part of a family's social and relationship capital. In a survey of adults' views on what contributed to quality of life, relationships with family and relatives were named most frequently as most important (Bowling, 1995). Findings from the British Social Attitudes Survey showed that a high value is placed on three-generational family life, particularly by grandparents (Dench and Ogg, 2002). Nine out of ten grandparents in that survey agreed that grandparenting was a very important part of their life. There is a growing interest in intergenerational relationships and in particular the role of grandparents (Mooney and Statham, 2002; Brannen et al, 2003;). Earlier cohort study findings have also shown that the extended family is alive and well with parents of children born in 1958 and 1970 often helping to look after their grandchildren (Ferri et al, 2003). Forty per cent of men and 60% of women born in 1970 said their parents offered some sort of childcare help.

Money and wealth also transfer within wider families both while grandparents are alive as well as after death through inheritances, making grandparents contributors to the physical capital and wealth of families. Indeed, there is a case to be made that, with the weakening of horizontal household ties via divorce, vertical intergenerational transfers and transmission are becoming more not less important.

Here we consider the extent to which the cohort baby's grandparents were involved with the baby's household, how often they saw each other and if they helped financially with the baby.

Frequency of contact with grandparents

Studies have found that grandparenting tends to be most intense during grandchildren's pre-school years, and especially for the first grandchild. The intensity and frequency of shared activities lessen when grandparents have more than one grandchild and also as grandchildren get older. In the ONS Omnibus Survey, the majority of mothers with a child under 5 received help from their own mothers (such as help with domestic tasks, childcare, money, paperwork/maintenance, shopping and lifts), particularly when it was their first child (Grundy et al, 1999).

Almost two thirds of MCS mothers saw their own mother at least once a week with almost a quarter seeing them every day (Table 3.9). Whereas more than a half said that, since the baby's birth, there had been no change in the frequency of contact, almost a third saw their mother more often. Grandmothers were seen more frequently than grandfathers, which may be indicative of closer ties between mothers and daughters at this time and certainly there was greater involvement of grandmothers compared with grandfathers in childcare (Table 3.10).

Fathers saw their own mothers less frequently than mothers did, although a similar proportion of these partners said they saw their mothers more often following the baby's arrival. There was little difference between seeing their mothers and seeing their fathers, possibly because they are seen together. Other surveys have also found women see their parents more often than men and, within the grandparent generation, grandmothers see their children and grandchildren more often than grandfathers do (Grundy et al, 1999).

There were differences between countries and between non-disadvantaged and other disadvantaged wards in the frequency with which cohort mothers saw their own mothers, but few differences for fathers. The highest proportion of cohort mothers to see their mothers every day was in Northern Ireland (39%) and the lowest in England (22%). Cohort mothers in other disadvantaged wards compared with non-disadvantaged wards were more likely to see their own mothers

Table 3.9: Frequency cohort mother sees her own mother by ethnic group

Maternal ethnic group (collapsed)	Mother: frequency sees own mother						
	Every day	At least once a week	At least once a year	Less than yearly	Not alive	Total	Unweighted sample size
White	24.7	41.7	24.5	2.7	6.5	100.0	15518
Indian	12.2	19.1	32.8	28.7	7.2	100.0	478
Pakistani	26.9	16.2	14.5	34.6	7.9	100.0	888
Bangladeshi	18.5	14.5	20.2	37.0	9.8	100.0	371
Black Caribbean + Black African	17.1	18.1	18.3	31.5	15.0	100.0	675
Mixed and other	11.8	18.5	25.9	33.7	10.1	100.0	558
All	23.9	39.1	24.2	6.0	6.9	100.0	18488

Base: All UK MCS mothers when baby was 9-10 months old. Weighted percentages.

Table 3.10: Frequency cohort mother sees her own father by ethnic group

Maternal ethnic group (collapsed)	Mother: frequency sees own father						
	Every day	At least once a week	At least once a year	Less than yearly	Not alive	Total	Unweighted sample size
White	12.6	34.6	28.3	8.8	15.7	100.0	15517
Indian	8.1	17.1	26.1	25.5	23.2	100.0	478
Pakistani	19.6	13.6	12.4	33.9	20.5	100.0	886
Bangladeshi	10.9	10.3	13.8	28.2	36.8	100.0	371
Black Caribbean + Black African	5.6	9.4	19.4	34.2	31.5	100.0	675
Mixed and other	5.9	9.7	23.2	34.3	26.9	100.0	558
All	12.3	32.1	27.3	11.4	16.9	100.0	18485

Base: All UK MCS mothers when baby was 9-10 months old. Weighted percentages.

every day. More daily contact between cohort mothers and their own mothers in other disadvantaged wards may be attributable to closer proximity, but it may also be influenced by a stronger feeling that grandparents ought to be involved in rearing children. Mothers and their partners in wards with high minority ethnic populations were the most likely to see their parents less than once a year. This is reflected in frequencies of seeing parents by ethnic group.

Minority ethnic mothers were much more likely to see their mothers less than once a year (28.7-37.0%) than white mothers (2.7%) (Table 3.9). However, Pakistani mothers were also the most likely to see their mothers every day (26.9%) where they were alive. Similarly, minority ethnic mothers were more likely to see their own fathers less than once a year (25.5-34.3%) than white mothers (8.8%) (Table 3.10). This pattern was repeated for partners. This relatively high frequency of little if any contact with parents may indicate that minority ethnic parents are more likely to have their own parents living outside the UK, and so find more frequent contact difficult and expensive.[8] However, fathers of South Asian ethnic origin were much more likely to see their own mothers and fathers than fathers from other ethnic groups. This reflects the high rates of co-residence with the partner's parents, already noted in Chapter 2. White mothers were the most likely to report that they had contact more often with their own mothers since the birth of the baby (31.3%) (Table 3.11) and with their fathers (25.0%). Similarly, white partners were the most likely to report that they had contact more often with their own mothers since the birth of the baby (25.4%) (Table 3.12) and with their fathers (21.1%).

Contact with cohort grandparents where separation or divorce occurred

The frequency of contact between the cohort grandparents and the cohort parents may have been affected where a divorce or separation occurred in the grandparent generation.[9] On the whole, daily contact with cohort grandfathers only occurred in very few cases, regardless

Table 3.11: Mother: change in frequency of contact with own mother by ethnic group

Maternal ethnic group (collapsed)	Mother: change in frequency of contact with own mother since birth				Sample size (N) unweighted
	... more often,	about the same as before,	or less often?	Total (%)	
White	31.3	58.6	10.1	100.0	14457
Indian	18.2	63.2	18.6	100.0	442
Pakistani	15.3	63.9	20.8	100.0	817
Bangladeshi	11.0	67.7	21.3	100.0	339
Black Caribbean + Black African	18.9	69.0	12.0	100.0	569
Mixed and other	22.8	58.2	19.0	100.0	506
All	29.9	59.2	10.9	100.0	17130

Base: All UK MCS mothers with grandparent alive when cohort baby was 9-10 months old.
Weighted percentages.

Table 3.12: Father: change in frequency of contact with own mother by ethnic group

	Father: change in frequency of contact with own mother since birth				Sample
Paternal ethnic group (collapsed)	... more often,	about the same as before,	or less often?	Total (%)	size (N) unweighted
White	25.4	63.5	11.1	100.0	10173
Indian	9.8	76.1	14.1	100.0	306
Pakistani	8.6	79.2	12.1	100.0	507
Bangladeshi	7.5	81.3	11.2	100.0	220
Black Caribbean + Black African	12.1	78.8	9.1	100.0	212
Mixed and other	12.8	71.4	15.9	100.0	326
All	24.1	64.6	11.3	100.0	11744

Base: All UK MCS fathers with grandparent alive when cohort baby was 9-10 months old. Weighted percentages.

of the status of the cohort grandparent's past partnerships. Where grandparents had experienced a separation or divorce, 44.3% of the cohort mothers reported seeing their own mothers a few times a week and 49.9% reported very rarely seeing their own fathers; and 40.5% of cohort fathers indicated that they had contact with their own mothers a few times a week (Table 3.13). In other respects, contact between the cohort father and his own mother or father was with roughly equal frequency: 47.1% said they very rarely visited their own mothers and 53.8% said the same about their own fathers. A further 23.9% of cohort mothers and 21.6% of cohort fathers reported that they 'never' saw their own fathers when there had been a parental separation or divorce. It is clear from these findings that contact between cohort mothers and their own mothers is relatively unaffected by a parental separation or divorce, whereas contact between cohort fathers and their own fathers drops significantly. Chapter 2 considered other relationships between cohort parents' experiences and the marital status of their own parents.

Among the Millennium Cohort parents, those without any qualifications or with only low levels of qualification were more likely than those with higher levels of education to report that they never saw their own fathers after a separation or divorce had occurred.[10] This lack of contact may be one of the unfortunate side effects of divorcing or separating parents. The younger the age at which their own parents separated, the higher the likelihood that these cohort parents (either mothers or fathers) were out of contact with their own fathers. It is not surprising that it is a child's contact and relationship with the father that suffers most when parents split up. The father is

Table 3.13: Cohort parents' frequencies of contact with their own parents by whether those parents had ever separated or divorced

Cohort parents frequency of contact with cohort grandparents*	Cohort mothers (%)				Cohort fathers (%)			
	Contact with own mother		Contact with own father		Contact with own mother		Contact with own father	
	Grandparent separated or divorced	Never separated or divorced	Grandparent separated or divorced	Never separated or divorced	Grandparent separated or divorced	Never separated or divorced	Grandparent separated or divorced	Never separated or divorced
Every day	21.2	22.9	3.8	15.9	6.4	8.6	4.9	9.5
Few times a week	44.3	43.6	22.3	47.9	40.5	47.6	19.6	46.6
Very rarely	29.8	31.5	49.9	34.1	47.1	42.4	53.8	42.5
Never	4.7	1.9	23.9	1.9	5.9	1.4	21.6	1.4
Total	100.0	100.0	100.0	100.0	100.0	100.0	100.0	100.0
Unweighted sample size	4726	11371	4473	10079	2751	8626	2417	7521
P value	0.0000	0.0000	0.0000	0.0000	0.0000	0.0000	0.0000	0.0000

Base: All UK MCS mothers and fathers with relevant own parent alive when cohort baby was 9-10 months old. Weighted percentages.

*Frequency of contact with grandparents is only asked if the grandparent is still alive.

often the person who leaves the family home after a partnership dissolves. He may have difficulties in maintaining a stable relationship with the child due to the distance of his new residence; on-going or unsettled conflict between him and his former partner; and the pressures of needing to raise additional income to support two households. Non-resident fathers' relationships with the cohort child are also considered in Chapter 7.

Providing financial support

Cohort parents were asked whether their own parents would help if they had financial problems. A large majority of cohort mothers agreed that they would get help from their own parents. Overall, 50.4% agreed strongly and 35.7% agreed that their family would help if they had financial problems; 6.7% either disagreed or strongly disagreed that their family would help. There were few differences by country or type of ward. However, there were more differences by ethnic group although not large (Table 3.14). White mothers were slightly more likely than mothers with other ethnic identities to agree strongly (51.4%) that their family would help. Black mothers were the most likely to disagree or disagree strongly (14.1%) that their family would help financially.

Mothers were asked a factual question concerning financial help since the birth (Table 3.15). Financial help, where available, was most likely to take the form of buying gifts and 'extras' for the baby, reported by 72.1% of mothers and 69% of partners, followed by buying essentials such as baby food, clothes, nappies and so on (25.0% of mothers and 19% of partners), and lending money (18.0% of mothers and 16% of partners). It was rare for financial support to take the form of paying for household costs (8.9% of mothers and 6% of partners) or giving money or cash gifts (1.0% of both mothers and partners). Few grandparents contributed to the costs of childcare but many of them were doing childcare themselves, as noted later in this chapter as well as in Chapter 8. Approximately 21.7% of mothers and 25% of their partners said they had received no financial help from their family

There were marked differences in financial support received by ethnic group. White mothers were the least likely to report no financial support from parents (19.5%). Nearly half of Black mothers (49.4%) and Bangladeshi mothers (45.5%) reported no financial support (Table 3.15). This in part, at least, may reflect the relatively disadvantaged economic situation of these groups in the UK and in some cases grandparents living overseas. The differences were most pronounced

Table 3.14: Family would help if financial problems by ethnic group

Maternal ethnic group (collapsed)	Mother: family would help if financial problems							
	Strongly agree	Agree	Neither agree nor disagree	Disagree	Strongly disagree	Can't say	Total (%)	Unweighted sample size
White	51.4	35.5	5.1	3.4	2.8	1.8	100.0	15313
Indian	44.8	36.9	6.3	5.4	3.8	2.8	100.0	426
Pakistani	43.1	36.8	5.8	6.3	3.1	4.9	100.0	754
Bangladeshi	37.6	42.1	9.0	4.5	3.8	3.0	100.0	282
Black Caribbean + Black African	38.9	35.3	7.9	7.6	6.5	3.8	100.0	608
Mixed and other	37.4	40.1	6.5	5.8	6.0	4.2	100.0	486
All	50.4	35.7	5.2	3.7	3.0	2.0	100.0	17869

Base: All UK MCS mothers when cohort baby was 9-10 months old. Weighted percentages.

in the category of buying gifts and extras for the baby, which was highest for the parents of white mothers (74.3%). The pattern of financial support from fathers' parents by ethnic group was the same as for mothers. The level of support from cohort fathers' parents was mostly lower than for cohort mothers' parents except in the case of Indian and Pakistani fathers, whose parents were most likely, of all groups, to buy essentials for the baby and to pay other household costs: 23.9% of Indian and 24.7% of Pakistani paternal grandparents were reported by the cohort father to buy essentials for the cohort baby compared with 18.8% of all paternal grandparents. In the case of paying for other household costs, 23.0% of Indian and 20.0% of Pakistani compared with 6.1% of all paternal grandparents gave this type of help.

Cohort parents who never saw their own mother were approximately six times more likely to indicate that they did not receive any help from that grandmother compared with cohort parents who had daily contact with the baby's grandmother. Grandfathers who were not in contact with the cohort parent were more likely to fail to provide any financial help compared with grandfathers who were in contact, especially compared with those who were in daily contact with the cohort parent (Table 3.16). However, cohort grandfathers who were not in contact nevertheless provided a relatively high level of support compared with cohort grandmothers who were not in touch.

Table 3.15: Mother: financial help from parents by ethnic group

Mother: financial help from own parents	Mother's ethnic group (collapsed)						
	White	Indian	Pakistani	Bangladeshi	Black	Mixed and other	All
No, does not help in any of these ways	19.5	33.3	34.7	45.5	49.4	39.9	21.7
Buying essentials for the baby - food, clothes, nappies, etc	26.0	12.5	18.3	12.8	20.9	14.7	25.0
Paying for other household costs - e.g. bills, shopping etc	9.0	5.0	7.9	4.1	10.1	7.4	8.9
Buying gifts and extras for the baby	74.3	62.0	59.7	48.8	42.3	53.5	72.1
Lending money	19.0	4.7	10.8	7.0	12.8	10.0	18.0
Paying for childcare	0.7	0.1	0.5		0.3	0.4	0.7
Other/buying or paying for large capital items	0.5		0.1		0.1	0.4	0.5
Other/giving money or cash gifts	1.1	0.4	0.4	0.2	1.1	1.0	1.0
Other/trust fund or savings account for baby	0.2				0.5	0.2	0.2
Other financial help	0.5	0.5	0.5	0.7	1.4	1.4	0.5
Sample Size unweighted	15151	465	867	358	607	533	17981

Base: All UK MCS mothers with grandparent alive when cohort baby was 9-10 months old. Weighted percentages.

Support systems

As noted in Chapter 1, the extent of family breakdown has raised questions about how far families are still effective private systems of social support. Whether public systems of support will be needed to compensate for any decline in effectiveness of private support systems is a contingent issue. We are able to explore the interaction of private and public support systems with the MCS data. Parents were asked about their access to grandparent support for childcare and in other ways. They were also asked about the extent of emotional support and advice from friends, about their use of local state health services and the Sure Start early years programme, and about any receipt of state benefits. We can examine whether, as might be expected, lower levels of private support from parents, wider family and friends are related, possibly inversely, to levels of state support. We can also examine, in part, whether these relationships are the same across families of varying minority ethnic identities.

There is an interesting mix of support for families, according to their family circumstances (Table 3.17). Most striking, although predictable, is the range in receipt of means-tested state income support across these types of families: from 87.8% of lone-parent families, through 39.1% of cohabiting to 18.0% of legally married couples. One could argue that this is a direct compensation from the state for the absence of a second parent in private support systems of families. The variation in extent of accessing other state services since the new baby's birth is less and in the opposite direction to accessing IS. Legally married couples were most likely to be accessing health and other services (63.4%) compared with cohabiting (59.6%) and lone parents (52.7%).

Private support levels varied to a much smaller extent across the family types. Grandparent support was ubiquitous and high in all family types, slightly higher in cohabiting than in the other family types. Doing childcare, while mothers were at work or at any other time, was a grandparent contribution in the case of 33.2% of MCS families. Other emotional support and advice was at a broadly similar extent across these family types (42.9 to 47.7%). The partner doing childcare (while mother was employed) was generally less frequent, particularly among lone parents. Its prevalence among legally married (16%) and cohabiting couples (17%) was not high.

Comparisons by mother's ethnic identity (Table 3.18) show that there were differences in the extent of support (where sample sizes allow an analysis) in a way that is difficult to generalise. Black African

Table 3.16: Cohort parents' frequencies of contact with their own parents and the reported financial assistance received from them

Financial assistance given by cohort grandparents*	Cohort mother's contact with cohort grandparents (%)				Cohort father's contact with cohort grandparents (%)			
	Every day	Few times a week	Very rarely	Never	Every day	Few times a week	Very rarely	Never
Cohort grandmothers								
Does not help	12.7	16.0	29.0	76.5	12.6	15.9	29.2	74.1
Buys essentials	35.2	26.5	15.7	6.4	33.1	24.7	12.3	2.8
Buys gifts	79.1	77.8	66.9	19.1	75.0	77.6	66.5	21.8
Other help with bills, money	33.4	23.4	13.9	6.9	34.7	24.7	14.9	8.9
Unweighted sample sizes	4320	6663	4730	564	1246	5355	4527	349
Cohort grandfathers								
Does not help	12.7	15.2	25.1	36.6	15.7	16.7	27.9	41.2
Buys essentials	35.7	27.9	19.1	21.1	29.5	24.9	13.6	14.1
Buys gifts	78.3	78.7	69.9	57.2	72.6	76.4	67.2	54.2
Other help with bills, money	32.8	24.8	18.6	22.3	33.2	25.8	16.5	15.7
Unweighted sample sizes	2278	5594	5330	1456	1044	4080	4146	718

Base: All UK MCS mothers and fathers with living parents when cohort baby was 9–10 months old. Weighted percentages.

*Financial assistance was a multiple response variable based on column, therefore values do not add to 100%

Table 3.17: Prevalence of varying types of support to families

Marital/family status	Support (%)					
	Grandparent support	Partner does childcare	Other emotional support/advice	State services support	State income support	Maximum unweighted sample sizes
Legally married	70.5	16.0	47.2	63.4	18.0	10910
Cohabiting or part-time resident father	76.5	17.9	42.9	59.6	39.1	4447
Lone parent	72.4	2.8	47.7	52.7	87.8	3191

Base: All UK MCS mothers when cohort baby was 9-10 months old. Weighted percentages.

Have you turned to any of the following for help or support since the 'cohort baby' was born?

Definitions: 'Grandparent support' is based on grandparents who are still alive and; care for baby at any time, or reside in household, or whether cohort mother believes that grandparents would assist financially if required, or whether grandparent has provided financial assistance to family excluding buying gifts for cohort child.

'Partner does childcare' includes partner listed as offering childcare while mother employed or at other times.

'Other emotional support/advice' includes cohort mothers who strongly agree that they can talk to other parents, or cohort mothers who spend time with their friends at least 3 times per week.

'State services support' includes cohort mothers who have sought support since the birth of their cohort baby from GP (doctor) or a drop in centre for families, or mothers who have used Sure Start or mothers who have found it easy or very easy to access support services.

'State income support' includes mothers who are in receipt of Income Support or Working Families Tax Credit.

families tended to have lower levels of private support which is probably related to their families being less likely to be in the UK. However, this group also tended to access state support to a lesser extent than families of other minority ethnic origins, and this may be due to a preference or to their more recent arrival in the UK and an associated ignorance about state services. It was noted in Chapter 2 that Asian grandparents were more likely than white grandparents to live with their children and grandchildren. Nonetheless, when it comes to grandparents' contributions to families taken as a whole, white families were not less supported by grandparents than Asian families. The low level of partner childcare among Pakistani families partly reflects the low participation of these mothers in paid work, although cultural traditions were likely to be playing a role, as discussed further in Chapter 7.

In conclusion, therefore, state support kicks in as a compensatory device through the important element of income support. Families without two parents are heavily reliant on state income support. But,

Table 3.18: Mothers' extent of support by selected ethnic origin

Marital/family status	Grandparent support	Partner does childcare	Other emotional support/ advice	State services support	State income support
Legally married					
White	71.8	17.1	49.5	64.4	16.0
Indian	72.6	13.0	24.5	59.4	16.0
Pakistani	65.5	4.1	30.1	55.3	48.5
Black Caribbean	79.4	17.2	50.0	65.6	21.9
Black African	45.3	15.0	42.5	43.7	23.3
Cohabiting or part-time resident father					
White	77.1	18.0	42.9	59.8	39.1
Black Caribbean	(82.1)	(9.8)	(34.1)	(46.3)	(34.1)
Black African	(48.7)	(18.6)	(27.9)	(47.6)	(35.7)
Lone parent					
White	75.3	3.0	49.5	53.1	88.6
Black Caribbean	66.7	1.1	43.5	57.6	85.9
Black African	30.6	3.9	26.5	44.7	78.6

Base: All UK MCS mothers when cohort baby was 9-10 months old. Weighted percentages.

Definitions as in Table 3.17 above.

( ) based on under 50 cases.

as far as other elements of private and public support are concerned, there is no evidence of any compensatory relationships. While there was some variation by the mother's ethnic identity and marital status, this dimension of variation did not change the basic conclusions.

Conclusions

This chapter has examined the resources, mainly financial, of the families in which Millennium Cohort babies started out their lives. Along with the topics covered in Chapter 2, they are another part of the origins of these cohort babies, and some would argue the most important part. We have not taken a narrow view of financial resources. As well as covering income from earnings and benefits, it has been widened out to consider socioeconomic status and education as the potential for income generation; consumer durables; other assets; subjective feelings about finances; savings; material and non-material support from grandparents; and access to some publicly provided services.

Babies most at risk of being brought up in poverty are those born to lone mothers, workless couples, and mothers who are not in the labour market and have no or low qualifications. Having a young mother, being Black, Pakistani, Bangladeshi or of mixed ethnic origin, or living in an area of high minority ethnic population or other disadvantaged area were associated with a higher risk of poverty. There is particular reason to be concerned about first-time mothers who became pregnant while in receipt of JSA. Many of these, as we have seen, subjectively felt their financial circumstances had improved from this very low base, as a result of having the cohort baby. As the literature shows, however, being in poverty at this stage of life is associated with poor outcomes for both the child and the mother.

The government's targets for reducing child poverty are challenging. It will depend in large part on getting more mothers including lone mothers into employment. This analysis supports the idea that being out of employment is associated with poverty. In this sense, getting into employment should be a route out of poverty. However, employment is not the whole story. Also associated with mothers' poverty are lack of qualifications, being in certain minority ethnic groups, large family size, and starting to have children at younger ages. Some of these additional characteristics are also associated with being out of the labour market, but they are less easy to address through targeted government policies, and may even be associated with a positive choice to be at home and not employed.

In any case, employment is variable and not necessarily a panacea if it is vulnerable and insecure compared with a definite and reliable benefits cheque, as qualitative studies have pointed out (Baines et al, 2003). Also, there needs to be a consideration of whether we should focus on the symptoms, poverty resulting from lone parenthood, or the causes of that poverty, entering the state of lone parenthood, mothers choosing to live alone, or fathers failing to live with or support the mothers of their children.

Given that 40% of cohort families felt financially worse off than before the cohort baby was born, the extent of poverty may be at its greatest at this juncture, over the childbirth period. The loss of earnings at this point was the largest single reason for feeling worse off. The time of having a new baby may be one, therefore, when families are particularly vulnerable to entering poverty. Government policy needs to consider this phase of life for particular attention if it is seeking to address family poverty.

Despite societal family changes and claims of more individualistic relationships, grandparents remain a very important source of family resource in the new millennium. The vast majority of grandparents, especially grandmothers, are involved with their children and grandchildren and supply much practical, time and some monetary assistance and transfers to the younger generations. To this extent, we have not retreated to the more individualised or nuclear family. It is, however, predominantly mothers who are maintaining these intergenerational relationships.

The government has singled out one-parent families for particular state support, and the incidence of Income Support receipt by this group in this survey (75%) reinforces the extent of this support. However, when other forms of private family support were examined, lone parents were not significantly worse off than other family units. State support compensates, therefore, for the loss of income from the absence of one parent in lone-parent families, but it does not need to compensate for lower levels of other forms of support which were generally similar in all family types, although varying by ethnic origin. Cohort mothers, whether lone or partnered, saw and kept in touch with the baby's maternal grandmother regularly. Cohort fathers were far less likely to keep in touch and see their own parents. Many mothers had friends to turn to for help. Lone mothers differed from couple mothers in the extent to which they called on fathers to do childcare while they were at work. However, it is not clear whether this difference from couple mothers is because lone mothers were not working to the same extent and did not need this help, or were not working because they did not have the help, or did not get the help because they were not even in contact with absent fathers. Probably something of all these explanations applies to some extent.

The key element of division between babies born into lone and couple families is in the amount of financial and social capital with which they start out. Future sweeps of the survey will reveal how much this matters.

If any further case were to be made for state support to compensate for a lower level of private family support, it is only Black African families where the statistics suggest there may be a need. However, while Black African mothers had lower rates of grandparent help, they also had lower rates of support from state services. It is possible that both of these findings rest on this group's more recent migration history and a consequent lack of familiarity with available services. If so, the elapse of time may be sufficient to change their patterns of service use, although not necessarily the availability of grandparents in situ.

Table A3.1: Selected educational and socioeconomic characteristics of MCS mothers by ethnic identity

Characteristics	White	Mixed	Indian	Pakistani	Bangladeshi	Black Carib-bean	Black African	Other ethnic groups*
% with tertiary level academic qualifications	28.3	25.3	36.8	11.2	7.9	22.9	38.6	36.2
% with no qualifications**	10.4	18.3	15.1	40.5	41.7	11.6	25.5	23.6
Median/mean age at leaving full time education	17/17.6	17/17.6	19/19.0	16/17.1	16/16.8	17/17.4	18/18.9	19/18.9
% currently not working or on leave and who have not actively sought work after birth of cohort child	40.9	58.7	41.6	80.7	83.6	38.5	46.7	59.4
% in managerial and professional social classes***	33.9	31.3	34.0	16.3	19.2	31.4	30.2	33.8
% in semi-routine and routine social classes***	36.0	40.4	35.6	59.2	61.9	31.7	37.8	34.8
% in couples where both not in work/on leave	6.4	19.2	4.7	16.3	21.7	10.7	14.9	9.7
% in households with below 60% equivalised median income****	25.3	48.0	27.3	63.8	74.2	47.3	49.1	31.1
% in households receiving one or more means-tested benefit(s)*****	34.1	51.0	23.2	57.1	62.3	55.9	51.8	27.9
% with self-perceived financial difficulties	9.3	20.2	10.1	12.9	21.4	15.7	34.7	16.6
Maximum unweighted sample size******	15545	191	480	893	371	264	379	382

Base: All UK MCS mothers when baby was 9-10 months old. Weighted percentages.

Statistical tests on figures in each row rejected null hypotheses of similarity between ethnic groups at level of p = 0.001 for all rows.

* A heterogeneous category comprised of women of all other backgrounds.

** Existing derived variable giving NVQ equivalence of respondent's highest academic or vocational educational qualification.

*** Based on current or past occupation.

**** Below 60% of the median equivalence household income scale.

***** These are: Income Support, Jobseekers' Allowance, Working Families Tax Credit, Disabled Persons Tax Credit.

****** Unweighted sample of all main respondent mothers (natural, adoptive, foster, step) before missing cases on particular variables were dropped.

Table A3.2: Log odds from models of whether mother living in poverty, using different definitions of poverty

	Means-tested benefits*		Low-income poor**	
	Model 1	Model 2	Model 1	Model 2
Parents' marital status				
Married natural parents	1.00	–	1.00	–
Cohabiting natural parents	3.47***	–	2.07***	–
Lone natural mother	38.56***	–	14.03***	–
Mother's highest qualification				
None on the list shown	1.00	1.00	1.00	1.00
NVQ Level 1	0.67***	0.77*	0.88NS	1.14NS
NVQ Level 2	0.46***	0.62***	0.53***	0.70***
NVQ Level 3	0.41***	0.58***	0.43***	0.59***
NVQ Level 4	0.24***	0.39***	0.24***	0.35***
NVQ Level 5	0.16***	0.21***	0.17***	0.24***
Employment during pregnancy				
No	1.00	1.00	1.00	1.00
Yes	0.18***	0.67***	0.34***	0.91NS
Mother's age at birth				
14 to 19	1.00	1.00	1.00	1.00
20 to 29	0.43***	0.56***	0.41***	0.54***
30 to 39	0.23***	0.33***	0.22***	0.32***
40 plus	0.22***	0.25***	0.22***	0.30***
Mother's ethnicity				
White	1.00	1.00	1.00	1.00
Mixed	2.29***	1.72NS	2.07**	1.64NS
Indian	0.32***	0.44*	1.61*	2.01***
Pakistani or Bangladeshi	0.72*	0.95NS	3.56***	4.37***
Black or Black British	1.96***	2.44***	1.68***	1.77**
Other	1.01NS	1.29NS	1.54*	1.85**
Number of siblings of baby				
Only child	1.00	1.00	1.00	1.00
1 sibling	1.12*	1.30**	1.86***	2.14***
2 siblings	1.54***	1.63***	3.63***	4.15***
3+ siblings	2.88***	2.41***	7.53***	7.65***
Country				
England	1.00	1.00	1.00	1.00
Wales	1.10NS	1.08NS	1.19*	1.21*
Scotland	1.18NS	1.31NS	1.40***	1.52***
Northern Ireland	1.10NS	1.34*	1.58***	1.84***
Type of ward				
Non-disadvantaged	1.00	1.00	1.00	1.00
Other disadvantaged	1.76***	1.53***	1.72***	1.60***
Minority ethnic	2.27***	1.61**	2.11***	1.86***
Combined marital & employment status				
Married, both employed	–	1.00	–	1.00
Married, one earner	–	7.48***	–	3.77***
Married, zero earners	–	315.68***	–	38.88***
Cohabiting, both employed	–	3.29***	–	1.68***
Cohabiting, one earner	–	39.32***	–	7.59***
Cohabiting, zero earners	–	655.49***	–	74.87***
Lone, earner	–	38.12***	–	7.01***
Lone, not employed	–	1867.17***	–	137.20***
Unweighted sample size	16908	16877	16407	16373
F statistic	159.91	128.08	141.32	119.93
Chi Square	0.000	0.000	0.000	0.000

Base: All UK MCS natural mothers. $p < 0.001$***, $p < 0.01$**, $p < 0.05$* NS = Not Significant. Standard errors corrected for cluster sample design. * Dependent variable = 1 where all natural mothers were identified as means-tested benefit poor, zero otherwise. ** Dependent variable = 1 where all natural mothers were identified as low-income poor, zero otherwise.

Table A3.3: Household income bands used in MCS sweep 1 for UK couple and lone parents

Couple parents	UK responses (%)	Lone parents	UK responses (%)
Less than £1600	0.3	Less than £1050	1.2
£1600 to < £3100	0.4	£1050 to < £2100	1.5
£3100 to < £4700	0.8	£2100 to <£3100	2.0
£4700 to <£6200	1.6	£3100 to <£4200	7.4
£6200 to <£7800	2.1	£4200 to <£5200	19.7
£7800 to <£10400	4.1	£5200 to <£7000	23.8
£10400 to <£13000	6.6	£7000 to <£8600	12.2
£13000 to <£15600	8.1	£8600 to <£10400	9.4
£15600 to <£18200	8.8	£10400 to <£12200	5.9
£18200 to <£20800	8.4	£12200 to <£13800	3.8
£20800 to <£26000	13.9	£13800 to <£17400	3.1
£26000 to <£31200	10.3	£17400 to <£20800	1.4
£31200 to <£36400	7.4	£20800 to <£24200	0.8
£36400 to <£41600	5.4	£24200 to <£27800	0.7
£41600 to <£46800	3.5	£27800 to <£31200	0.2
£46800 to <£52000	2.9	£31200 to <£34600	0.1
£52000 to <£80000	5.0	£34600 to <£52000	0.2
£80000+	2.8	£52000+	0.1
Don't know	5.4	Don't know	4.0
Refused	2.1	Refused	2.5
Total %	100	Total %	100
Unweighted sample size	14928	Unweighted sample size	3588

Base: All UK MCS main respondents. 'Which of the groups on this card represents you (and your husband's) total take-home income from all these sources and earnings after tax and other deductions. Just tell me the number beside the row that applies to your income/s.'

Notes

[1] McClements equivalence scale = 1 for a childless couple

Number of people in family	Equivalence scale
Head	0.61
Spouse	0.39
Each additional adult (over 16)	0.45
Each child	0.09–0.36

[2] See Table A3.3 for complete set of income bands.

[3] For top and bottom categories of the income bands the thresholds were used as the income level. The survey does not include enough information to adjust for housing costs.

[4] This is indeed a more restrictive definition of claiming means-tested benefits than one which merely sums all those claiming at least one of the following: Income Support, Jobseekers' Allowance, Disabled Persons Tax Credit or Working Families Tax Credit, which includes 35.3% of families (see Plewis et al, 2004, Table A2.11). The latter is nearly double the measure used in the text. The difference between the two measures consists largely of families eligible for WFTC but with too high an income to qualify for Housing Benefit (or other non-claimants of Housing Benefit).

[5] The next waves of the MCS include questions that will help to refine this measure.

[6] The analyses by Hawkes at al (2004) confirm that low education and unemployment of a partner contribute to low income in two-parent families.

[7] Although all Models (1,2, 3 and 4) were estimated on both of these two alternative and more objective dependent variables, for interest it is arguable about how far entering variables capturing mothers' earnings into the model of being on means-tested benefits is a sensible or valid thing to do.

[8] The survey did not ask about the residence in the UK of grandparents of the cohort baby.

[9] This contact is recorded as 'your mother' and 'your father', which we assume was interpreted by respondents as meaning their biological parents. This limits any analysis of the relationship between the cohort parent and step-parents.

[10] Research by Ermisch (2004) suggested that adult sons and daughters who are more affluent have less frequent contact with their parents.

FOUR

Pregnancy and childbirth

Hiranthi Jayaweera, Heather Joshi, Alison Macfarlane,
Denise Hawkes and Neville Butler

The Millennium Cohort Study (MCS) collected information about pregnancy and delivery retrospectively at 9–10 months after the child's birth. For this and other reasons, midwives and other clinical staff were not involved in the data collection, unlike the 1946, 1958 and 1970 cohort studies which started as birth surveys. This limited the potential for collecting reliable detailed information about topics such as complications in pregnancy and at delivery. Clearly, pregnancy and childbirth have got safer over time. In the 1946 birth cohort, 4.0% of babies died in the first week after birth, 3.3% in the 1958 cohort and 2.4% in the 1970 cohort (Williams, 1997). On the other hand, the MCS covered some issues not included in the earlier, more clinically oriented birth cohort surveys.

Many but not all of the topics in this chapter are monitored through routine data systems in the four countries of the UK. Birth registration and NHS maternity statistics systems collect information about trends in demographic structure and patterns of care at delivery, although the ways in which they do so differ between countries. What these routine systems do not provide, however, is much information about the social factors which lie behind these changes in care and in the population giving birth. In addition, NHS maternity systems are largely based on information about hospital care. They do not contain information about encounters which usually take place in the community, notably women's first NHS consultations about maternity care and their use of other services such as antenatal classes. The NHS records also contain only limited information about births outside hospital. The aim of this chapter is both to analyse the data about pregnancy and mothers' use of services in their social context, and to relate them to the trends documented elsewhere.

The national service framework for children, young people and maternity, published in 2004, has a social as well as a clinical agenda (DfES and DH, 2004): 'Women have easy access to supportive, high quality maternity services, designed around their individual needs and those of their babies.' *Standard 11, maternity'* emphasises choice for women in planning their own care and choosing the place to give birth. It also prioritises the needs of marginalised women, particularly those from disadvantaged groups. Fieldwork for the first sweep of the MCS took place before most of these policies were implemented. The data provide, therefore, a useful baseline against which the new policies could be assessed in future. Comparison with previous birth cohorts and other surveys as well as routine data can inform other policy issues.

The MCS enables us to pay special attention to families from minority ethnic groups with new births on whom little reliable information was previously available, especially on their socioeconomic circumstances (see Table A3.1). We do know from the Family Resources Survey that children in households in which the head was of minority ethnic origin in 2001-02, the period in which the MCS sweep 1 interviews took place, were more likely than those in white households to be on low income. Forty-one per cent of children in Black Caribbean households compared to 24% of those in white households, rising to 68% of children in Pakistani and Bangladeshi households, were in the lowest quintile of the income distribution in Britain after housing costs (DWP, 2003b). Membership of a minority ethnic group clearly affects life chances as well as living standards. For some groups there is a higher than average rate of poor health outcomes for mothers and babies, as reflected in infant deaths and maternal mortality and morbidity (Parsons et al, 1993). Studies of low-income families with young children have shown how living on a low income, with limited access to money, resources and services such as transport, childcare and healthcare, and a healthy diet, lead to poor health outcomes for family members (Kempson, 1996; Jayaweera and Garcia, 2000; Millar and Ridge, 2001). There is also local study evidence that women of Bangladeshi origin, and particularly those with limited English fluency, have difficulty in gaining information about and accessing aspects of antenatal care and screening for anomalies (Hemingway et al, 1997; Sandall et al, 2001).

Estimates from the Confidential Enquiry into Maternal Deaths (Lewis and Drife, 2004) covering the period 2000-02 for the UK, suggested that on average women in non-white ethnic groups had three times the risk of maternal mortality of women in white groups. Black African women, including refugees and asylum seekers, were seven times more likely than white women, and nearly three times more likely than Black Caribbean or Bangladeshi women, to die in pregnancy or within 42 days after the birth. Rates for Indian and Pakistani women were no higher than those of white women. Generally, there is evidence of a lower level of access to care among non-white women who died, compared to white women, including late booking (>22 weeks) and poor or no antenatal clinic attendance (Lewis and Drife, 2004).

Plan of this chapter

In the rest of this chapter, we review the process of giving birth in the Millennium. First, we examine the timing of motherhood. We look at the age of motherhood, whether it was planned and whether fertility was assisted. The chapter follows with a consideration of the use and experience of the health services related to maternity and delivery. Finally, we consider mothers' intentions about future fertility.

A few of the 18,553 MCS families have been excluded from some or all of the tabulations in this chapter. As the focus is on mothers' experiences, the 50 households where the main informant was not the baby's natural mother have been excluded and most of the detailed analyses are restricted to singleton births, with a few analyses of multiple births, as numbers allow. As parents' experiences, clinical complications and their use of services differ radically between first and subsequent births, they have been analysed separately in many cases.

We make particular use of the data on mothers from ethnic minorities throughout this chapter. Details for ethnic groups in England are reported in Table A4.2 and some regression analyses of the ethnic differences in several perinatal outcomes in Table A4.3. Scotland and Northern Ireland have their own birth registration systems. Information on country of birth was only available to the MCS by linking administrative data into the survey. At the time of writing, this linkage had only been completed for England, making country of birth data unavailable for analysis for Wales, Scotland or Northern Ireland. Although these tables include some information on low birthweight, defined as below 2,500g, the analysis of this (and breastfeeding) is postponed to the next chapter.

Mother's age at birth and its demographic context

The children in the Millennium Cohort were born at the end of a period of falling birth rates, when they reached an all-time low, as noted in Chapter 1. Overall fertility had been falling in England and Wales since 1990 although it rose in 2002 and 2003 (ONS, 2004a).

Fertility rates in Scotland had fallen to a level below that of England and Wales (Graham and Boyle, 2003) but there was an increase in 2003. In Northern Ireland, where rates were above those for the other countries, the fertility rate also reached a minimum in 2002 and rose slightly in 2003 (General Register Office, Northern Ireland, 2004).

The other marked demographic trend was the increasing age at childbirth which has been a common feature in most developed countries. Birth rates have been declining for women in their 20s and rising for women in their 30s and early 40s. In England and Wales as a whole, over the last quarter of the 20th century, the proportion of babies with mothers aged 25-29 declined and became smaller than the increasing proportion with mothers aged 30-34 *(*Maher and Macfarlane, 2004a). This is also the case in Scotland and Northern Ireland, but the two groups are of almost similar size in Wales, where there are proportionately more births to women in their teens compared with the rest of the United Kingdom. Furthermore, in England and Wales as a whole, the 30-34 age group now has the lowest proportion of low-weight babies and the lowest rates of infant mortality (Maher and Macfarlane, 2004b).

The age distribution of mothers of all births is reflected in the age distribution of the mothers in the sample. Overall, nearly a third of all natural MCS mothers were in the 30-34 age group, while only around a quarter were under 25. When the data in the MCS sample were compared with those from birth registrations in Table 4.1, the survey appeared to under-represent mothers in their early 20s and the much smaller group of mothers aged 40 and over. Wales had a higher

Table 4.1: Comparisons of age distributions of percentages of registered maternities occurring in 2001 and weighted percentages of natural mothers in Millennium Cohort sample

		Mother's age, years						
Country		Under 20	20-24	25-29	30-34	35-39	40 and over	Total %	Number of observations (unweighted)
England	Registration	7.3	18.3	26.9	30.1	14.6	2.8	100.0	558,271
	MCS	7.1	15.9	27.7	31.6	15.4	2.2	100.0	11,496
Wales	Registration	10.4	21.3	27.4	26.8	11.8	2.2	100.0	30,325
	MCS	9.5	18.9	26.9	31.2	11.6	1.9	100.0	2,755
Scotland	Registration	8.6	17.5	26.3	30.8	14.6	2.4	100.0	52,018
	MCS	8.1	16.6	25.0	31.8	16.1	2.4	100.0	2,327
N Ireland	Registration	7.0	17.0	27.8	31.2	14.4	2.7	100.0	21,722
	MCS	6.8	15.7	28.0	31.7	15.6	2.2	100.0	1,919
UK	Registration	7.6	18.3	26.9	30.1	14.5	2.7	100.0	662,608
	MCS	7.3	16.2	27.4	31.6	15.3	2.2	100.0	18,503

Base: All MCS natural mothers and registered maternities in 2001. MCS weighted percentages.

proportion of registered births to younger mothers compared with the other countries.

While the mean age of the mother at the birth of the cohort child was 29 for the study as a whole, Pakistani and Bangladeshi mothers were distinctly younger with mean ages of 26 and 25 respectively (Table A2.2). Those of Black African identity were on average older with a mean age of 31. Similar patterns can be seen in data from birth registrations in England and Wales when data for births to migrant women are analysed by the mother's age and country of birth (Collingwood Bakeo, 2004).

There were major differences by age in cohort mothers' marital/cohabitation status. While over half of mothers under 18 were neither married nor cohabiting at the time of the birth, this was true of less than 10% of mothers in their 30s and 40s, three quarters of whom were married. While a quarter of women in their early 20s were neither married nor cohabiting, this was the case for just over 10% of those in their late 20s.

The social profile of the timing of motherhood

The diversity of socioeconomic circumstances of families with mothers of different ages reflects a marked difference between women who

Table 4.2: Parents' marital status and mother's social class by mother's age

	Mother's age, years							
	Under 18	18-19	20-24	25-29	30-34	35-39	40 and over	All UK total
Marital status at time of birth								
Spouse	4.9	11.5	35.0	65.0	76.7	74.7	73.0	61.5
Cohabiting	42.6	43.6	39.8	24.2	16.5	18.3	18.9	24.7
Neither	52.5	44.9	25.3	10.8	6.8	7.0	8.2	13.9
Total %	100.0	100.0	100.0	100.0	100.0	100.0	100.0	100.0
Unweighted sample size	487	1099	3555	5113	5345	2513	391	18503
Woman's NS-SEC, three class								
Managerial and professional	1.9	3.7	8.9	26.3	43.4	47.2	47.4	30.9
Intermediate	5.7	11.0	17.6	24.9	24.5	24.6	25.0	22.4
Routine and manual	51.5	69.1	60.0	42.1	27.7	23.6	23.3	38.8
No stated occupation	40.9	16.2	13.5	6.7	4.5	4.6	4.4	7.9
Total %	100.0	100.0	100.0	100.0	100.0	100.0	100.0	100.0
Unweighted sample size	487	1099	3555	5113	5345	2513	391	18503

Base: All UK MCS natural mothers when cohort baby was 9-10 months old.
Weighted percentages.

have their first child early and late. Early motherhood was most likely for those from and in disadvantaged circumstances, and very uncommon among those with higher qualifications. Delaying motherhood towards and beyond age 30, which has become more and more frequent towards the turn of the century, is particularly common among those with higher status careers. The contrasts between early and late mothers are partly due to differences which pre-date parenthood, but are compounded by various disadvantages in adult life: a poorer chance of having or keeping a partner; of having or keeping a job; of having or gaining qualifications; of attaining home ownership; of living in a more congenial neighbourhood; of higher income, higher life satisfaction and good mental health. Early motherhood is a marker for a whole set of disadvantages, for the mother and the cohort child, without necessarily being their cause (Hawkes et al, 2004; Joshi and Wright, 2005).

Around one quarter of Bangladeshi mothers, and those of mixed origins (25.8%) and Black Caribbean (23.5 %) mothers were teenage mothers for their first ever child, not necessarily the cohort child (Table A2.2). Among other Asian mothers, proportions of teenage mothers at first birth were far lower among Indians (5.5%) than among Pakistanis (15.2%). Other recent research has found similar ethnic patterns in teenage motherhood (Berthoud, 2001a).

We explored, through multivariate analysis, the relationship between age at motherhood and some background factors for the subset of women who had their first birth in the MCS (Table A4.1). The most common (and median) age band was 28-30, but there is quite a range extending either side: teenagers up to age 18 accounted for 9% of these first births and women aged 34 and over for 14%. We present a model of mothers' age and timing of a first birth in age bands over the whole of the age span, rather than focusing on either early or late births specifically. The explanatory variables were selected as likely to be largely pre-existing circumstances, rather than the result of the timing of the cohort child's birth. These included some known features of the mother's childhood (including the stability of her own parents' partnership as discussed in Chapter 2), her ethnic identity, and the country and type of area in which she was living at the time of the survey.

The 41% of mothers who left school at the minimum age had a strong and significant tendency to have their first child relatively young (as shown by the negative coefficient), as did those whose parents who had split up (30% before the cohort child's birth) and the minority who had been in care as children. As these factors are correlated with each other (and other variables in the model), the impact of each when all factors are adjusted for each other is moderated but not eliminated. Belonging to a minority ethnic group certainly pre-dates entry to motherhood, but the association with the age at which motherhood happened is diverse. Only three groups were significantly more likely to become mothers when young: mothers of Bangladeshi, Pakistani and mixed ethnic identity. Other groups had birth timing similar to whites. This pattern is little changed whether or not other factors are controlled. Residence in a ward of high minority ethnic population in England had an additional association with early childbearing. The other controls for type of area show that mothers living in disadvantaged areas in all four countries had a higher likelihood of childbearing at young ages. This, to a lesser extent, was also the case for mothers living in non-disadvantaged areas in Wales and Northern Ireland, when compared with those in the rest of England.

The follow-up of these families will help in due course to see whether the spread of these sociodemographic starting points is compounded or compensated in the development of family circumstances as the new century progresses.

The decision to have a child

Overall 58.1% of mothers said that their pregnancy was planned. This varied widely by age, with only 15.7% of women aged under 20 and 39.3% of those aged 20-24 saying their pregnancy was planned. In contrast, over two thirds of mothers aged 30-34 and nearly two thirds of other mothers aged 25 or over said they had planned their pregnancy (Table 4.3).

Of the mothers for whom the cohort baby was her first, 57.4% said the pregnancy was planned, while planning was the case for 58.7% of mothers having their second or subsequent babies. Despite this overall similarity, there were marked differences between age groups, as Table 4.3 shows, with over three quarters of first births to women aged 30 or over being planned.

Among women who had planned their pregnancy, 82.4% said they had been very happy to be pregnant and a further 16.1% said they were happy to be pregnant; fewer than 2% reported ambivalent feelings or unhappiness. Women aged under 20 were slightly less likely than older women to report that they were very happy rather than just happy. Within each age group, women with planned pregnancies were more likely to report that they were very happy for first births than for subsequent births.

Table 4.3: Mothers' views about becoming pregnant

	Mother's age						Unweighted sample size	P value
	Under 20	20-24	25-29	30-34	35 and over	All ages		
Whether pregnancy was planned								
Weighted percentage who said pregnancy was planned								
All	15.7	39.3	62.9	69.9	64.7	58.1	18,216	0.0000
First births	14.6	37.9	68.3	77.1	76.0	57.4	7,457	0.0000
Not first birth	21.8	40.4	58.7	66.0	60.9	58.7	10,532	0.0000
Mother's feelings about unplanned births								
Weighted percentage of all unplanned births								
Mother was:								
Very happy	16.4	24.9	28.9	30.5	32.9	27.1	2,197	0.0000
Happy	39.1	39.4	38.3	36.9	31.9	37.4	3,114	
Not bothered either way	16.9	13.8	12.3	11.7	11.0	13.0	1,118	
Unhappy	20.5	14.9	14.9	12.9	16.7	15.5	1,320	
Very unhappy	7.2	7.0	5.5	8.1	7.4	7.0	591	
First births:								
Weighted percentage of unplanned first births								
Very happy or happy	56.2	68.5	78.0	76.7	84.0	69.0	2,348	0.0000
Unhappy or very unhappy	26.6	20.1	14.2	12.8	11.5	19.2	702	
Subsequent births:								
Weighted percentage of unplanned subsequent births								
Very happy or happy	51.3	59.0	60.3	63.7	60.7	60.9	2,876	0.0000
Unhappy or very unhappy	33.2	24.2	24.6	24.0	26.8	25.1	1,188	

Base: All UK MCS natural mothers when cohort baby was 9-10 months old. Weighted percentages

Not surprisingly, the picture was somewhat different for women who had not planned their pregnancies. But even here, 69.0% of mothers with first births and 60.9% of those with subsequent births said they were happy or very happy, although mothers under 20 were far less likely to be happy (Table 4.3). While a fifth of all first-time mothers and a quarter of other mothers said they had been unhappy or very unhappy, this was true of a quarter of first-time mothers aged under 20 and a third of other mothers in this age group. It should be noted that these reports are of feelings about an event up to 18 months before the interview. Views about an unplanned pregnancy may well have been modified in the light of a decision not to terminate the pregnancy or of the relationship with the baby once born.

Of course, these data need to be set in the context of unwanted pregnancies which did not continue. The Office for National Statistics combines data from birth registration with those from notification of abortion under the 1967 Act to derive estimated conception rates (ONS, 2004a). Miscarriages are not included as there are no data collected routinely about them. An estimated 22.7% of the 767,000 known conceptions in 2000 in England and Wales ended in a termination of pregnancy. The proportion was 39.3% among women aged under 20, 35.4% among women over 40 and lower in the age groups in between. In Scotland, where conception rates are estimated only for mothers under 20, the percentage of conceptions in 2000-01 ending in termination was very similar to that in England and Wales – 40.9% (ISD Scotland, 2004a). Estimates are not constructed for Northern Ireland as the 1967 Abortion Act does not apply so most terminations take place outside the province. Among conceptions which end in a registered live birth, about 0.5% would have died before 9 months of age when sampling for the cohort took place.

Multiple births and use of subfertility management

Overall 3.1% of women used some sort of procedure for subfertility management. This included not only those who had IVF or some other form of assisted conception, but also those who used drugs to stimulate ovulation. Not surprisingly, given that fertility problems are more likely among older women, assistance with fertility varied markedly by age, being very uncommon in women aged under 25, while 5.8% of women aged 35 and over used one or more of these procedures. Women in professional, managerial and intermediate occupations were more likely to use assisted fertility methods than others. This is a consequence not only of their older age at childbirth, but also of the fact that assisted conception was not available under the National Health Service at the time the survey took place. Only more affluent women and their partners would have been able to afford it at that time. There was also a difference between first-time mothers, 4.7% of whom used subfertility management, and other mothers, of whom only 1.9% used it.

The cohort sample includes 246 sets of twins and 10 sets of triplets. Mothers with multiple births formed 1.5% of all births, which is in line with data from birth registration. As expected, the proportions were higher among older mothers, as older women are more likely to have multiple births spontaneously, as well as being more likely to have them as a consequence of using subfertility management. Some form of assisted fertility had been used by half of the women who had triplets and 26% of those who had twins, compared with only 2.7% of mothers who had just one baby. The social class differences in the percentages of multiple births reflect this variation along with differences in the age at childbearing.

The incidence of multiple births varied by ethnic identity. It was lower among the Asian than among the white mothers, and higher among the mixed (1.9%) and especially Black African (3.0%) compared to 1.5% among white mothers. Similar patterns can be seen in data from birth registration (Collingwood Bakeo, 2004). The higher proportion of multiple births among cohort babies born to Black African mothers may be related to the fact that they were slightly older than mothers in other ethnic groups at the birth of the cohort baby. However, it is more likely to arise from longstanding and well-established ethnic difference (MacGillivray et al, 1988).

Pregnancy experiences and use of antenatal services

Pregnancy confirmation

In the sample as a whole, over half of the women said they had their pregnancy confirmed by a doctor or midwife before the eighth week of pregnancy. This included the 5.0% who reported having it confirmed before four weeks. Most women had their pregnancy confirmed before 16 weeks, but 3.4% said they had it confirmed at 16 or more weeks and 1.0% said it had not been confirmed. The percentages whose pregnancy was confirmed at 12 or more weeks are shown in Table A4.2 (row 2). Pregnancy was reported sooner for first-time mothers than for others and there were marked age and socioeconomic classification differences. The youngest women and those in manual and routine occupations or with no stated occupation reported pregnancy being confirmed later than others.

There were differences by ethnic identity in the timing of confirmation of pregnancy (Table A4.2, rows 2 and 3). Generally, differences between mothers from white and other ethnic identities were wider for the first antenatal visit compared with confirmation of pregnancy, although not all these differences were statistically significant (Table A4.3, columns 5 and 7).

Overall, relatively few mothers in any ethnic group reported confirming their pregnancy after 12 weeks, and ethnic group membership was associated significantly with late confirmation of pregnancy only for Black Caribbean mothers, after allowing for potential confounders (Table A4.3). Additionally adjusting for whether English was spoken at home made no further difference to these results.

Antenatal care

The vast majority of women (97.1%) received antenatal care. This is a similar proportion to the 98% reported in the UK Infant Feeding Survey conducted in 2000 (Hamlyn et al, 2002). Over 7% of women under 20 and around 5% of women aged 20-24 reported that they had not had antenatal care. The proportions were similar for first-time and other mothers in each age group. We must bear in mind that some of the reports of lack of antenatal care may be due to differential ability to recall experiences reliably, 9 months or more later, which might vary by age.

Among those who reported receiving antenatal care, 4.2% did not start it until 20 weeks or more of pregnancy and a further 7.1% started at 16-19 weeks, while 44.5% reported starting at 12-15 weeks. Overall, 11.0% of mothers (n=1,085) reported they had not had an antenatal visit until after 16 weeks of pregnancy. We considered 16 weeks and over as a suitable marker for a first antenatal visit being defined as 'late', given the recommendation in the NICE Antenatal Care Guidelines that most antenatal tests and screening should take place before 16 weeks of pregnancy (NCCWCH, 2003).

Overall, there was little difference between first-time and other mothers in the timing of starting antenatal care, although this did differ by age group. Overall, a fifth of mothers under 20 and around 10% of older mothers reported starting antenatal care after 16 weeks. Mothers in managerial and professional occupations tended to start sooner than mothers in lower status occupations or those without an occupation.

Ethnic identity was strongly associated with not receiving antenatal care (Table A4.2, row 1). Twelve per cent of Bangladeshi and 10.0% of Pakistani mothers reported that they had never had any antenatal care. The proportions of mothers in the other groups, particularly of mixed, other, Indian and Black African identities, who had not received antenatal care were smaller but still quite marked. These patterns are not consistent with other evidence that suggests that the uptake of antenatal care nationally is near universal. In the 1994–95 Infant Feeding in Asian Families Survey, 97.0% of Bangladeshi mothers, 98.0% of Pakistani mothers and 99.0% of Indian mothers, compared with 100.0% of white mothers, said that they had at least one antenatal check up (Thomas and Avery, 1997, p 53). In that survey, mothers were interviewed for the first time when their babies were a few weeks old – much earlier than the MCS interviews. Therefore, the differences may in part lie in difficulties of recall over time among the MCS mothers. It is also possible that being recent migrants may explain some of the difference. [1] This was not possible to analyse as there were no data in the MCS on the date of migration of non-UK born respondents. There is also the possibility that some women may, for example, have been moving between Bangladesh and Britain while they were pregnant, and therefore not getting antenatal care in Britain. Negative attitudes to being attended by male GPs and hospital doctors, particularly if they are from the women's own ethnic communities, may also play a part in explaining the lower rate of antenatal care for mothers in some minority ethnic groups (Katbamna, 2000). Practical difficulties in accessing care, such as the need to find someone who can help women communicate in English with health professionals, and the need to arrange for the care of older children while on antenatal visits, may also be important elements of the explanation.

After allowing for potential confounding influences in a multivariate analysis, (Table A4.3), mothers of mixed and Pakistani ethnic identities were around twice as likely not to receive antenatal care compared with white mothers (Odds Ratio=2.4 and 1.9, respectively), and this was statistically significant ($p<0.05$). However, when further adjustment was made for whether English was spoken at home, these effects were weaker and no longer significant at the 5.0% level (data not shown). Receiving antenatal care was also associated significantly but separately with ethnic group, no English being spoken at home and the individual's birthplace being outside the UK. While all were significant when associated separately in turn, they were no longer significant when adjusted for each other. This suggests that it is difficult to separate out these effects.

Ethnic identity was strongly associated with a late first antenatal visit. After allowing for potential confounders, including whether born in the UK or not (Table A4.3), Bangladeshi and Black African mothers were about twice as likely (Odds Ratio=2.0 in both cases), and those in the 'other' ethnic grouping were nearly three times as likely (Odds Ratio=2.7), to be late attenders for antenatal care. Black Caribbean mothers were also at increased risk of late attendance (Odds Ratio=1.8, p=0.015). These results were statistically significant (p<0.05). Some of these effects were due to language since, when further adjustment was made for whether English was spoken at home, they became weaker for mothers of all ethnic groups and only the results for Black Caribbean mothers and mothers in the 'other' ethnic group remained significant at the 5% confidence level.

Antenatal classes

The use of antenatal classes was markedly different by birth order, with 69.1% of first-time mothers and only 15.0% of other mothers reporting that they had attended classes. These percentages are slightly higher than those reported in the UK Infant Feeding Survey conducted in 2000 (Hamlyn et al, 2002). Among first-time mothers, usage was much higher among older mothers and mothers in managerial and professional occupations, while for mothers having subsequent births usage was much lower and differences were far less marked.

There were wide differences by mothers' ethnic identity in whether the MCS mothers attended antenatal classes (Table A4.2 row 4). Around three quarters of Bangladeshi and Pakistani mothers, whose cohort baby was their first child, reported not attending classes compared with just under one third of white mothers. Indian mothers' experiences were closest to those of white mothers in their attendance patterns. However, between 42.0% and 46.0% of mothers in the other groups did not attend classes. The findings, particularly for Bangladeshi and Pakistani mothers, fit in with evidence from other studies (Katbamna, 2000).

Preterm birth

In the past, the term 'premature' was used to describe babies who were born too soon or too small. As the underlying factors for these are different, since the late 1970s, a distinction has been made between preterm birth and low birthweight. Babies born before 37 completed weeks of pregnancy are defined as 'preterm', those born between 37 and 41 weeks as 'term' and those born after 42 or more completed weeks as post-term (WHO, 1992). As many of the very preterm babies will have died before the age when interviews took place, they have not been included in the sample. This limits the scope for using the first sweep of MCS to look at preterm birth in the population, although not of course to follow up the survivors in successive sweeps.

Gestational age is notoriously difficult to measure, even when based on the most modern ultrasound techniques. 'Expected dates of delivery', when the duration of pregnancy is estimated to be 40 weeks, are of varying reliability. In addition, our examination of the MCS data on gestational age suggests that data gathered from mothers on this topic may also be unreliable.[2] The extent to which the problems are attributable to errors in recall or because mothers did not ever know the information accurately is not clear.[3] The linkage of survey data to administrative sources will in due course help to fill this gap and offer the potential for further analysis of the nature of the problem. We feel more confident about the data if we define 'preterm' as lying from 28 to 36 completed weeks of pregnancy and some analysis of this experience was undertaken.[4] On this basis, 6.8% of all births, and 7.3% of first births in this sample were preterm.

Overall, preterm births showed differences by mother's age which are similar to those in the national data for Scotland (ISD Scotland and Scottish Programme for Clinical Effectiveness in Reproductive Health, 1998) and elsewhere. The highest rates of preterm births were among the youngest mothers under 20 and the oldest mothers. This pattern was particularly marked among births which were not to first-time mothers. The reported percentages of preterm births were 15.8% for mothers aged under 20 with existing children and 7.5% for those over 35. Among first-time mothers, however, rates of very preterm births were higher among women aged 30-34 (7.7%) than among older mothers. No differences between socioeconomic circumstances or ethnic groups were detected (Table A4.3). Analyses in the West Midlands and East London have shown high rates of preterm birth among West African and Caribbean mothers (Aveyard et al, 2002; Macfarlane et al, 2004), but this was not replicated in the MCS data possibly because of their high mortality. These findings should be regarded as provisional and should be revisited once the linkage to hospital records is complete.

Care at delivery and postnatally

Place of birth

Overall, 2.3% of mothers had their babies at home and 0.2% had them in places other than hospitals. Hospital maternity care was not subdivided by type, so it was not possible to distinguish the use of birth centres, in hospitals with or without a consultant obstetric unit or other types of midwife-led care. Over 2% of MCS births in England and Wales were at home, 1.8% of those in Scotland and 0.2% of those in Northern Ireland, roughly the same pattern seen in national statistics. Only 0.6% of first-time births but 3.6% of subsequent births took place at home. Mothers aged 20-24 were less likely than others to have births at home and mothers in managerial, professional and intermediate occupations were more likely than others to do so.

Home births were even less common for mothers of Asian ethnic identity. All the Bangladeshi mothers had their babies in hospital and 99% of Indian and Pakistani mothers did so. To some extent, this reflects the clustering of home births and the fact that the places with the most proactive home birth policies are less likely to be those in areas with significant minority ethnic populations.

During the 20th century, there was a radical change from home to hospitals and other institutions as the usual place of birth. The percentage of births in hospitals and maternity homes rose from 15% in 1927 to 24% in 1932 and 35% in 1937 (Campbell and Macfarlane, 1994). In the post-war era, political concern was about meeting the rising demand for hospital care and 42.4% of singleton babies in the 1946 cohort and 36.1% of those in the 1958 cohort were born at home (Chamberlain et al, 1975). Analyses of the 1958 British Perinatal Mortality Survey, which were interpreted as suggesting that home births were unsafe, contributed to these policies (Butler and Bonham, 1963; Fedrick and Butler, 1978), although their interpretation was subsequently challenged (Cochrane, 1972; Campbell and Macfarlane, 1994). During the 1960s, the number of births declined and the number of beds increased so that, by 1970 when only 12.4% of singleton births in the cohort were born at home, birth in a district general hospital became official policy (Campbell and Macfarlane, 1994). This remained the case until the early 1980s, but the policies set out in Changing Childbirth (DH, 1993) have not led to a substantial increase in the proportion of home births nationally. Another major change which took place steadily over the second half of the 20th century has been the declining length of postnatal stay. Most MCS mothers stayed in hospital for no more than two days and many went home in under 24 hours while the mean hospital stay in 1946 for women, who did give birth there, was 13 days (Campbell and Macfarlane, 1994; Williams, 1997).

Who was present at the birth?

Only 4% of the mothers gave birth with no one other than health professionals present. In 86% of cases overall, the baby's father was present. In 16% of cases, the mother's own mother or mother-in-law was there, possibly in addition to the partner. In two-parent families, the baby's father was present at the birth in 93% of cases, and in 47% of lone-mother families. There were few differences across the countries of the UK in this, but striking differences by ethnic group, as shown in Figure 4.1.

Higher percentages of Black African and Black Caribbean mothers than those in other groups had no one present at the birth except health professionals (Table A4.2, row 7; Figure 4.1). Fewer Black Caribbean and Black African mothers had their baby's father present at the birth. This is not surprising given the higher rates of single parenthood in these groups. Alongside Pakistani mothers, Black

Figure 4.1: Whether no one, the baby's father or the respondent's mother (in-law) were present during the birth

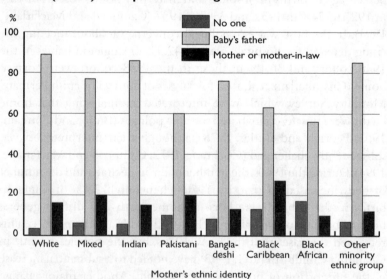

Base: MCS natural mothers in England.
Note: It is possible to be counted in both baby's father and mother (in-law) categories.
Weighted percentages.

Caribbean mothers were also the most likely to have their mothers or mothers-in-law as birth partners.

Induction of labour

Overall, just under 30% of mothers said they were 'induced' compared with 26% in the 1970 cohort. Rates had risen in the 1960s and continued to rise in the early 1970s in response to high perinatal mortality rates found in prolonged pregnancies in the 1958 British Perinatal Mortality Survey (Butler and Bonham, 1963). The interpretation of these findings was already being questioned in the early 1970s, and induction rates fell in the late 1970s in response to major doubts and criticisms about over-use of the practice (Chamberlain et al, 1978; Chalmers, 1978). This experience made a major contribution to the later decision to focus on evaluation of healthcare through randomised trials rather than undertaking a further birth survey in 1982 (Williams, 1997).

'Induction' should mean rupturing membranes and/or the use of oxytocin or prostaglandin to start labour. It could also incorrectly include the use of these drugs to speed up labour, as has been reported in other data collection systems and surveys (Macfarlane et al, 2000). Official sources suggest 21.5% of all labours in England and 26.8% of live births in Scotland in 2000-01 were induced. It would appear that the induction rates in the MCS are higher than average and this may be due to the definitions varying (DH, 2003; ISD Scotland, 2004b). Most inconsistently, 13% of MCS mothers who had elective caesareans reported that they had been 'induced'.

There were no differences by age in induction rates for either first-time or other mothers, nor according to whether the definitions of induction were narrowly or more widely defined. The differences in the overall induction rate reflect the differences between the age distributions of the two groups. In contrast, mothers having second or subsequent babies appeared to have been less likely to be induced if they were in managerial, professional or intermediate occupations. Mothers of mixed ethnic origin were the most likely to be induced for the cohort baby; just under 50% compared with 23% of Indian mothers and between 30% and 40% of mothers in the other ethnic groups. There was a significant difference in induction rates according to ethnicity only if the cohort baby was the first born (p=0.036) (Table A4.2).

Method of delivery

Just over two thirds of mothers of singleton babies in the cohort had a spontaneous vaginal birth without having either an assisted birth or a caesarean. One tenth of women had an assisted birth with either forceps or, more usually, the ventouse or vacuum extractor, which is now the preferred method of assisted vaginal birth. The remaining 21.3% had caesarean sections.

Rising rates of caesarean section have followed the move to hospital birth in the latter half of the 20th century. Only 2.7% of mothers of singleton babies in the 1958 cohort and 4.5% of those in the 1970 cohort had their babies delivered by caesarean section. In both England and Scotland, caesarean section rates rose through the 1970s, flattened off in the early 1980s and then rose again from the late 1980s onwards (Macfarlane and Mugford, 2000). Concern about the rise led to national audits in Scotland in the mid 1990s (McIlwaine et al, 1998) and in other countries of the UK at the turn of the century (National Sentinel Caesarean Section Audit, 2001). Although some clinicians have claimed that the rise in caesarean section rates has occurred in response to women's requests for elective caesarean sections, the National Sentinel Caesarean Section Audit found that mothers' requests were the primary indication in only one in 7.3% of caesarean sections and that this included cases where there were complications concerning the mother or the baby.

In the Millennium Cohort, 9.2% of singleton babies were born by elective caesarean and 12.1% by emergency caesarean. The rates for each country were similar to those reported in other sources (National Sentinel Caesarean Section Audit, 2001; Northern Ireland Perinatal Information Project, 2001; DH, 2002b; National Assembly for Wales, 2002; ISD Scotland, 2004b).

There were significant ethnic differences for all methods of assisted delivery, including caesarean sections, among women having first-born and non-first-born singleton cohort babies (p=0.0156 and p=0.0098). Pakistani mothers were the least likely to have an assisted delivery (just under 30%), and white, Indian and Black African mothers were the most likely (a little over 40%) for a singleton first-born cohort baby (Table A4.2, row 6). In a pattern similar to inductions, there was a considerable reduction in proportions of mothers in all ethnic groups, apart from those of mixed ethnic origin, experiencing an assisted delivery if their baby was not a first born. The highest proportion of mothers with previous births having an assisted delivery was among the mixed origin mothers, one third of whom had assisted deliveries.

The lowest proportions, slightly under 20%, were among the Bangladeshi and Pakistani mothers. Evidence from other studies found that some minority ethnic women in the UK experienced higher rates of interventions in delivery, including caesareans, than white women (Parsons et al, 1993). This finding is not straightforwardly replicated in the MCS. As we have seen, white mothers had higher rates of both induction and assisted delivery than women in some minority ethnic groups.

Across the board, assisted births and caesareans were more common for first-time mothers than for other mothers. The youngest mothers were least likely, and the oldest mothers most likely to have an assisted birth or a caesarean. Given the differences in age, it is therefore not surprising that mothers in managerial and professional occupations, and also those in intermediate occupations, were most likely to have caesareans. However, the differences were relatively small.

Increases in caesareans have been characterised in terms of middle-class women being 'too posh to push', but the situation is more complicated. Despite their greater affluence and better general health, the fact that middle-class women tend to delay childbearing means that they are more likely to encounter obstetric complications as well as reduced fertility.

Feelings about birth and future family intentions

Mothers were asked at the 9-month interview if they planned to have any more children. Half said no, just over one third (35%) said they did plan to have more children and one sixth (15%) said they did not know. Our analysis treats those who said they did not know as being more inclined to have further births than those who said no, but less so than those who said yes.

Older mothers and those who already had more than one child were more inclined to stop with the children they already had. Not having a partner also reduced the likelihood of planning more children. If the cohort birth had not been planned or was seen not to have been wanted, mothers were also less likely to want more children. In particular, young mothers, who were not happy about the cohort pregnancy, were least inclined to claim they wanted more children. Among minority ethnic groups, and before controlling for other factors, only Pakistani mothers were significantly more likely than average to be inclined to have further births.

Data from other sources show that many women experience backache, incontinence and pain during intercourse to a varying extent after childbirth. Such problems could well affect their decisions about having a further child, but were not in the interview schedule. There has been a considerable body of other research on this subject in recent years. Data from the General Household Survey for the years from 1979 to 2001 showed that there has been a fall in women's intended numbers of children over this period, along with a decline in actual family size (Smallwood and Jefferies, 2003). The data suggest, however, that intentions stated by young women in the 1980s appear to have been poor predictors of their final level of fertility. Analyses of linked data from the British Household Panel Study showed that women tended to overestimate their future fertility (Berrington, 2004). They showed consistency within couples between men's and women's fertility intentions. Conflicting responses were more likely when the woman already had two or more children and intended to have a further birth. An analysis of data from the ONS Longitudinal Study showed that women with higher qualifications were more likely to postpone childbearing. Once they did start, they were more likely than other women to have another child and to do so more quickly (Rendall and Smallwood, 2003).

Conclusions

The data collected in the MCS on mothers' ages, marital status and type of delivery on the whole[5] corresponded well with other sources. The MCS data adds to what is already known by having asked a number of questions not collected in routine systems. The survey can show that the growing spread of ages at childbearing is associated with social, economic and educational inequalities existing before early or postponed motherhood. It also shows that differences in whether births are planned, and whether unplanned pregnancies are welcome, vary along social lines.

Around 1 birth in 30 was the result of successful management of subfertility, particularly to older and more affluent women, who also experienced above average rates of multiple births. The uptake of antenatal care was generally high, but it was lowest for less advantaged young women who did not plan to be pregnant. The vast majority of babies were born in hospital, representing the culmination of a trend away from home births and accompanied by the increasing medicalisation of childbirth, typified by the growth of caesarean section rates from 2.7% in 1958 to 21.3% in 2000–01.

This chapter has explored only a small subset of the information collected about pregnancy, labour, pain relief and the postnatal period.

The survey amplifies other evidence of poorer experiences of pregnancy and birth for some minority ethnic groups. Most perinatal characteristics of MCS mothers that were examined were associated with ethnic differences, although the significance of some of these differences was partly or entirely accounted for by their demographic and socioeconomic characteristics. The role of language as a barrier to services and health knowledge was striking. Cultural diversity was also apparent in the chances of the baby's father being present at the birth. While there has been a general trend in the UK for fathers (even if they don't live with the mother) to attend the delivery, there are big differences among the minority ethnic groups which, in this respect, are most likely due to different cultural traditions.

Note

[1] Very recent migrants are likely to have been under-sampled in the MCS if it took time to establish their entitlement to Child Benefit, especially if they were asylum seekers who would not have been included in the Child Benefit sampling frame.

[2] In the MCS, mothers were not asked directly how many weeks pregnant they were when the baby was born. Instead they were asked what date the baby was due.

[3] Scotland is the only country for which reliable national data on gestational age are routinely published, and these data helped to show the unreliability of the MCS gestational data.

[4] Clearly, a few eligible babies would have died before they could be included in the MCS sample, and cannot be included in the analysis.

[5] With the exception of gestational age and induction.

Table A4.1: Factors associated with age at motherhood: MCS mothers having a first birth

	Impact on chance of a later first birth		
	Association of each factor in turn	Adjusted for all other factors	Mean (weighted)
Dependent variable: first birth			
<18			0.093
19-21			0.139
22-24			0.111
25-27			0.151
28-30			0.210
31-33			0.159
34-36			0.091
37 plus			0.046
Childhood background			
Left school at the minimum school leaving age	−0.646 **	−0.548 **	0.409
Own parents separated before birth of cohort child	−0.478 **	−0.413 **	0.288
In care at some point in childhood	−0.791 **	−0.374 **	0.011
Ethnic group of mother			
White	0	0	0.912
Mixed	−0.447 **	−0.419 **	0.009
Indian	0.027 (ns)	−0.097 (ns)	0.017
Pakistani	−0.531 **	−0.539 **	0.020
Bangladeshi	−0.680 **	−0.639 **	0.005
Black Caribbean	0.027 (ns)	0.124 (ns)	0.010
Black African	0.113 (ns)	0.138 (ns)	0.010
Other ethnic group	0.257 *	0.173 *	0.017
Type of area			
England			
Non-disadvantaged	0	0	
Other disadvantaged	−0.539 **	−0.417 **	0.510
Minority ethnic	−0.566 **	−0.421 **	0.270
Wales			
Non-disadvantaged	−0.185 *	−0.187 *	0.036
Other disadvantaged	−0.734 **	−0.636 **	0.028
Scotland			
Non-disadvantaged	−0.043 (ns)	−0.082 (ns)	0.024
Other disadvantaged	−0.524 **	−0.441 **	0.060
Northern Ireland			
Non-disadvantaged	−0.064 (ns)	−0.170 *	0.039
Other disadvantaged	−0.716 **	−0.725 **	0.018
Cut points for age groups (adjusted model)			
19		−2.053 **	
22		−1.331 **	
25		−0.932 **	
28		−0.507 **	
31		0.061 (ns)	
34		0.611 **	
37		1.196 **	
Base: UK MCS natural mothers with first child	7563	7563	
F(18, 372)		88.47	
Prob > F		0.0000	

* significant at 5%; ** significant at 1% (ns) not significant at 5%.

Ordered probit estimates are unweighted as controls included for each of the nine stratum/country groups.

Standard errors were adjusted for the cluster sampling design.

Table A4.2: Selected perinatal characteristics of MCS mothers in ethnic groups, England

Characteristics	White	Mixed	Indian	Pakistani	Bangladeshi	Black Caribbean	Black African	Other ethnic groups*	p-value
% who did not receive antenatal care	2.3	7.7	5.2	10.0	12.0	2.1	4.5	7.8	<0.001
% who confirmed their pregnancy after 12 weeks	6.9	6.9	6.1	8.0	9.1	12.0	8.9	7.2	0.1849
% whose first antenatal visit was at over 16 weeks	9.9	17.0	14.0	19.0	26.0	17.0	21.0	21.0	<0.001
% first time mothers who did not attend antenatal classes	29.0	46.0	33.0	74.0	77.0	42.0	45.0	43.0	<0.001
% who smoked during pregnancy	22.0	25.0	2.0	3.0	2.2	20.0	2.4	6.1	<0.001
% who had an assisted** delivery if first-born singleton baby	44.0	31.0	42.0	29.0	38.0	36.0	42.0	39.0	0.0081
% who had no birth partner	3.4	6.1	5.6	10	8.2	13.0	17.0	6.9	<0.001
% where cohort baby was preterm (singletons only)***	6.8	9.3	9.5	5.3	6.6	8.6	7.5	7.4	0.282
% where cohort baby was low birth weight (singletons only)****	5.5	9.7	13.0	13.0	13.0	9.4	7.9	8	<0.001
Median birth weight (kgs)	3.4	3.4	3.0	3.1	3.1	3.2	3.4	3.3	
% multiple (twins or higher order) births	1.5	1.9	0.8	0.8	0.4	1.2	3.0	0.4	0.1447
Maximum unweighted sample size (N)*****	8664	169	458	866	359	255	366	339	

Base: All England's MCS mothers when cohort baby 9-10 months old. Weighted percentages.
* A heterogeneous category comprised of women of all other backgrounds.
** Includes all vaginal assisted methods (forceps, ventouse, breech) and planned and emergency caesareans.
*** Preterm birth is defined as less than 259 days (37 weeks).
**** Low birth weight is defined as less than 2.5 kilogram.
***** Unweighted sample of natural mothers before missing cases on particular variables dropped.

Table A4.3: Odds ratios for no antenatal care, late confirmation of pregnancy, late first antenatal visit, and preterm birth, England

Ethnic group	No antenatal care		Late confirmation of pregnancy+		Late first antenatal visit++		Preterm birth+++	
	% (total*)	Adjusted** odds ratio (95% CI) p-value	% (total*)	Adjusted** odds ratio (95% CI) p-value	% (total*)	Adjusted** odds ratio (95% CI) p-value	% (total*)	Adjusted** odds ratio (95% CI) p-value
White	2.3 (8579)	1.0	6.9 (8581)	1.0	9.9 (8581)	1.0	6.8 (8581)	1.0
Mixed	7.7 (109)	2.4 (1.1-5.3) p = 0.037	6.9 (109)	1.1 (0.5-2.2) p = 0.849	17.0 (109)	1.4 (0.8-2.4) p = 0.276	9.3 (109)	1.6 (0.7-3.6) p = 0.286
Indian	5.2 (216)	1.8 (0.8-3.8) p = 0.148	6.2 (217)	1.3 (0.7-2.4) p = 0.433	14.0 (217)	1.4 (0.8-2.5) p = 0.245	9.5 (217)	1.2 (0.7-2.2) p = 0.527
Pakistani	10.0 (337)	1.9 (1.2-3.0) p = 0.008	8.0 (339)	0.8 (0.4-1.3) p = 0.311	19.0 (339)	1.1 (0.82-1.5) p = 0.505	5.3 (339)	0.7 (0.4-1.4) p = 0.302
Bangladeshi	12.0 (110)	1.9 (0.7-5.2) p = 0.231	9.1 (110)	1.6 (0.8-3.0) p = 0.167	26.0 (110)	2.0 (1.19-3.37) p = 0.009	6.6 (110)	0.8 (0.3-1.8) p = 0.586
Black Caribbean	2.1 (124)	0.3 (0.1-1.3) p = 0.119	12.0 (124)	1.7 (0.9-2.4) p = 0.078	17.0 (124)	1.8 (1.12-2.77) p = 0.015	8.6 (124)	0.5 (0.2-1.4) p = 0.210
Black African	4.5 (168)	0.8 (0.4-1.8) p = 0.612	8.9 (169)	1.5 (0.9-2.4) p = 0.086	21.0 (169)	2.0 (1.27-3.25) p = 0.003	7.5 (169)	1.5 (0.8-2.9) p = 0.189
Other	7.8 (186)	2.0 (1.0-4.2) p = 0.058	7.2 (186)	1.6 (0.8-3.2) p = 0.189	21.0 (186)	2.7 (1.61-4.61) p<0.001	7.4 (186)	1.4 (0.5-3.8) p = 0.499

Base: All MCS England's natural mothers when cohort baby was 9-10 months old.

Standard errors adjusted for cluster sample design.

+ over 12 weeks gestation

++ Over 16 weeks gestation

+++ less than 259 days (37 weeks)

*Weighted sample size for each particular variable

**adjusted for mother's age at birth of cohort baby, parity, health problems in pregnancy or not, birthplace (UK/not UK), mother's highest qualification, and household income in all variables; and in addition for the baby's weight/gestational age at birth, mother's height at interview, mother's weight before pregnancy, mother's body mass index before pregnancy, mother's smoking status in pregnancy, and mother's partnership status, in the case of preterm birth and low birth weight. Adjusted also for sample design.

CI – confidence interval

FIVE

Children's health

*Carol Dezateux, Lucy Foster, Rosemary Tate, Suzanne Walton,
Lamiya Samad, Helen Bedford, Suzanne Bartington,
Catherine Peckham, Tim Cole and Neville Butler*

Children in the UK are growing up against a background of changing family size and structure as well as changing demographic, economic and societal circumstances, which together have important implications for their health (Peckham, 1998). It is important to understand how the changes in patterns of caring for children and family context influence health in early childhood and the adoption of child health promoting behaviours by parents and carers. In recent years, there has been increasing interest in the contribution of these changes to obesity, asthma and related allergic diseases, autoimmune conditions, and disorders of social communication and behaviour (Gent et al 1994; Bach, 2002; Lobstein et al, 2004). The factors underlying these trends remain poorly understood, although they are clearly of great public health and human importance. The importance of an interdisciplinary perspective combining social, environmental and biological approaches to elucidate their causes is increasingly recognised.

Plan of this chapter

In this chapter, after considering the data sources in more detail, we describe the health during infancy of the cohort children through investigating the baby's birthweight, its infant weight at 8-9 months, and the early nutrition and patterns of breastfeeding. A range of parental and community influences on the baby's health are then considered – namely, parental smoking and alcohol use, immunisation, health problems and other use of services. Finally, the chapter examines indicators of good health in infancy and concludes with the implications of the findings for child health policy.

Data sources

At the first contact with the families when the children were aged around 9 months, information was obtained by parental (usually maternal) report on a wide range of measures. This included those relevant to the prevention of illness and promotion of health in the child, such as breastfeeding, parental smoking and immunisation status, and to conditions and illnesses that have implications for growth and development. Also included were measures which provide a baseline for examining later patterns and trajectories which will change with increasing age – for example, birthweight and bodyweight.

Data were also enhanced with respect to child health information by verifying maternal reports at the time of interview from information recorded in the personal child health record (Walton et al, 2005) and, subsequently, by linkage to routine birth registration records and health service information either at the individual or health service level (Bartington et al, 2005; Tate et al, 2005). In this chapter, we have been able to use these additional data sources to examine social, ethnic and maternal factors influencing the accuracy of maternal report of birthweight. We also examine the social, ethnic and maternal factors influencing mothers' use and access to their child's personal child health record, which verified maternal report of the child's last weight and immunisation status. Linkage to information on policies to support breastfeeding at the maternity unit where the child was born has, in addition, enriched understanding of the contribution made to breastfeeding practices through health services.

The personal child health record (sometimes called the 'red book') is a record of a child's health, growth and development which is issued to all new parents. Parents and health professionals are encouraged to use it with the aim of improving communication, enhancing continuity of care and increasing parental understanding of their child's health and development (Hall and Elliman, 2003). In recognition of this, the personal child health record is endorsed in *The national service framework for children, young people and maternity services* (DfES and DH, 2004). Furthermore, within the National Programme for Information Technology, it is planned that the personal child health record will link to the NHS Care Record Service with the intention of providing a complete electronic health record from birth to adulthood. The use of the record within the cohort thus provided an opportunity to enhance the data reported by mothers, but also, uniquely, to examine the accessibility and effective use of the record within a nationally representative cohort of mothers.

Parents were given advance warning that the interviewer might wish to refer to their child's personal child health record and were encouraged to produce and consult it in order to answer questions regarding their child's last weight, immunisation status and hearing test. Overall, 93% of mothers were able to produce their child's record and 88% consulted it to verify information on the child's last weight. Of the records consulted, 97% contained information relating to the child's last weight. Thus, 85% of mothers demonstrated 'effective use' of the personal child health record (defined as production, consultation and information regarding the child's last weight recorded). All these outcome measures were highest in England and lowest in Scotland (Figure 5.1)

The proportion of mothers able to produce their child's personal child health record was significantly less in other disadvantaged wards

Figure 5.1: Proportion of mothers 'effectively' using their child's personal child health record*

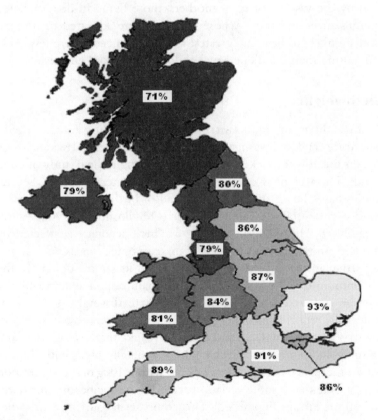

* Effective use was defined as production, consultation and the child's last weight was recorded.
Base: All UK MCS mothers when cohort baby was 9-10 months old. Weighted percentages.

(89%) compared with non-disadvantaged (95%) and wards containing high concentrations of minority ethnic populations (94%). In addition, mothers living in the south of England were more likely to produce their child's personal child health record than those living in the north. Production of the personal child health record increased with increasing maternal age, socioeconomic status and educational level. Production of the personal child health record decreased for those whose children had been admitted to hospital.

A number of factors were found to be independently associated with 'effective use' of the personal child health record, as defined earlier. In a multivariate analysis, effective use of the personal child health record was reduced in association with living in one of the other disadvantaged wards; being a young mother; having a large family; low maternal educational attainment; lone-parent status; maternal longstanding illness; and unplanned pregnancies, as well as admission of the child to hospital. Although the personal child health record was used by the vast majority of mothers, those living in disadvantaged circumstances and those whose children were admitted to hospital (and are likely to have the greatest health care needs) were less likely to be using their child's personal child health record effectively.

Birthweight

Birthweight is an important measure for assessing future growth trajectories, and for investigating both immediate health risks and those in later life. It is thus a key variable in any longitudinal study of child health. The weight is often obtained from maternal report. Several studies have shown that mothers' recall of birthweight is reasonably good, even several years after the birth (O'Sullivan et al, 2000; Walton et al, 2000). However, the extent to which accuracy is affected by ethnicity and social class in socially mixed populations is unclear and of particular relevance to this cohort, given its sample design. In the Millennium Cohort Study (MCS), the main respondent, usually the mother, was asked to report her baby's birthweight. Linkage of maternally reported birthweight to information available in the birth registry data in England and Wales revealed that consistency, and presumably accuracy, of birthweight is generally high, with 92% of cohort mothers reporting the weight to within 100g of the registration weight, albeit with some variation according to socioeconomic status and ethnic group (Figure 5.2). This compares favourably with other UK studies on parental report of birthweight, suggesting that future analyses can reliably be based on respondent (usually maternal) report.

Figure 5.2: Differences in maternally reported birthweight and birthweight at birth registration by selected ethnic group*

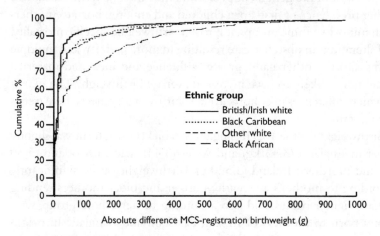

Ethnic group
——— British/Irish white
··········· Black Caribbean
– – – – Other white
— — · Black African

*Most other groups were intermediate, though the curve for Bangladeshis overlay that for Black Africans
Base: UK MCS unweighted natural mothers where possible to match survey data to linked hospital routine data on birth registration. Weighted.
Cohort babies were born at a median gestational age of 40 weeks, with 93% of babies (94% of singletons) being born at term (37 weeks or more).

When compared to babies in previous British birth cohorts, the Millennium Cohort babies were on average heavier at birth than the 1970 birth cohort, and lighter than babies from the 1946 and 1958 cohorts (Figure 5.3). The reasons for this may be complex. Over the

Figure 5.3: Mean birthweight (kg) in the four UK birth cohorts (including multiple births, except 1946)

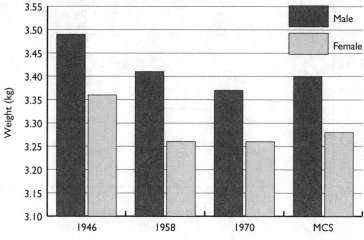

Base: All UK MCS babies, weighted.

last 50 years, various influences are likely to have decreased average birthweight in the general population. These include trends towards a higher prevalence of first-born children and children born to mothers from minority ethnic groups, improved birthweight-specific mortality, and alterations in obstetric care resulting in more preterm and multiple births. On the other hand, greater affluence and increased maternal body mass is likely to have increased average birthweight. The extent to which differences in cohorts' average birthweight reflects these trends is uncertain.

Birthweight for the 16,915 singleton babies born at term was slightly lower in England (3.43 kg) and Wales (3.44) than in Scotland (3.50 kg) and Northern Ireland (3.52 kg). Birthweight varied significantly according to mother's age, with younger and older mothers tending to have lighter babies, and also according to her ethnic group, with babies born to mothers of Indian, Pakistani and Bangladeshi origin being on average 300g lighter than their white counterparts (Figure 5.4). Mothers who smoked during pregnancy had lighter babies (by 150g on average), as did mothers who were lone parents at the time of interview (by 125g) and those with first-born infants (by 100g). Significant differences in mean birthweight for all these factors still remained after controlling for the baby's sex, gestational age, country, ward type and the mother's age, academic qualifications, smoking during pregnancy, ethnicity, lone parenthood, parity and Body Mass

Figure 5.4: Predicted* birthweight by ethnic group and maternal age for first-born singleton babies born at term (37 weeks or later)

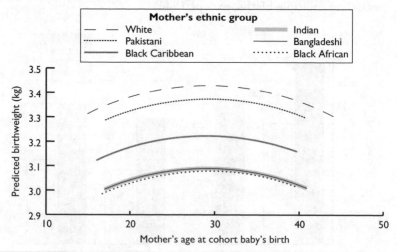

* Prediction based on regression
Base: All UK MCS singleton babies. Weighted.

Index (BMI). Some of the differences became smaller after adjustment: the gap between countries became smaller; the difference between white and Pakistani mothers narrowed to 235g, between white and Black Caribbean mothers from 180g to 100g; and the difference for lone mothers became 40g. All other differences remained broadly the same after controlling for the other factors, suggesting that socioeconomic factors do not account for all the differences in birthweight according to ethnic group and mother's age, which may also have biological explanations. Mothers' alcohol consumption during pregnancy was not associated with birthweight. There was a slight but significant positive correlation between birthweight and the mother's BMI (r=0.15).

Weight in infancy

Mothers were asked to report their child's most recent weight at this first interview, as there was not an opportunity to weigh the child. In the first year of life mothers have an option of attending child health clinics to monitor their baby's weight. Babies are also usually weighed when they attend for immunisations or for routine child health surveillance, including the routine hearing test (the infant distraction test) offered at around 8 months of age. Personal child health records were used in the cohort interview as previously described to verify maternal report of last weight as well as immunisation status.

The mean weight for term babies who had been weighed at 8-9 months of age (the age at which the majority of children were last weighed) and whose weight had been recorded in the red book (N=9,617) was just under 9kg. Boys were heavier than girls by around 700g on average. Babies in Scotland (9.06kg) and Wales (9.05kg) were heavier than those in England (8.96kg) and Northern Ireland (8.94kg), with a difference of 100g between babies living in England and Scotland. Weight in later infancy was significantly related to the mother's age if the child was first born, being highest for those born to mothers in their late 20s, and showed marked variation by ethnic group, with children born to Black African mothers being the heaviest and those born to Pakistani and Bangladeshi mothers the lightest (Figure 5.5).

At 8-9 months, infants who were first born or of mothers who smoked or were lone parents at the time of interview had caught up in weight. Their average weight (after adjusting for baby's age and ethnicity) was now no different from other infants. Infants of mothers who had never breastfed or who had stopped breastfeeding by 4 months were on average about 130g heavier than those who were still being

Figure 5.5: Predicted infant weight by ethnic group and maternal age for singleton babies born at term (37 weeks or later)*

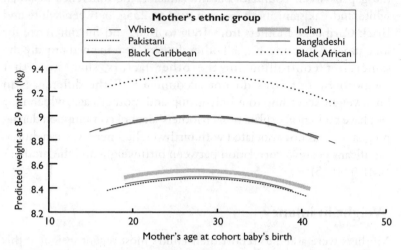

* Prediction based on regression. Includes only infants who were weighed between 8-9 months and for whom weight was recorded in the red book.
Base: All UK MCS singleton babies. Weighted.

breastfed at this age. This weight difference increased to 335g when compared to babies whose mothers had exclusively breastfed – that is, they had not given the baby any other type of milk or solid food before 4 months of age. This supports previous reports of breastfed infants showing slower growth in infancy than those fed formula (Ong et al, 2002). There is increasing evidence that this slower growth may have a protective effect on cardiovascular diseases in later life (Singhal and Lucas, 2004).

Early nutrition and patterns of breastfeeding

The policy context for breastfeeding in the UK

British breastfeeding rates are among the lowest in Europe, and social inequality in the UK in starting and continuing to breastfeed is well recognised. There is substantial evidence to support the health benefits of breastfeeding for mothers and their children. Consequently, as part of a commitment to reduce mortality and health inequalities among babies and children, a number of government policies have been proposed aimed at increasing the initiation and duration of breastfeeding in the UK (DH, 1998, 1999, 2004). For example, in England, a three-year Infant Feeding Initiative was launched in 1999, targeted at groups of the population who were least likely to breastfeed. More recently, the Department of Health's *Priorities and planning framework 2003-06* set a UK target to increase breastfeeding initiation by 2% per annum, while focusing on women from disadvantaged groups (DH, 2002a). Similar initiatives are under way in the other UK countries: the Welsh breastfeeding strategy, 'Investing in a better start', was launched in 2002 followed by the appointment of an All Wales Breastfeeding Coordinator in 2003. In Northern Ireland, breastfeeding targets were set in 1995 for 50% of women to initiate breastfeeding and 35% to still be breastfeeding at six weeks (DHSS, 1996). Scotland has demonstrated a national commitment to improving infant feeding practices over the past decade; in 1994, the Scottish Office set a target rate of 50% of mothers to be breastfeeding their babies at six weeks by 2005 and, since 1994, Scottish health policy documents have all highlighted the importance of breastfeeding (Management Executive Letter, 1994). Globally, the World Health Organisation (WHO) recommends that wherever possible infants should be fed exclusively on breast milk from birth to 6 months (WHO, 2002).

The MCS offers an important opportunity to examine breastfeeding patterns in the United Kingdom, and factors operating at the individual, family, community and health service levels which might influence these patterns. The importance of early nutrition on a range of later child and maternal health outcomes is well recognised (Howie et al, 1990). Furthermore, it is important to understand its relation to early growth trajectories and the potential pathways to later childhood obesity.

Breastfeeding patterns in the MCS

Overall in the UK, 70% of MCS mothers initiated breastfeeding, defined in the National Infant Feeding Survey as the proportion of all mothers who put their baby to the breast, even if this is on one occasion only (Hamlyn et al, 2002). This was highest in England (72%) and lowest in Northern Ireland (51%). However, within England there was considerable regional variation with the lowest initiation rates in the North East (51%) and highest in London (83.4%) (Figure 5.6). A significant proportion of mothers discontinued breastfeeding in the early weeks. Of those who initiated breastfeeding, only 71% continued to breastfeed for at least one month, 47% for four months and 33% for six months, with fewer women in Northern Ireland breastfeeding for as long (Figure 5.7). Thus, in the cohort as a whole, 48%, 33% and 22% of all infants were still breastfed for at least one, four and six

Figure 5.6: Proportion of mothers who initiated breastfeeding by UK country or English region

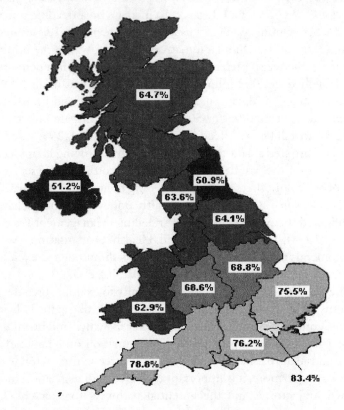

Base: All MCS natural mothers in each region. Weighted percentages.

months, respectively. The proportion of all babies breastfed for at least one month was only 30% in Northern Ireland and in the North East of England, whereas around twice that proportion were still being breastfed in southern England, rising to 69% in London. Only 6,816 (40%) of babies were exclusively breastfed for at least one month, 2,719 (16%) for at least four months and 208 (1%) for at least six months.

The figures for the Millennium Cohort are, perhaps unsurprisingly, similar to those obtained from the National Infant Feeding Survey carried out in 2000. They were also higher than those reported for the 1958 and 1970 cohort, but not for the 1946 cohort (Table 5.1); this reflects the success of public health and health service interventions to increase breastfeeding since the very low rates prevalent in the 1970s.

However, marked inequalities in breastfeeding remained, with rates

Figure 5.7: Proportion of mothers who, having started to breastfeed, continued to give breast milk by weeks since birth and by country

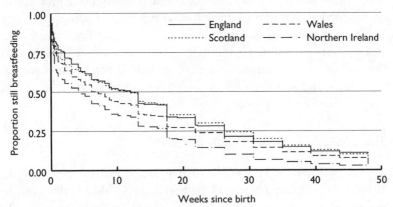

Base: All MCS natural mothers. Weighted.

being lowest in younger mothers, lone parents, those without educational qualifications and white mothers. White mothers were further categorised as either 'British/Irish-white' or 'Other-white', with 68% of the latter being from other countries in Europe: British/Irish-white mothers were less likely to breastfeed than mothers from all other ethnic groups, including the 'Other-white' group. In British/Irish-white mothers, characteristics of area of residence were important, notably for lone parents, with women living in non-disadvantaged wards or wards with high minority ethnic populations being more likely to initiate breastfeeding, although not to continue beyond one month, than mothers living in other disadvantaged wards. By contrast,

Table 5.1: Breastfeeding rates for boys and girls in the four British birth cohort studies

	1946 cohort		1958 cohort		1970 cohort		MCS[a] 2000	
	Boys	**Girls**	**Boys**	**Girls**	**Boys**	**Girls**	**Boys**	**Girls**
Never breastfed (%)	24	25	31	30	62	62	29	30
Breastfed for less than one month (%)	14	12	24	25	17	16	21	20
Breastfed for one month or more (%)	61	63	44	44	21	22	50	50
Total (%)	100	100	100	100	100	100	100	100
Unweighted N	5,841	5,426	4,862	5,049	4,325	4,557	9,337	8,810

[a] Weighted figures for MCS

Base: All UK MCS singleton babies with natural mothers interviewed. Weighted percentages.

Source: Ferri et al (2003)

British/Irish-white women with partners from different ethnic groups (those that are from minority ethnic groups or Other-white) were more likely to initiate and continue breastfeeding for one month than those with partners of the same ethnic group. These findings emphasise the importance of social and community support for breastfeeding and suggest that public health interventions to increase breastfeeding initiation and continuation need to address partners' attitudes and understanding, and the role of wider networks in the community, particularly for lone parents.

The UNICEF UK Baby Friendly Initiative

The Baby Friendly Hospital Initiative is a global campaign by the WHO and the United Nations Children Fund (UNICEF) that provides information, support and assessment for implementation of the evidence-based 'Ten steps for successful breastfeeding' in maternity services (WHO and UNICEF, 1989; WHO, 1998, 1992a). Best practice standards include training all staff in the techniques of successful breastfeeding, encouraging breastfeeding on demand, skin-to-skin contact, and allowing mothers and their babies to remain together 24 hours a day. Healthcare facilities that successfully fulfil the criteria may apply for a rigorous assessment and examination by professional staff to receive the prestigious full Baby Friendly accreditation award. Maternity hospitals that present a policy statement for best practice are awarded a certificate of commitment to demonstrate progress towards the standards necessary for the full Baby Friendly accreditation award.

The UK Department of Health worked in partnership with UNICEF UK Baby Friendly to develop a national programme for the implementation of the initiative in the hospital sector (DH and UNICEF, 1993). This was followed in 1999 by the 'Seven point plan' for introduction of the programme to the community-based healthcare sector (UNICEF, 1999). In recent years, all four countries of the UK have made considerable progress in engaging maternity hospitals with the initiative, reflected in a substantial increase in the proportion of births nationally which take place in participating facilities.

In March 2001, the midpoint of the period in which the Millennium Cohort babies were born, 31 maternity units in the UK held the full UNICEF UK Baby Friendly accreditation award, with a further 68 holding a certificate of commitment (Radford, 2001). The proportion of Millennium Cohort babies that were delivered in a UNICEF UK Baby Friendly hospital was highest in Scotland (21%), with equivalent percentages being 10.4% in Northern Ireland, 4.5% in Wales and 2.9% in England (Bartington et al, 2005). Scotland has demonstrated that commitment to implementing a breastfeeding policy at a national level has resulted in actual improvements in infant feeding practices (Tappin et al, 2001). In the MCS, delivery in a maternity unit that held the full Baby Friendly accreditation award was associated with a higher rate of breastfeeding initiation after adjusting for the social, demographic and other factors known to be associated with initiation (Bartington et al, 2005).

The MCS findings confirmed those of earlier studies that infants born to British/Irish-white women, especially younger mothers, without educational qualifications and from disadvantaged families and communities, were least likely to be breastfed, and that minority ethnic mothers achieved high levels of breastfeeding despite living in very disadvantaged communities. Several novel observations about breastfeeding have emerged from the MCS. A significant contribution to explaining variations in breastfeeding initiation and continuation came from partners' ethnic group among British/Irish-white women. Area of residence and its ethnic composition was found to be an important predictor of breastfeeding initiation among British/Irish-white lone mothers. In addition, there is some evidence from observational data that health service level interventions are associated with higher rates of breastfeeding initiation.

Parental smoking and alcohol use

Smoking during pregnancy is associated with substantial ill health for both the foetus and mother. There are also substantial adverse health consequences if the baby is exposed to tobacco smoke from household members after birth (British Medical Association, 2004). Established risks to the child of parental smoking include respiratory illnesses, impaired growth and development and Sudden Infant Death Syndrome (SIDS or cot death) (Blair et al, 1996; Cook and Strachan, 1999). While the government has introduced measures to reduce smoking in public places, recent evidence among older children suggests that exposure to tobacco smoke in the home (usually from parents) continues unabated (Jarvis et al, 2000).

The Millennium Cohort mothers were more likely to report smoking during pregnancy than currently at the time of interview, and this was highest at both time points for MCS mothers in Wales (40.1% and 33.5%) and Northern Ireland (37.5% and 33.4%), and lowest at both points for mothers in England (33.5% and 27.8%) and

Scotland (35.4% and 29.4%). This unexpected observation is likely to reflect a rather stringent definition of maternal smoking during pregnancy as any smoking, even in the early stages of pregnancy. Thus, even if mothers stopped smoking at some point during pregnancy, overall they were still categorised as smokers. This finding also suggests that many of the mothers did not start smoking again after birth. Within England, however, there was also significant variation between regions (Figure 5.8), with the highest levels of current smoking observed in the North East of England. Maternal smoking was strongly socially patterned: younger mothers, lone parents, white mothers, those living within other disadvantaged areas, with lower level occupations and with lower academic qualifications, were more likely to smoke in pregnancy. Similar patterns were observed for partners and, for both, for smoking during early infant life.

In contrast, alcohol use was less common during pregnancy than postnatally, with overall one third of mothers reporting some alcohol use in pregnancy compared with 82% reporting current alcohol use

Figure 5.8: Proportion of mothers who smoked at time of interview by UK country or English region

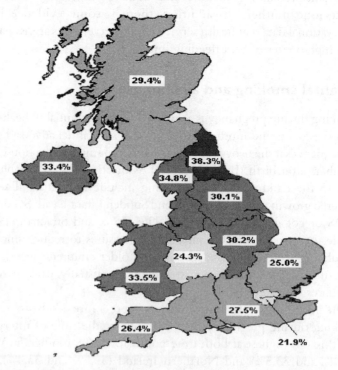

Base: All MCS mothers in region. Weighted percentages.

at the nine-month interview. As with smoking, alcohol consumption showed marked ethnic variation, with less than 2% of Pakistani and Bangladeshi mothers reporting alcohol use. As a further contrast to smoking, alcohol use was more common among women from managerial and professional occupations and of higher educational level. Lone parents were more likely to smoke and use alcohol (70%) than women who had a partner (53%).

Separate sections of this chapter describe the associations between maternal smoking during pregnancy and at time of interview, and alcohol use at time of interview, and specific child health measures. In summary, smoking was associated with a child's birthweight, immunisation status, and admissions to hospital with wheezing and asthma. Alcohol use was not associated with the child's birthweight but there were some associations with childhood injuries.

Immunisation

Childhood immunisation continues to be one of the most effective preventive health measures in both developing and developed countries (Hadler et al, 2004). Its value in protecting individuals as well as populations against disease has been highlighted in two recent government policy documents. (DH, 2004; DfES and DH, 2004). Both these reports emphasise the need to maintain high coverage in the general population as well as boosting uptake among subgroups where it may be less than optimal. The MCS provides a unique opportunity to investigate risk factors for sub-optimal immunisation in a large contemporary cohort and thus to identify where interventions to maximise uptake are best directed.

At the time of the survey interview, mothers were shown a card listing the following vaccines: diphtheria, tetanus, whooping cough, polio, Haemophilus influenzae type B (Hib) and meningococcal type C. They were asked if the infant had received any of the vaccines and, if so, whether they had received three doses of each of the listed vaccines. Mothers were encouraged to consult the personal child health record to confirm their response. Fully immunised infants were categorised as those who had received all three doses of the listed vaccines. Infants who had either one or more antigens omitted, or who had received all the vaccines listed but fewer than three doses, were grouped as incompletely immunised, whereas unimmunised infants had received none of the vaccines.

Overall, only 4% of infants were incompletely immunised for their age with 1.3% unimmunised. Immunisation uptake in England and

Wales was significantly lower than in Scotland and Northern Ireland (Table 5.2) and, within England, London had the lowest rates for complete immunisation (Figure 5.9). The patterns of completed primary immunisation for the Millennium Cohort is consistent with those for each country obtained from the Cover of Vaccination Evaluated Rapidly (COVER) programme (Figure 5.9) (Health Protection Agency, 2004). However, the higher rates among the cohort infants could result from differences in reporting immunisation status – that is, maternal self reports in the Millennium Cohort compared with computerised records on which the COVER programme depends.

In a multivariate analysis, mothers who were lone parents at interview, resident in wards with high minority ethnic populations or other disadvantaged wards or with large families, had smoked during pregnancy or were teenaged were all more likely to have incompletely immunised infants. Mothers of unimmunised infants were more likely to live in wards with high minority ethnic populations or other disadvantaged wards, be lone parents, have large families, and be 40 years and over, as well as more likely to have been educated to degree level or above. Mothers of incompletely immunised cohort children were similar to those of unimmunised infants, but were younger and less well educated. Medical reasons (47%) followed by health service and accessibility issues (34%) were the most frequent reasons cited by mothers for incomplete immunisation. Maternal concerns about, and beliefs around, immunisation (40%) were primarily cited as reasons for an infant being unimmunised. These findings confirm earlier research which has highlighted the need to ensure immunisation services are organised to facilitate access for socially disadvantaged families. However, the finding that more highly educated, older mothers are choosing not to immunise their infants is a novel and important

Table 5.2: MCS mothers' reports of immunisation uptake by country[a] (per cent of mothers reporting uptake)

Immunisation uptake	Country (%)				
	England	Wales	Scotland	N. Ireland	Total
Complete	95.1	95.6	96.5	97.1	94.9
Incomplete	3.6	3.5	2.8	2.5	3.9
None	1.3	0.9	0.7	0.4	1.2
Total %	100	100	100	100	100
Unweighted N	11495	2750	2325	1918	18488

[a] Weighted percentages, p < 0.05

Base: All natural MCS mothers when baby was 9-10 months old.

**Figure 5.9: Completed primary immunisations in UK:
The Millennium Cohort Study (MCS)[a,b] and Cover of Vaccination
Evaluated Rapidly (COVER) programme (by 12 months – 2001)**

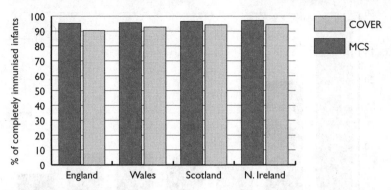

a Weighted percentages
b Base: MCS natural mothers, singletons and first order of birth in the case of multiple births

issue which has emerged from analysis of the Millennium Cohort. Different interventions may be required to address the concerns of this group of mothers and to ensure that their rejection of immunisation is a fully informed decision and based on accurate information.

Health problems and other use of health services

As the principal caregiver, parents are able to take an overall view of their child's health, and most acute episodes of ill health are managed in the home without recourse to professional advice (Neill, 2000). Previous research has shown that parents who are more likely to consult the family doctor with acute childhood illness are those with lower socioeconomic status and from minority ethnic groups (Neill, 2000). Parents seek advice from general practitioners and health visitors, accident and emergency departments and the telephone helpline NHS Direct, established in 1998.

During the MCS interview, mothers were asked if they had taken their child to the GP, health centre, Casualty, or called NHS Direct for any health problem(s). They were also asked to report the number and type of health problems. Overall, 78% of the Millennium Cohort mothers reported their baby had at least one health problem. The median number of health problems was 1 with an interquartile range of 1-2 health problems. In 171 of the cohort families, babies were reported to have more than nine reported health problems. Based on the maternal response, families with a cohort boy were more likely than those with a girl (80% and 76%, respectively) to have a baby with

Figure 5.10: Maternal report of health problems in the Millennium Cohort

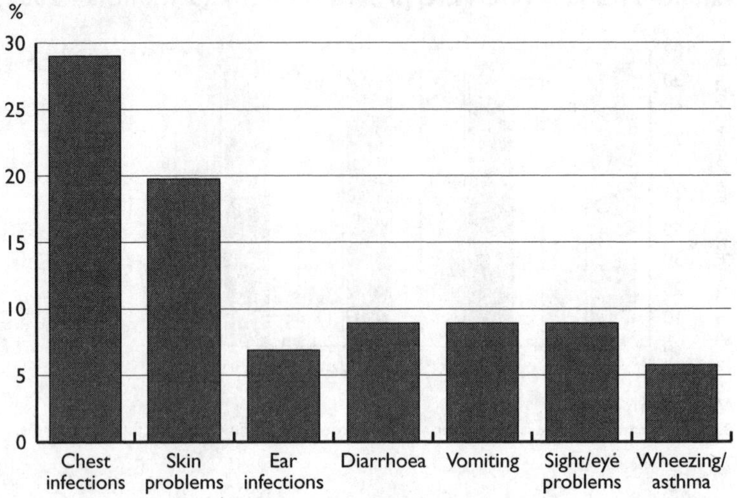

Base: All UK MCS mothers when baby was 9-10 months old. Weighted percentages.

at least one health problem, and this difference was statistically significant (p<0.001).

Overall, the single most commonly reported health problem was a chest infection: at least one such episode was reported for 29% of the cohort children. Skin problems (20%), ear infections (10%), persistent or severe diarrhoea (9%), persistent or severe vomiting (9%), sight or eye problems (9%), and wheezing or asthma (6%) were the next most common health problems reported (Figure 5.10).

Admissions to hospital

Fifteen per cent of families with a cohort boy and 13% with a girl had had the baby admitted to hospital on at least one occasion. Hospital admissions of children were more likely among families living in other disadvantaged wards, for children of younger mothers, lone parents and mothers who reported depression or longstanding illness. They were also higher among families of lower socioeconomic status and for mothers with few or no academic qualifications.

The most common reasons for first admissions to hospital were a chest infection or pneumonia (25%); gastroenteritis (9%); wheezing or asthma (6%); a high temperature (5%); vomiting (3%); convulsions, fits or loss of consciousness (3%); and meningitis (3%). Although unusual, 0.5% of families had children who had been admitted at least once for an injury at this age.

Overall, 4% of mothers had their baby admitted to hospital with a chest infection or pneumonia. Admissions for this reason were significantly more likely for those living in Wales (5.7%), in Northern Ireland (4.9%) and in other disadvantaged wards (4.7%). Children of younger mothers, those with few or no academic qualifications, lone parents, currently smoking mothers, or who lived in rented accommodation were also more likely to be admitted to hospital. Several characteristics of the child were also associated with an increased chance of hospital admission with a chest infection. These included male sex, premature birth, birth by caesarean section, incomplete immunisation, never having been breastfed and living with siblings. In multivariate analyses, admission to hospital with a chest infection or pneumonia was significantly more likely among families with a cohort boy, those living in Wales, families with a premature baby, those who never breastfed, had incomplete immunisations or where families were large.

Overall, more than 2 in 100 cohort children (1.5%) had been admitted to hospital with gastroenteritis prior to the nine-month interview. Without controlling for other factors, hospital admissions with gastroenteritis were significantly more likely among those living in other disadvantaged wards (1.8%) rather than in wards with high minority ethnic populations (1.0%). They were also more common among children of younger mothers, lone parents, mothers who were depressed, had no or minimal educational qualifications, had never breastfed their child, or where the child had not received all their immunisations. In a multivariate analysis, admission to hospital with gastroenteritis was more significantly likely among babies with younger mothers or mothers who reported themselves as depressed. This is an interesting observation since admission to hospital may not only be related to illness severity but also, for example, to a mother's confidence, and her ability to care for the child and offer social support.

Overall, less than 1% of families had a child admitted to hospital for wheezing or asthma. These admissions were significantly more common in Northern Ireland (1.6%) and Wales (1.4%), and in families who lived in other disadvantaged wards (1.2%). Within England, there were also significant differences according to region of residence. Children's admissions for wheezing or asthma were more common among children of younger mothers, lone parents, mothers with no or few educational qualifications, mothers with depression or longstanding illness and those who failed to initiate breastfeeding. Admissions were also more common among those whose mothers had a history of asthma (1.8%), had smoked during pregnancy (1.3%), or currently (1.5%), reported damp and condensation in the home (1.6%) and in areas where parents rated pollution, grime or environmental problems as 'very common'.

Injuries during infancy

Despite decreasing childhood mortality levels, a relatively high number of deaths still occur due to injuries in young children, albeit few of these are during infancy. However, injuries in infancy are socially notable and may be regarded with suspicion in view of concerns about child protection, especially now, in the light of recent high profile cases such as that of Victoria Climbié (Laming, 2003). A strength of the MCS is its heterogeneous and unselected population which allows for examination of the social and environmental correlates of maternally reported injuries in infancy.

An increasing proportion of deaths during childhood are due to injuries, and injuries are also a major cause of long-term disability and ill health. Every year, around 500,000 children under the age of five are taken to hospital after an accident or injury (DTI Home and Leisure Accident Surveillance System [HASS], 2003). Most injuries to children under the age of four occur in the home, and so risks associated with the quality of housing and use of safety equipment are important in this age group. Injuries in infancy reflect the child's physical and motor development, with independent mobility, exploratory behaviour and hand to mouth activity all increasing the possibility of injury. Very few studies have examined risk factors for injury occurring before the age of one, which is a critical period of development.

Mothers in MCS were asked whether their children had ever had an accident or injury for which they had been taken to the doctor, health centre or hospital. Interviewers recorded the sort of accident or injury, the age at which it happened, whether the child attended Accident and Emergency at hospital, and whether they were admitted for each incident separately.

Eight per cent of mothers reported that their child had sustained at least one injury. In total, 93 of these children were admitted to hospital as a result of an accident, which means that approximately 1 in 200 infants were admitted to hospital for an injury by the age of 9 months (Table 5.3). Reported accidents were higher in Wales compared to the other UK countries and, of those sustaining an accident, a higher proportion were admitted to hospital.

At this age, head injuries were the single most common cause of injury (58 % of injuries reported) of which 0.7% resulted in loss of consciousness, followed by soft tissue injuries (21%), burns and scalds (8%), fractured bones (2%) and swallowed objects (2%). Of those who were admitted to hospital as a result of their first accident, this was as a result of a head injury (63%), a burn or scald (11%), or soft tissue injuries (10%). Over all types of injury, the risk increased with increasing age of the child.

Mothers' reporting of injuries by 9 months of age was inversely associated with maternal age, lone parent status, maternal depression or long-standing illness, residence in one of the other disadvantaged wards and being born to a mother of white or mixed ethnic origin.[1] More serious injuries (those resulting in admission to hospital), were more likely among families where the baby was mobile or walking, who had younger mothers and among mothers with long-term illnesses or alcohol use during pregnancy, but not at the time of interview. The frequency, severity and pattern of injuries are likely to increase with increasing age in this cohort when further exploration of their relation to family, community and developmental status of the child will be possible.

Indicators of good health in infancy

It is important to develop some measures of positive health status in early childhood as a reflection of the quality of the environments in which children grow and as an indicator of early childhood circumstances. An understanding of the distribution of child health status, according to a range of social and familial factors, can also provide important information for fiscal and other policies aimed at maximising children's potential at the time and later.

Table 5.3: Injuries to cohort children by UK country

	England	Wales	Scotland	Northern Ireland	UK
% (n) children with an accident or injury *	8.0 (879/11501)	9.0 (270/2755)	7.8 (180/2327)	6.4 (125/1918)	8.0 (1454/18501)
% (n) of first injuries that resulted in a hospital admission**	5.6 (52/877)	8.5 (20/270)	6.0 (11/180)	6.7 (10/125)	6.0 (93/1452)
% (n) children requiring hospital admission for an injury *	0.5 (52/11499)	0.8 (20/2755)	0.5 (11/2327)	0.4 (10/1919)	0.5 (93/18500)

Base: ** All MCS singleton children with an injury. * All MCS singleton children.

Values are weighted percentages (and absolute numbers) for each outcome

There are no standard validated measures in this field on which to draw. The MCS data provided an opportunity to begin to develop such measures. We combined three factors considered to be particularly pertinent to 'positive child health status' – namely, being breastfed for at least one month, being completely immunised by the time of the interview and living with a non-smoking mother during infancy. These factors are recognised as important key child health indicators for children across Europe (Rigby and Kohler, 2004). Furthermore, they are potentially routinely available in the UK, making them good measures to apply to whole child populations. We examined 'positive child health status' in relation to area of residence and a selection of maternal characteristics, including minority ethnic status, family structure and lone-parent status.

Overall in the UK, only one third of children (37.7%) could be considered to have positive child health status, according to this measure. There was significant variation across the UK, ranging from 24.1% in Northern Ireland, 31.9% in Wales, 37.3% in Scotland to 42.0% in England (Figure 5.11). Within England, there was also significant variation from north to south, with the lowest proportion of children being in the North West and North East of England.

Children living in non-disadvantaged areas, or in wards with high minority ethnic populations, were more likely than those living in other disadvantaged areas to have positive child health status. There were also marked variations by maternal ethnic group, which ranged from 37.5% of infants of British/Irish-white mothers to 77.4% of Black African mothers. There was a significant difference between children of British/Irish-white and Other-white mothers, with 64.6% of children in the latter group having this child health indicator.

Socioeconomic status was also a significant factor in explaining positive child health status. There was a greater than two-fold difference between children with positive status whose mothers were in routine or semi-routine occupations and those in managerial and professional occupations. Similarly, highest maternal academic qualification was also influential: 71.9%, 50.9% and 19.4% of children with mothers holding degrees (undergraduate or higher), A/AS/S levels or O levels, respectively, had this positive health status indicator.

While maternal age was important, no significant difference in the extent of a child's positive health status was found for primiparous or multiparous mothers. Lone-parent status was perhaps the most striking factor, with only 15% of children in lone-parent households achieving positive health status, as defined earlier.

The strengths and limitations of this preliminary measure of good

Figure 5.11: Proportion of infants with 'positive child health status' by UK country or English region*

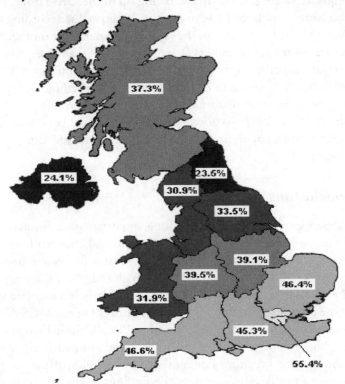

* 'Positive child health status' defined by presence of the following: breastfed to one month (four weeks), non-smoking mothers and completely immunised.
Base: All MCS natural mothers of singleton babies in region. Weighted percentages.

health should also be acknowledged. Importantly, the three variables included are effectively all measures of maternal health behaviours rather than direct measures of health. Furthermore, the figures presented do not control for other variables and it is recognised that the different variables can be confounded either positively or negatively. The social and ethnic patterns of breastfeeding were largely the inverse of that seen for maternal smoking, with smoking being rare but breastfeeding common among mothers of minority ethnic identities. Furthermore, the social patterning of immunisation uptake, as discussed previously, is complex with different relations to social disadvantage seen for unimmunised and incompletely immunised infants. In addition, uptake of immunisation was generally high across the UK and therefore the relative contribution of this measure to variability in the composite measure was small.

These findings demonstrate that there are some important and large inequalities between children growing up in the UK. Those children who were considered to have positive health status according to this measure varied according to the characteristics of their mother, family and area of residence. However, we have shown that lone parenthood and maternal ethnic group were particularly influential correlates of a child's health status. While children of minority ethnic groups were often brought-up in disadvantaged settings, mothers of these children were far more likely to adopt behaviours that are beneficial for the positive health of their child, in particular breastfeeding and not smoking.

Conclusions

In this chapter, we have reviewed some important dimensions of health and illness in infancy among more than 18,000 children born in the new century and living in diverse social and family circumstances across the UK. We conclude this chapter by considering these dimensions from the perspective of different family and social structures.

One interesting finding from this first analysis of the MCS relates to children from minority ethnic groups, especially those living in wards with high minority ethnic populations or other disadvantaged wards. Although the literature contains many examples of poorer health among minority ethnic groups, the findings of the MCS show that children from minority ethnic groups have opportunities for health which their British/Irish-white counterparts are denied. The mothers of such children are less likely to smoke, use alcohol either in pregnancy or postnatally, and their children are more likely to be both breastfed at all and breastfed for longer. This is despite mothers from ethnic minorities being less likely to have an academic or educational qualification, less likely to be in skilled occupations and more likely to be, on average, younger than their white counterparts. Of particular interest is the observation that both partners' ethnic identity and community ethnicity were associated with a greater likelihood of breastfeeding initiation among white mothers. Developing an understanding of the family, social and cultural influences which help sustain these opportunities for health in the face of marked social and economic disadvantage is crucial. Patterns of early size and growth were strongly associated with ethnic identity and it will be important to examine ethnic variation in these growth trajectories in the preschool years.

Some measures of health service use such as uptake and completion of immunisations and effective use of personal child health records did not differ by ethnic group. However, significant discrepancies between birthweight reported by mothers and that recorded in birth registry records were more prevalent among children whose mothers were from minority ethnic groups.

We have reported some important geographic variations in health in infancy. Mothers in Northern Ireland and the North East of England were least likely to start or continue to breastfeed, and, together with mothers in Wales, most likely to smoke during pregnancy and postnatally. Mothers in Wales and Northern Ireland were more likely to report that their child was admitted to hospital with respiratory illnesses of some kind. Mothers in Wales were more likely to report that their child experienced an injury in the first nine months of life. By contrast, immunisation uptake and completion was lowest in England, being particularly poor in the London area. A preliminary evaluation of existing maternity unit policies in relation to breastfeeding demonstrated higher breastfeeding initiation rates among mothers whose babies were born in Baby Friendly accredited facilities.

A preliminary evaluation of a simple measure of 'good health' – incorporating measures of breastfeeding, maternal smoking and immunisation status – was presented. Area of residence, socioeconomic status, social support and maternal education were all associated with wide variation in health status in infancy.

Our understanding of the social, environmental and biological influences on child health in this cohort will be enhanced by the collection of biomedical information, which was not possible logistically in this first survey. This will be particularly important in relation to two priorities for child public health – namely, early origins of childhood obesity and allergic disease. This first analysis has identified significant variations in body size and weight gain, early nutrition and their association among the cohort members. Analysis of measures of ill health, including those identified through maternal report or use of health services, highlight the importance of respiratory and infectious illnesses in infancy.

In conclusion, these analyses of health in the first nine months of life among the Millennium Cohort children lay a firm foundation on which to build in future surveys of this cohort. It will be important to continue the existing strong interdisciplinary approach, comprising social, environmental and biological perspectives. This will enhance public health understanding and the development of interventions aimed at reducing inequalities in child health and supporting families to achieve optimal health and development for their children.

Note
[1] Based on bivariate analysis.

SIX

Children's development in the family environment

Ingrid Schoon, Amanda Sacker, Steven Hope, Stephen Collishaw
and Barbara Maughan

The first year of life is increasingly regarded as a 'critical' stage of a child's development and of emerging family relationships (Carnegie, 1994). The most frequently studied early indicators of child development include biological factors such as illness at birth, low birthweight and physical disability. In this chapter, we focus on indicators of early child development as measured by developmental delays in gross motor and fine motor development, as well as the development of communicative gestures. The questions used to identify milestones in these domains of development are set out in Table 6.1. Gross motor skills include sitting up, standing and walking; fine motor skills reflect ability to use hands and fingers; communicative gestures include smiling, waving goodbye and other signals to other people. Motor development is generally considered to be an important indicator of the overall rate and level of development during the early months and years after birth (Gesell, 1973; Illingworth, 1975). It influences the nature and sequence in which certain perceptual and cognitive abilities unfold, and the lack of motor competence may hinder the development of those abilities (Bushnell and Boudreau, 1993). There are rapid improvements in locomotor and manipulative skills during the first year of life while gestural language develops at around 9 or 10 months when babies begin to use gestures to ask for things (Bates et al, 1987; Bee, 1994).

Child development is assessed by a set of functional skills or age-specific tasks, called developmental milestones, that most children can do at a certain age range. The study of child development in the MCS is based on a socioecological model of human development (Bronfenbrenner, 1979; Sameroff, 1983). Such models underscore the role of multiple influences on children's development, and they conceptualise human development as the active interaction between a child and its context or environment. Developmental capacities,

Table 6.1: Developmental milestones by age of baby and delayed development in percentages

	Per cent reaching development stage by age				Delayed development	
	8 mths	9 mths	10 mths	11+ mths	N unweighted	%
Gross motor coordination						
S/he can sit up without being supported	92	96	98	99	18798	4.21
If baby is put down on the floor, s/he can move about from one place to another	88	92	94	97	18798	7.33
S/he can stand up while holding onto something such as furniture	55	69	79	91	18798	0.20
S/he can walk a few steps on his/her own	01	04	09	21	18798	0.00
Fine motor coordination						
S/he grabs objects using the whole hand	99	99	99	100	18799	0.70
S/he passes a toy back and forth from one hand to another	93	95	96	98	18781	4.79
S/he can pick up a small object using forefinger and thumb only	83	89	92	94	18747	1.61
S/he puts his/her hands together	76	84	89	94	18788	0.13
Communicative gestures						
S/he smiles when you smile at him/her	99	99	100	100	18799	0.48
S/he extends arms to show s/he wants to be picked up	76	81	85	92	18798	0.18
S/he reaches out and gives you a toy or some other object that s/he is holding	51	57	71	83	18793	0.00
S/he waves bye-bye on his/her own when someone leaves	27	35	48	65	18797	0.00
S/he nods his/her head for 'yes'	07	07	10	24	18789	0.00

Base: All UK MCS mothers when the cohort baby was 9-10 months old. Weighted percentages.

therefore, are thought to be shaped by the child's interactions with their parents and the wider context of which both are part.

Plan of this chapter

The aim of this chapter is to investigate the relationship between the child's development and the family environment, examining the relative influences of child, family and environmental factors in shaping individual development during the first year of life. The available data were used to address a number of specific research questions, namely:

* What is the degree of developmental delay in gross and fine motor development and communicative gestures among the cohort members after adjusting for variations in birth months?
* What is the association between characteristics of the child, the family and the environment, and early developmental functioning?
* What is the specific influence of these characteristics on a particular developmental outcome?
* Can the influence of biological child characteristics on early developmental functioning be moderated by characteristics of the family environment?

Due to missing data for some cases, the sample was reduced to 17,556 babies with complete data on the variables of interest. All analyses were based on these complete cases with appropriate methods which take account of the clustered sample design.

Child characteristics

Several kinds of differences among babies can affect their physical and cognitive development. For example, differences in a child's social behaviour may be explained by gender-specific physiological differences (Maccoby, 1990), although there are usually very few sex differences in physical development among young infants (Cossette et al, 1991). Delays in motor development are often associated with a number of serious health conditions. For example, preterm or low birthweight babies generally move more slowly through the developmental milestones. In a study comparing early physical development among normal and preterm babies, Den Ouden and her colleagues (1991) demonstrated that preterm babies are about 10-15 weeks behind their full-term peers in most physical skills, such as crawling or transferring objects from one hand to another. Other indicators of health, such as the number of illnesses the infant experiences and admission to hospital, will be included in the analysis, as well as the links of development with ethnicity. There is evidence to suggest that non-white babies, especially Black babies, are more advanced in their gross motor development than white babies (Tanner, 1990).

Socioemotional family environment

The characteristics of the family and their approach in relating to their children are other major influences on the child's development. The extent and form of parent-child interactions are influenced by family social class, maternal level of education, maternal psychosocial health and single-parent status. For example, parental education is sometimes considered as a proxy for the amount of stimulation and learning provided for the child (Melhuish et al, 2001), and maternal depression has been associated with less effective parent-child interactions (Corcoran, 1995). There is also evidence that characteristics of the socioemotional family environment are linked to early child functioning, and that the experience of adverse experiences in the early family context can have long-term consequences (Rutter and Madge, 1976; Conger et al, 1993; Werner, 1992; Duncan and Brooks-Gunn, 1997; Schoon et al, 2002;). Family structure – for example, particularly fragile marital status and living in a single-parent family – has been shown to affect children's physical development negatively (McLanahan and Sandefur, 1994).

However, any one family characteristic usually shows a rather weak effect on children's developmental outcomes. Usually it is the combination of these factors that pose a major risk to development (Rutter, 1990). For example, single parenthood, low levels of parental education, unemployment, psychological distress and lack of social support often co-occur, and it has been difficult to tease apart the effects of each upon children. Thus, it is important to investigate the effects of family structure on a child's development taking into consideration other coexisting factors.

Family and wider community factors may also have a positive impact on development. For example, informal support systems can play a vital role in helping disadvantaged children and their parents to cope with ongoing stressors of life in poverty. Social integration describes the embeddedness in the community, the social relationships and involvement with various groups within the community of which the family is part, including contact with relatives and friends (Coleman,

1988). Social relationships within the community have also been described in terms of family social capital, which can play an important role in a child's development (Coleman, 1988). The MCS data offer indicators of contact with grandparents and childcare provision as proxy measures of social integration, as described in Chapters 2 and 3. Parenting beliefs are explored further in Chapter 7.

Physical environment

Specific material environmental conditions in the family household could affect the baby's development – for example, conditions of overcrowding, damp or condensation; the absence of central heating in the household; or smoking near the baby (also described in Chapters 2 and 5). The wider environment of the neighbourhood, local authority or region is not explicitly modelled, but may have effects through these immediate conditions.

Developmental milestone measures

Developmental milestones are a set of functional skills or age-specific tasks that most children can do at a certain age range. MCS parents were asked to respond to selected statements from the Denver Developmental Screening Test, which is the most popular tool for screening for potential developmental problems (Frankenburg et al, 1967, 1990, 1992). Replies of the parents on their child's developmental status were grouped into two main areas: gross and fine motor skills.

In addition, items from a UK adaptation of the MacArthur Communicative Development Inventories (CDI) were used to identify early communicative gestures. The CDI is a checklist of words and gestures assessing the child's development of receptive and productive vocabulary through parental report (Fenson et al, 1993).

Although each milestone has an age level, the actual age when a normally developing child reaches that milestone can vary considerably. For example, some children may walk as early as 11 months, while others may not walk until they are 15 months old. Both cases are still considered normal. About 3% of children will not reach a milestone on time, but most of them will eventually develop normally over time. Thus, the assessment of developmental delay will be adjusted by the child's age in birth months.

Table 6.2: Summary of developmental delay in months (%)

| | Per cent of babies with stated months of delay | | | |
	Unweighted N	0	1	2+	Total %
Full sample					
Gross motor coordination	18795	89.0	10.3	0.7	100
Fine motor coordination	18715	93.3	6.3	0.4	100
Communicative gestures	18780	99.3	0.7	0.0	100
Analysis sample					
Gross motor coordination	17556	89.2	10.1	0.7	100
Fine motor coordination	17556	93.4	6.1	0.4	100
Communicative gestures	17556	99.4	0.6	0.0	100

Base: All UK MCS cohort babies when they were 9-10 months old. Weighted percentages.

Identification of developmental delay

Delay in the developmental milestones is defined according to whether the baby has not reached a milestone that 90% of babies in that age group can pass. For example, only 88% can move around the floor at 8 months but 92% can do this by 9 months. So an 8-month-old baby is not delayed if it cannot move around, but a 9-month or older baby is identified as showing delay. The age-weighted proportions of babies who mastered each of the items measuring gross motor and fine motor coordination as well as communicative gestures is presented in Table 6.1.[1]

Developmental delay for each of the specific developmental functions is summarised in Table 6.2. The greatest delay (11.0% of all babies) has been identified for items indicating gross motor coordination, followed by fine motor coordination (6.7%). We could identify least delay in the communicative gestures, which generally emerge only at around age 10 months. Yet, while most babies did smile, a delay in this function might have strong social implications, as the smile is an extremely potent social signal (Bee, 1994).

A description of the frequencies or mean values of the independent variables included in the analysis, covering characteristics of the child and the socioemotional and physical family environment, can be found in Table A6.1.

Predicting delay in gross motor functions

First we focus on delay in gross motor functions. As mentioned earlier, it is important to recognise the three sets of factors that are able to influence the extent of delay in development milestones. In order to investigate the relative importance of these three sets of predictive factors – the characteristics of the child, socioemotional factors and physical family environment – multivariate analyses were used. A series of nested logistic regression models were estimated with each set of factors being included initially by themselves. Finally, they were all included together (Table 6.3).

On examining the characteristics of the child, the strongest predictors of developmental delay were low birthweight and prematurity, followed by the number of hospitalisations and the event of multiple birth. Black, Indian and children of mixed ethnic identity were less at risk of delayed gross motor functions than white children. Bangladeshi/ Pakistani children were at an increased risk compared with white children.

Examination of the influence of socioemotional family characteristics on gross motor development of the child found that children born to older mothers were at an increased risk of delayed motor functioning, as were children born to a mother showing signs of psychological distress. Maternal education level, on the other hand, appeared to have a beneficial effect on a child's development of gross motor function.

When the physical characteristics of the family home were included, only overcrowding showed a significant association with delayed gross motor functioning of the child.

After controlling for all the three sets of explanatory variables together, the significant predictors of delayed gross motor functioning were mostly the same. Among the child characteristics, prematurity, low birthweight, number of hospitalisations and ethnicity were significant predictors. Among the indicators of the socioemotional family environment, mother's age and psychological distress remained significant risk factors, and mother's education was associated with a beneficial influence on gross motor functioning. However, none of the indicators of the physical home environment remained significant, after controlling for the other variables in the equation.

Further statistical tests were carried out to find out which of the models had the best fit (using a Wald statistic). These tests indicated that the characteristics of the child (some would call these the biological risk factors) explained most of the variation in delayed gross motor functioning and contributed most to our understanding of gross motor delay. The socioemotional environment also contributed to our understanding as the second most important explanation. However, the physical environment did not contribute directly to our understanding of gross motor delay in children, although overcrowding was associated with other risk factors.

Table 6.3: Odds of gross motor delay by measures of child characteristics, the socioemotional environment and the physical environment for MCS babies

		Model 1	Model 2	Model 3	Model 4
Child characteristics					
Female		0.98			0.98
Ethnic Identity	White	1.00			1.00
	Mixed	0.74 *			0.69 *
	Indian	0.55 *			0.51 **
	Bangladeshi/Pakistani	1.66 ***			1.36 *
	Black	0.34 ***			0.29 ***
	Other	0.98			0.80
Multiple birth		1.34 *			1.34
Low birth weight		2.31 ***			2.27 ***
Prematurity		2.22 ***			2.27 ***
Any illnesses		1.03			1.08
Hospitalisations		1.33 ***			1.32 ***
Socio-economic environment					
Mother's age at birth	Under 20		1.00		1.00
	20-24		1.14		1.18
	25-29		1.28 *		1.37 *
	30-34		1.32 *		1.45 *
	35-39		1.53 **		1.68 ***
	40+		1.89 **		2.05 ***
Employment status	Not in paid work		1.00		1.00
	Part-time		0.93		0.91
	Full-time		0.91		0.90
Qualifications	None		1.00		1.00
	NVQ 1		0.89		0.92
	NVQ 2		0.65 ***		0.65 ***
	NVQ 3		0.66 **		0.70 **
	NVQ 4		0.60 ***		0.63 ***
	NVQ 5		0.69		0.79
	Other		0.80		0.93
Lone parent			0.86		0.92
Number of siblings			1.05		1.02
Parenting beliefs scale			0.99		1.00
Maternal distress			1.04 **		1.03 *
Sees grandparents	None		1.00		1.00
	Maternal		1.00		0.95
	Paternal		0.89		0.83
	Both		0.88		0.83
Care while at work	Parent		1.00		1.00
	Relative		0.81*		0.90
	Nursery		0.86		0.91
	Other care		0.99		1.04
Physical environment					
Overcrowding				1.25 **	1.05
Smoking near baby				1.03	0.94
Damp or condensation				1.09	1.06
No central heating				1.13	1.08
Wald Test		$F_{(11,379)}$ = 49 $p < 0.00005$	$F_{(23,367)}$ = 6 $p < 0.00005$	$F_{(4,386)}$ = 3 $p = 0.027$	$F_{(38,352)}$ = 20 $p < 0.00005$
Unweighted N values		17556	17556	17556	17556

* $p < 0.05$; ** $p < 0.005$; *** $p < 0.0005$

Base: All UK MCS babies when they were 9-10 months old. Standard errors corrected for cluster sample design. Analysis weighted

Predicting delay in fine motor functions

The same method was used to examine the predictors of delay in dexterity, or fine motor function, in children.

When only the characteristics of the child were included, girls were at lower risk of fine motor developmental delays than boys, while Indian and Pakistani/Bangladeshi ethnic origin, low birthweight and prematurity were associated with an increased risk (Table 6.4). The influence of the socioemotional family environment revealed that lower age and mothers with no qualifications appeared to raise the risk of delayed fine motor functioning. Parenting beliefs suggesting laissez-faire parenting practices and psychological distress were significant risk factors. Among the indicators of the physical environment, overcrowding and smoking near the baby appeared as significant risk factors. After including all sets of factors as potential predictors, only low birthweight, prematurity, parenting beliefs and mother's psychological distress remained as significant risk factors. While mother's age and education appeared to have a direct impact on the risk of delayed fine motor functioning, in this case the influence would seem to work through other factors – for example, the fact that younger less educated mothers tend to have higher levels of psychological distress.

The Wald test used to distinguish which set of factors offered the most important predictors suggested that the socioemotional environment predicted fine motor delay better than either child characteristics or the physical environment. However, in the model with all predictors entered, only the socioemotional environment and child characteristics predicted fine motor delay. As with gross motor delay, the physical environment was less important and captured by the other characteristics.

Predicting delay in communicative gestures

Finally, the same approach was applied to identifying the predictors of the baby's delay in communicative gestures. Among the child characteristics, only one explanatory variable was a significant predictor of delayed gestures: being a twin or triplet was a significant risk factor (Table 6.5). Among the characteristics of the socioemotional family environment, the mother's age and contact with grandparents was associated with a reduced risk of delayed gestures, while laissez-faire parenting beliefs and mothers' psychological distress appeared as significant risk factors. Among the explanatory variables capturing physical characteristics of the family home, only overcrowding emerged

Table 6.4: Odds of fine motor delay by measures of child characteristics, the socioemotional environment and the physical environment for MCS babies

		Model 1	Model 2	Model 3	Model 4
Child characteristics					
Female		0.89*			0.90
Ethnic identity	White	1.00			1.00
	Mixed	0.89			0.83
	Indian	1.21 *			1.06
	Bangladeshi/Pakistani	1.78 **			1.38
	Black	1.16			1.07
	Other	1.71 *			1.60
Multiple birth		0.89			0.95
Low birth weight		1.51 **			1.43 *
Prematurity		1.66 ***			1.67 ***
Any illnesses		0.81			0.83
Hospitalisations		1.18			1.10
Socioeconomic environment					
Mother's age at birth	Under 20		1.00		1.00
	20-24		0.72 *		0.74 *
	25-29		0.59 ***		0.60 **
	30-34		0.53 ***		0.54 ***
	35-39		0.56 **		0.58 **
	³ 40		0.56 *		0.56 *
Employment status	Not in paid work		1.00		1.00
	Part-time		0.97		0.98
	Full-time		0.92		0.91
Qualifications	None		1.00		1.00
	NVQ 1		0.89		0.93
	NVQ 2		0.73 *		0.77 *
	NVQ 3		0.82		0.86
	NVQ 4		0.84		0.90
	NVQ 5		0.80		0.86
	Other		0.96		0.97
Lone parent			1.06		1.08
Number of siblings			1.03		1.03
Parenting beliefs scale			1.10 ***		1.10 ***
Maternal distress			1.11 ***		1.10 ***
Sees grandparents	None		1.00		1.00
	Maternal		0.90		0.92
	Paternal		1.09		1.10
	Both		0.85		0.89
Care while at work	Parent		1.00		1.00
	Relative		0.97		0.99
	Nursery		0.90		0.95
	Other care		1.12		1.15
Physical environment					
Overcrowding				1.26 *	1.01
Smoking near baby				1.28 *	1.04
Damp or condensation				1.06	0.91
No central heating				1.24	1.12
Wald Test		F(11,379) = 9 p < 0.00005	F(23,367) = 7 p < 0.00005	F(4,386) = 4 p = 0.002	F(38,352) = 8 p < 0.00005
Unweighted N values		17556	17556	17556	17556

* p < 0.05 ** p < 0.005*** p < 0.0005

Base: All UK MCS babies when they were 9-10 months old. Standard errors corrected for cluster sample design. Analysis weighted

Table 6.5: Odds of delayed gestures by measures of child characteristics, the socioemotional environment and the physical environment for MCS babies

		Model 1	Model 2	Model 3	Model 4
Child characteristics					
Female		0.83			0.86
Ethnic identity	White	1.00			1.00
	Mixed	2.28			1.91
	Indian	1.63			1.12
	Bangladeshi/Pakistani	3.43 ***			1.78
	Black	1.17			0.69
	Other	1.12			0.69
Multiple birth		2.62 *			2.86 *
Low birth weight		1.58			1.43
Prematurity		1.03			1.08
Any illnesses		0.63			0.67
Hospitalisations		1.19			1.06
Socioeconomic environment					
Mother's age at birth	Under 20		1.00		1.00
	20-24		0.67		0.64
	25-29		0.55		0.57
	30-34		0.55		0.60
	35-39		0.31 *		0.33 *
	40+		0.04 **		0.04 **
Employment status	Not in paid work		1.00		1.00
	Part-time		1.42		1.48
	Full-time		1.59		1.63
Qualifications	None		1.00		1.00
	NVQ 1		0.76		0.86
	NVQ 2		0.53		0.58
	NVQ 3		0.62		0.66
	NVQ 4		0.49		0.53
	NVQ 5		0.51		0.56
	Other		0.83		0.82
Lone parent			1.12		1.21
Number of siblings			1.20		1.08
Parenting beliefs scale			1.15 **		1.16 **
Maternal distress			1.16 **		1.16 *
Sees grandparents	None		1.00		1.00
	Maternal		0.46 *		0.47 *
	Paternal		0.50		0.49
	Both		0.31 ***		0.33 ***
Care while at work	Parent		1.00		1.00
	Relative		0.97		1.05
	Nursery		0.24		0.28
	Other care		0.82		0.90
Physical environment					
Overcrowding				2.01 **	1.31
Smoking near baby				1.08	0.81
Damp or condensation				1.45	1.26
No central heating				1.70	1.64
Wald Test		F(11,379) = 6 p < 0.00005	F(23,367) = 4 p < 0.00005	F(4,386) = 4 p = 0.002	F(38,352) = 6 p < 0.00005
Unweighted N values		17556	17556	17556	17556

* p < 0.05 ** p < 0.005 *** p < 0.0005

Base: All UK MCS babies when they were 9-10 months old. Standard errors corrected for cluster sample design. Analysis weighted

as a significant risk factor. Investigating the combined effect of all explanatory variables in one multivariate model confirmed the relative and independent effect of these variables, except for overcrowding.

Further tests to identify the relative importance of different sets of predictors (Wald tests of the model) suggested that the baby's gestures, like its fine motor delay, were best predicted by the socioemotional environment. Child characteristics also made a contribution to the predictors, but secondary to the socioemotional environment.

Conclusions

In the first year of a baby's life, delay in gross motor functioning is more prevalent than delay in fine motor functioning or in development of communicative gestures.

The multivariate analyses of the various delays in development stages of babies suggested that there were different combinations of predictor variables that accounted for any specific developmental outcome. While biological risk factors (i.e child characteristics) were most important in predicting delay in gross motor functioning, their relative effect was less pronounced in predicting delay in fine motor functioning and gestures over and above the influences of the socioemotional family environment.

Among the child factors, low birthweight and prematurity were the strongest predictors of both gross and fine motor development, but these factors played no significant role in the development of communicative gestures, after controlling for family and environmental variables. Black and Indian babies, and babies from mixed ethnic origin, showed more advanced gross motor development than white babies, confirming findings reported by Tanner (1990). Bangladeshi/Pakistani babies, on the other hand, showed an increased risk of delay in gross motor development, after controlling for all other predictor variables. However, the baby's ethnicity was not a significant explanatory variable for understanding these babies' delays in fine motor functioning or gestures after controlling for other characteristics of the child and the socioemotional and physical environment. These findings confirm the relative importance of biological risk factors for motor development. However, biological risk factors were less important for explaining the development of communicative gestures. One caveat is that we are unable to exclude any effects from either real cultural differences between these families or possible response biases in their answers to the questions. This means that cultural and biasing factors could be influencing the results.

From among the indicators of the socioemotional family environment, a mother's age and her psychological distress were two factors influencing developmental delay across all three developmental functions. Maternal psychological distress appeared as a significant risk factor in all three development domains, confirming the important role of psychological distress in influencing parent–child interactions as well as child adjustment (Corcoran, 1995). However, in models of this kind based on cross-sectional data at one point in time, one cannot be sure whether the causal direction runs from a mother in psychological distress causing a development delay in the child, or a child with a development delay causing psychological distress in a mother.

Increased maternal age was a risk factor for delay in gross motor functioning, but it was associated with a reduced risk of delay in fine motor functioning and gestures. This finding might suggest that increased maternal age can be understood as a biological risk factor for gross motor development. However, on the other hand, older mothers might show more maturity and patience in interacting with their child, leading to a reduced risk of delayed fine motor functioning and communicative gestures.

Maternal education was associated with a reduced risk of delayed gross and fine motor functioning, but was not significantly associated with delay in communicative gestures after controlling for the other indicators of child, family and physical characteristics. This is a surprising finding, as mother's education is generally understood as a proxy for cognitive stimulation and learning provided to the child (Melhuish, et al, 2001). Possibly at this early age, appropriate stimulation is concentrated on motor development. Mother's increased education is also highly correlated with being employed.

Parenting beliefs were significantly associated with delay in fine motor development and gestures, but not with gross motor development. This finding could indicate that in order for children to develop their fine motor and communicative skills they need the structured attention of their parents, and that a laissez-faire style is counterproductive.

After controlling for all the other variables, lone parenthood was not significantly associated with delay in any of the three developmental functions. This is an interesting finding given the current policy focus on lone parents and their children. Number of siblings, on the other hand, was a significant risk factor for delayed gestures, possibly indicating that lack of parental attention due to a large family size might delay the development of communicative skills. Contact with grandparents was also significantly associated with development of communicative gestures but not with motor development. This suggests that regular contact with grandparents reduces the risk of delayed gestures. This again could be interpreted as underlining the importance of adult attention for the development of communicative skills. These results run counter to some of the relationships found between grandparent care and child development for pre-school children (Gregg and Washbrook, 2003).

Interestingly, neither maternal employment status, nor the experience of childcare for children whose mother was in paid employment, showed a significant association with any of the three developmental functions after controlling for the range of other variables. There is thus as yet no evidence for the concerns mentioned in Chapter 8 that poor quality day care may harm child development. There is also no investigation of the possibility of a child's delayed development affecting the mother's decision to go out to work. Likewise, the characteristics of the physical environment in which the baby develops showed no significant independent effect on the three domains of child development under investigation. This suggests that more adverse socioemotional environments are located within more adverse physical environments.

The findings suggest the importance of biological risk factors in shaping early development, particularly in regard to delays in motor development. They also illustrate the independent effect of parent-child and social interactions in shaping developmental outcomes during the first year of life. This is in addition to, but more important than, biological risk factors, especially with regard to the development of fine motor skills and communicative gestures.

The finding of an independent association between maternal psychological distress and delays in motor functioning are theoretically of interest because it extends previous research showing strong links between maternal depression and child cognitive and emotional development (for example, Hay et al, 2001; Murray et al, 2003). The results are interesting in demonstrating strong links between maternal distress and a stage-salient developmental task in children in the first year of life. We must await further data to address issues of causality and the directionality of effects within a longitudinal framework. The findings suggest that health visitors and GPs should investigate mothers' mental health when delays in a child's motor development are identified.

Table A6.1: Description of the independent variables used in the analysis (unweighted N = 17556)

		%
Socioemotional		
Mother's age at birth:	Under 20	7.2
	20-24	15.6
	25-29	27.5
	30-34	31.9
	35-39	15.5
	40+	4.3
Employment status:	Not in paid work	50.6
	Part-time	33.3
	Full-time	16.1
Qualifications:	No qualifications	10.9
	NVQ 1	8.1
	NVQ 2	30.2
	NVQ 3	14.4
	NVQ 4	30.5
	NVQ 5	3.8
	Other	2.0
Lone parent		15.3
Sees grandparents:	None	22.3
	Maternal	36.2
	Paternal	10.2
	Both	31.2
Care while at work:	Parent	
	Relative	16.8
	Nursery	8.1
	Other care	8.1
Child characteristics		
Female		48.6
Ethnicity:	White	89.1
	Mixed	3.1
	Indian	1.6
	Bangladeshi/Pakistani	2.9
	Black	2.4
	Other	0.9
Singleton birth		97.1
Low birthweight (<2500)		7.2
Premature (<37 weeks)		8.3
Any illnesses		78.2
Any hospitalisation		14.5
Physical environment		
Overcrowding		8.3
Smoking near baby		11.8
Damp or condensation		13.0
No central heating		7.8
		Mean (s.d)
Number siblings		0.90(1.64)
Parenting beliefs[1]		5.35(2.31)
Maternal distress[2]		1.60(2.50)

Cluster sample adjustments made; percentages weighted
Base: All UK MCS babies when baby was 9-10 months old

[1] 4 items gauging what parents think about child-rearing practices. Whether the child needs a more structural or laissez-faire environment.

[2] Assessed with a modified 8-item scale based on Rutter's et al (1970) Malaise Inventory.

Note

[1] The standardisation of the individual items is based on the complete sample of Millennium singleton babies.

SEVEN

Parenthood and parenting

Lisa Calderwood, Kathleen Kiernan, Heather Joshi,
Kate Smith and Kelly Ward

Learning to be responsible and involved with one's child is a new experience for parents of a first child. We can explore something of what this is like for the Millennium Cohort Study (MCS) parents, both mothers and fathers, as well as the impact of a new baby on families who already have children. The data provide some direct evidence from mothers and fathers about their involvement with their new baby and in family life, uniquely, for a very large sample of UK fathers.

Plan of this chapter

In this chapter, we first examine the effect of the baby. The spotlight is then turned on an under-researched group – fathers – as they appear in the existing literature, followed by a report on the division of domestic work between mothers and fathers. We then present what the survey finds about fathers' involvement with the cohort child, irrespective of whether they are living in the same home. Parenting beliefs and attitudes are reviewed as well as the overlaps in mothers' and fathers' views about parenting, and some of the mothers' feelings about having a new baby.

Baby shock

Having a new baby can come as a shock. The upheaval is probably greater when it is the first baby than for second or later children. There are sleepless nights, learning to feed and care for this infant who is totally dependent on its parents, and the financial implications. There are many one-off fixed costs for the first baby: a buggy, baby clothes, a cot, and then the regular expenses of nappies, clothes and toys. Where mothers have been employed before giving birth, they have more resources with which to meet these costs. Partnered parents are likely to find it easier than lone parents. Apart from the additional costs, there is the loss of income for employed mothers, where they do not have a generous maternity leave scheme, or they decide to have a career break to care for their own baby. This, for many, means learning to live at a lower standard of living. The MCS provided some information about the adjustment to having a new baby, as described later.

When asked what was the most difficult thing about having their cohort baby, 14.0% of the first-time mothers and 11.3% of their partners said that adjusting to parenthood had been the main challenge. Mothers who already had children faced the different challenge of looking after more children and the interactions between siblings (8.9%). Both parents also mentioned lack of sleep and, if employed, lack of time with the baby. However, for the vast majority these difficulties were offset and apparently compensated by very positive reports of how they were enjoying parenthood.

Among the more negative experiences were those reported by first-time lone mothers about poor relationships with some of the absent fathers (11.1% of lone parents). It was also possible that the stresses of parenthood could have harmed the relationships of couples who were still together. However, the majority of the mothers and fathers in couples felt that their relationship had become closer. This question was put to each parent, confidentially in self completion mode, so the partners did not know what each other had replied. Taking couples who both answered this question, in only 2% of cases did both partners think they had become less close, but there were 12% where at least one partner thought the relationship had worsened. Typically, parents reported the 'bundle of joy' as consolidating a happy family. This pattern was not affected by whether or not the mother had given up paid work, or by whether this was her first child.

It has become usual to think of the entry to motherhood as the time when a woman leaves the labour force. This would imply a first-time mother would stop going out to work during pregnancy, have a break, and in many cases return to employment later, often not until she had finished having children. This pattern was first noted in longitudinal data collected in the 1980 Women and Employment Survey (Martin and Roberts, 1984). The evidence from the Millennium Cohort mothers, admittedly an incomplete record of these mothers' labour market experiences, suggests patterns of working and not working over childbirth that are increasingly diverse. Among the Millennium Cohort mothers with a first birth, 59% were in paid work at the time the child was 9–10 months old. One in six (15%) had no job in pregnancy and no job at the time of the survey. This leaves just over one quarter (25.8%) who could be following the 'classic' pathway, taking a break from paid work at their entry to motherhood. Employment experiences are described in more detail in Chapter 8.

Fathers' employment sequences are even more dominated by continuity in employment. Four per cent of resident fathers had left a job since the time before the baby arrived, predominantly in couples where the woman was not employed either. It is unlikely that many fathers were induced to leave employment by the need to look after the baby. Taking the employment transitions of the mother and father together across the 12-18 months between the time of the pregnancy and the interview, there was no change in a two-earner couple in about half of all couples (55%), no change in having a one earner in about one fifth (21%) and no change in a zero-earner situation in 3.4% of couples. There was a loss of a woman earner in one sixth of couples (17.9%), and of a man earner in 1 in 20 (4.3%). In 1 in 100 couples, both had stopped earning (0.7%). There was a gain of at least one earner in 4.2% of couples.

With so much continuity in employment status, one wonders if the nature and amount of paid work done had changed. Parents with a job before and after the birth were asked if anything had changed about their work. First-time mothers were most likely to mention reductions in hours, associated with taking up part-time work after working full-time previously. Fathers might be expected to change their hours of work in both directions – to increase them to make up for the loss of the mothers' earnings, or to reduce them in order to spend more time with the family. In practice, relatively few parents reported either kind of change. Other changes mentioned (not overlapping with changed hours) included pay rises, changes in the timing of work, and a few changes in occupational status, either higher or lower status than previous occupation.

Spotlight on fathers

Fathers have traditionally been ignored in literature about infants and their mothers, or else received rather a bad press. In sociological studies of parents and the domestic division of labour, mothers have appeared to be shouldering the brunt of housework, caring for children, doing other emotion work and managing the home. Fathers feature as being employed for longer hours than mothers, doing a bit of DIY or some gardening, and with more hobbies and personal time taking them out of the home than mothers (Hochschild, 1990, 1997; Dunscombe and

Marsden, 1993; Warin et al, 1999). While there has been some basis in time budget studies for some of these generalisations, and in the evidence from the MCS discussed later, stereotypes and caricatures have not always been based on straight facts and certainly have tended to devalue or discount fathers' contributions to the family in comparison with those of mothers. In part, this has been due to information about fathers emerging from interviews with mothers rather than being heard from the men themselves. It also seems to be related to mothers, as managers of home life, feeling they have the greater responsibility even if men were to spend the same time doing domestic work as them.

A recent flurry of research projects on fathers and their roles in the family have started to move beyond the earlier simplified stereotypes. Mostly, the research is on resident fathers. Studies have described in fathers' own words what it is like to be a good father – namely, meeting the financial needs of the family; helping with the emotional needs of children and their wives; and 'being there' or spending time with the family. The breadwinner role, fathers feel, has been recognised longest (Burghes et al, 1997; Warin, et al, 1999). But the other roles are relatively new to be noted (Hatter et al, 2002; O'Brien and Shemilt, 2003).

Fathers in lower socioeconomic groups have been found to be more likely than those in high socioeconomic groups to spend time caring for their children, in some cases while the mother is at work (La Valle et al, 2002; Ferri and Smith, 1996). This is especially the case when mothers work at atypical times of day, although not where mothers work as self employed (Bell and La Valle, 2003; Baines et al, 2003). The long working hours of fathers in higher socioeconomic groups were clearly a factor that limited their involvement and time commitment in family life. The same findings were evident in early cohorts: 59% of fathers born in 1970 who had no qualifications shared childcare, while higher qualified fathers did much less.

A number of new insights have been learnt about fathers from more recent studies. Fathers see the need for parents, including themselves, to spend time with their children (Hatter et al, 2002). Some fathers, faced with the conflict between the breadwinner role and time with the family, had chosen the former, although not necessarily without feelings of regret or guilt at neglecting time with the child (Reynolds et al, 2003). In some cases, spending time with children was seen as the mother's role, so less of a problem if the father was not present. However, some fathers thought they had made sacrifices in their own careers in order to spend more time with their children at a certain point in their lives (Dex, 2003; Hatter et al, 2002).

Fathers felt constrained by the norms and culture of their workplace (La Valle et al, 2002; Reynolds et al, 2003). More than a few fathers across studies expressed the view that men were not expected to take time off work for family, or expressed a wish to have flexibility. Some jealousy was expressed that women got a better deal in the workplace because it was expected that they could arrange work to suit family life, and it was accepted that mothers could do this but not fathers.

Fundamental to fathers' views about their own roles was the claim that having a family and children had changed them. The impression given is that they changed from the 'laddish' culture of being single to being a responsible adult, and that this changed their attitude towards work and a career (Hatter et al, 2002; Reynolds et al, 2003). This fits with earlier evidence from sociologists and criminologists about the socialising and civilising effects of women and families on men (e.g. Furedi, 2001).

Division of domestic labour and childcare

Many studies have shown that the domestic division of labour within families is highly related to employment patterns with domestic tasks divided more equally in dual-earner families in which both partners work full time compared with dual-earner families in which the mother works part time and families in which the father is the sole earner. Findings from the 1991 sweep of the National Child Development Study (NCDS) reported by Ferri and Smith (1996) found a similar pattern of division of childcare among working parents.

In the MCS, mothers in families in which the father was the sole earner were more than twice as likely to be mainly responsible for looking after the children, compared with mothers in dual-earner families who were employed full time (78% compared with 35%). Mothers in dual-earner families who were working part time occupied a position between these two family types with 63% of such mothers reporting that they were mainly responsible for childcare (Figure 7.1).

The MCS figure reported for full-time employed mothers in dual-earner families was very similar to the equivalent figure from the British Household Panel Survey (BHPS). However, in the BHPS a higher percentage of mothers who lived in families where the partners were the sole earners (86%) and part-time employed mothers in dual-earner families (77%) reported that they were mainly responsible for childcare (Figure 7.1).

As the BHPS figures are based on all families with children, these comparisons might suggest that there is a more equal distribution of

Figure 7.1: Proportion of mothers saying they have main responsibility for childcare by couple working status

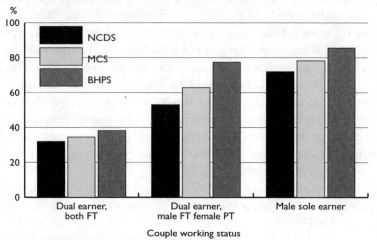

Base: All UK MCS families in which both natural parents are resident full time and both interviewed in person when cohort baby was 9-10 months old (n = 13150).
Analysis excludes 331 dual earner families with other combination of employment/hours not known, 342 mothers sole earner couples, 1248 non-working couples and 3 couples in which working status is not known.
Source: BHPS figures taken from Harkness (2003). NCDS figures taken from Ferri and Smith (1996). Weighted percentages.

childcare between parents in dual-earner families in which the mother is working part time and in sole father-earner families when the youngest child is very young.

However, for all three family types, both the MCS and BHPS found higher proportions of mothers reporting that they were mostly responsible for childcare than those found for 33-year-olds with children in the NCDS in 1991 (Figure 7.1). This comparison might suggest that families with children actually became less egalitarian in their division of childcare between the early 1990s and the beginning of the 21st century for a given number of earners, although the overall trend was in the opposite direction due to the increasing proportion of couples with two earners (Gershuny, 2000). Comparison of the 1970 and 1958 cohort studies by Ferri et al (2003) also suggested that the proportion of couples sharing equally in their responsibility for children, given the number of earners, had fallen between 1991 and 2000, although it should be borne in mind that the children were younger in the later survey.

The relationship between couples' employment status and the domestic division of cleaning and laundry/ironing, although following the same general pattern, is slightly more complex (Figures 7.2 and 7.3).

Figure 7.2: Division of cleaning by couple working status

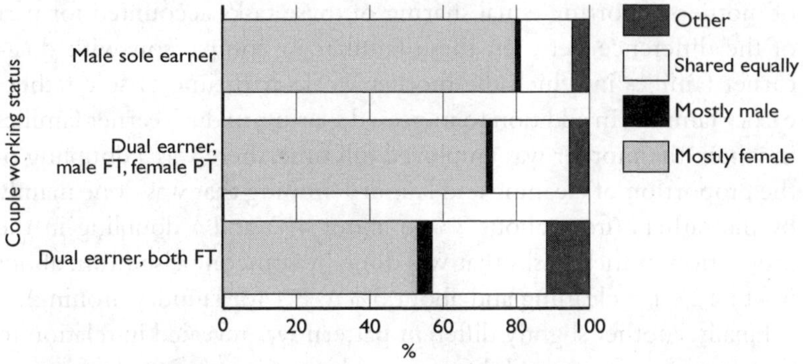

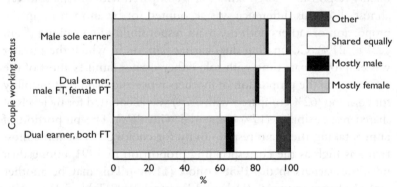

Base: All UK MCS natural mothers and natural fathers who were resident full time when cohort
baby was 9-10 months old.
Weighted percentages.

Figure 7.3: Division of laundry/ironing by couple working status

Base: All UK MCS natural mothers and natural fathers who were resident full time when cohort
baby was 9-10 months old.
Weighted percentages.

The comparison between fathers in sole-earner families and dual-earner families in which the mother works part time is straightforward: the proportion of mothers reporting that they had main responsibility for these tasks was lower in the latter family type where the mother works part time (72% compared with 80% for cleaning and 80% compared with 86% for laundry/ironing). The proportion of mothers reporting that these tasks were shared equally was correspondingly higher where she worked part time compared with where she did not work (21% compared with 14% for cleaning and 15% compared with 10% for laundry/ironing).

Mothers in dual-earner families employed full time were, as expected, the least likely to report that they had the main responsibility for cleaning (53%) and laundry/ironing (64%). Increases in proportions of mothers reporting equal sharing of these tasks accounted for part of the difference between these families in comparison with dual-earner families in which the mother works part time or sole father-earner families. In addition to increased sharing, in dual-earner families in which the mother was employed full time, there was a doubling of the proportion of cleaning and laundry/ironing that was done mainly by the fathers (from about 2% to about 4%) and a doubling in the proportion of these tasks that was done by someone else (from about 5% to 12% for cleaning and about 3% to 8% for laundry/ironing).

Finally, another slightly different pattern was revealed in relation to the division of responsibility for cooking. Comparing dual-earner families in which the mother was employed full time with dual-earner families in which the mother worked part time, there was, as expected, a big difference in the proportion of mothers reporting that they were mainly responsible for cooking (50% compared with 62%). However, almost all of this difference was accounted for by an increase in the proportion of fathers with the main responsibility for cooking (from 12% to 21%). Comparing dual-earner families in which the mother was employed part time with sole father-earner families, most of the difference in the proportion of mothers reporting main responsibility for cooking (62% compared with 75%) was accounted for by levels of shared responsibility (17% compared with 26%). The proportion of fathers taking the main responsibility for cooking (21%) was almost twice as high as the corresponding proportion in 1991 among dual full-time earners in the 1958 cohort (11.6%). This may be another sign of changing times[1] (Dale and Egerton, 1997, Table 5.1).

Despite this, it is striking that among the families with children born at the start of the 21st century, even where both parents work full time, according to the mother she was still mainly responsible for cleaning, laundry/ironing and cooking in over half of families and for childcare in 4 in 10 families (Figures 7.2 and 7.3).

Since these data were reported by mothers, it is possible that they may be over-reporting their own contribution and under-reporting the contribution of their partners as suggested by earlier studies. There is evidence that, within couples, fathers reported higher levels than mothers of equal sharing and correspondingly lower levels of mothers being mainly responsible (Ferri and Smith, 1996; Laurie and Gershuny, 2000). Laurie and Gershuny judged that the correlation between fathers' and mothers' reported shares of domestic work (0.77) was still reasonably high. They also compared self-reported shares with shares calculated from time diary data, and actually found that the mothers' reported shares correlated more highly with this measure than fathers' reported shares (0.69 compared with 0.65).

However, women may be reluctant to cede their position of responsibility in the domestic sphere to their partners. Mothers may be 'managing' their partners' involvement, or be gatekeepers of that involvement and feel thereby that they are doing more (Hochschild, 1990; Warin et al, 1999).

An alternative economic explanation for this apparently persistent inequality in the domestic sphere might be that, even among couples in which both partners are working full time, there is still a relatively large degree of inequality in the respective labour market positions of the fathers and mothers. For example, although both partners may be working full time, there may be a large disparity between their average weekly hours of paid work and their rates of pay. Among MCS families in which both partners were working full time, fathers worked on average 47 hours per week compared with 39 hours for mothers. In families in which the mother worked 90% or more of the hours the father worked, there was greater equality in the division of domestic tasks and childcare (Figure 7.4).

The relative timing of work patterns may also be a factor in explaining differences in the domestic division of labour/childcare. Are both partners at work and at home at the same times of day or week as each other? Or do fathers stay at home to look after the children while the

Figure 7.4: Proportion of full-time working mothers in dual-earner couples reporting equal sharing of domestic work/ childcare by relative working hours

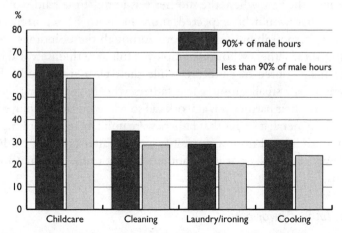

Base: All UK MCS natural mothers and natural fathers who were resident full time, in dual-earner couples where
the mother worked full-time when cohort baby was 9-10 months old. Weighted percentages.

mother goes out to work (and vice versa)? If so, does this mean they are also doing more domestic work while they are looking after the children?

This kind of shift-parenting is relatively rare among families in which both partners are working full time. Fathers were the main source of childcare while the mother was at work in only 11% of couple families in which both parents were employed full time. Shift parenting arrangements were much more common in dual-earner families in which the mother was working part time. Fathers were the main source of childcare while the mother was at work in over a quarter (28%) of these families. This proportion rose to almost 4 in 10 where the father was in a lower supervisory or technical (36%) or semi-routine/routine manual (40%) occupation, and fell to 2 in 10 (20%) where the father was in a managerial/professional occupation. This finding overlaps with those of LaValle et al (2002).

Among dual-earner couples, there was no real difference in the distribution of cleaning, washing and ironing whether or not the father was the main source of childcare when the mother was at work (according to the mother). For couples in which both partners were employed full time, fathers were much more likely to have main responsibility for cooking if they were the main source of childcare while the mother was at work (32% compared with 20%). However, there was no difference for couples in which the mother was employed part time. Oddly, mothers in dual-earner couples who were in part-time paid work did not report that fathers were any more involved in generally looking after the children when they were the main source of childcare although, where the mother was in full-time paid work, fathers were, as would be expected, more likely to be reported as having main responsibility for childcare. Although these findings are interesting, these fathers who were employed full time themselves and were the main source of childcare while their partner worked full time were a very small group. Most fathers who looked after their children while their partner was at work did so while she was employed part time. In general, it seems that fathers were unlikely to be cooking, cleaning, washing and ironing as well as looking after children while mothers were at work, or at least mothers do not think that they are doing this.

Resident fathers' involvement

Fathers who are living with their baby can be involved in looking after them to a greater or lesser degree. Overall, 53% of resident fathers fed their 9–10-month-old baby at least once a day, 57% changed their baby's nappy at least once a day and 60% looked after the baby on their own at least a few times a week.

Indian, Pakistani and Bangladeshi fathers were less likely than fathers in almost all other ethnic groups to feed or change their baby's nappy at least once a day (Figure 7.5). Pakistani fathers were particularly unlikely to change nappies – only 1 in 10 did this at least once a day. There were some differences between other groups but they are not statistically significant. In relation to looking after the baby on their own at least a few times a week, there was much less difference between fathers across ethnic groups. Pakistani fathers were less likely and Black African fathers more likely than white fathers to do this, but the differences between other groups were not statistically significant.

The involvement of the resident fathers with their babies is strongly related to labour market status and hours spent in paid work. Feeding the baby at least once a day and looking after the baby on their own at least a few times per week varied most with employment status and hours. Fathers who were not in paid work were the most likely to have this higher level of involvement. For fathers who were in paid

Figure 7.5: Fathers' involvement by ethnic identity

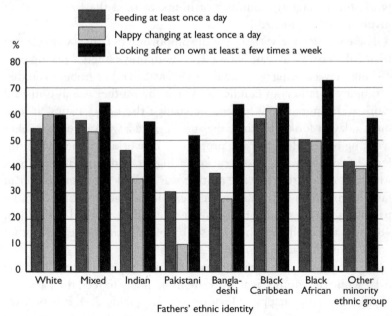

Base: All UK MCS natural fathers living in a natural two parent family and both interviewed in person when cohort baby was 9-10 months old. Weighted percentages.

Figure 7.6: Fathers' involvement by father's working status and hours

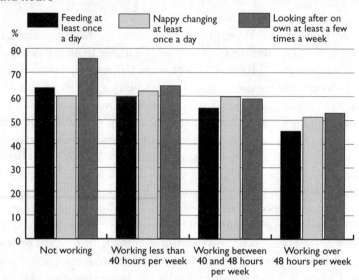

Base: All UK MCS families in which both natural parents were resident full-time and both were interviewed in person when cohort baby was 9-10 months old (n = 13150). Analysis excludes 151 families in which fathers' working hours were not known and 3 families in which working status was not known. Weighted percentages.

work, the greater the number of hours worked the lower level of involvement (Figure 7.6).

There is much less variation in the proportion of fathers who change their baby's nappy at least once a day – with only fathers working over 48 hours a week being significantly less likely than other groups to do this.

Employed fathers in families in which the mother was also in paid work were more likely to feed or change the baby's nappy at least once a day or look after the baby at least once a week, at each level of working hours. However, the proportion of working fathers with this level of involvement was very much higher if they were the main source of childcare while the mother was at work. About a quarter of families in which both parents were employed had this kind of 'shift-parenting' arrangement. Even where the father worked more than 48 hours a week, he was the main source of childcare while the mother was at work in 1 in 5 families.

It is, of course, unsurprising that fathers who are looking after the baby while the mother is at work are more likely to feed the baby and change the baby's nappy at least once a day (Table 7.1). It is perhaps more surprising that among fathers who were the main source of childcare while the mother was at work, 10.4% of those working less

Table 7.1: Fathers' involvement by father's working status, hours and carer status

	Father working less than 40 hours a week (%)**			Father working 40-48 hours a week (%)**			Father working more than 48 hours a week (%)**		
	Father main carer*	Father not main carer*	All	Father main carer*	Father not main carer*	All	Father main carer*	Father not main carer*	All
Feeding at least once a day	78.6	60.6	64.8	70.9	59.3	61.2	62.5	48.8	50.7
Nappy changing at least once a day	80.6	64.5	68.5	75.1	65.8	67.3	70.3	55.5	57.9
Looking after on own at least a few times a week	89.6	62.5	67.9	84.1	61.1	65.7	81.8	56.0	60.5
Unweighted sample size	307	829	1237	566	1904	2645	410	1653	2242

Base: All UK MCS families in which both parents were resident full time, both were interviewed in person and both were in paid work when cohort baby was 9-10 months old (excludes 331 dual-earner couples with other combination of employment/hours not known). *Main carer is only defined for families who reported childcare used; therefore total columns do not sum to total of care columns. Weighted percentages.

** Difference between less than 40 hours and 40-48 hours is only significant for the 'looking after on own' category comparison. Difference between more than 48 hours and other hours significant in all comparisons.

than 40 hours a week, 15.9% of those working 40–48 hours and 18.2% of those working 48 or more hours a week said that they did not look after the baby on their own at least a few times a week. Only the comparison between over 48 hours and hours less than 48 hours points to the difference being statistically significant. Again this may be because fathers were looking after the baby with someone else, or perhaps because they provided childcare while the mother was at work less than a few times a week.

Lone mothers and non-resident fathers' involvement

Across most developed societies, there have been noticeable increases in having children outside marriage with most of this increase being due to the rise in births to cohabiting couples. However, intriguingly in Britain there has also been an increase in the proportions of all babies born to parents who are not living together at the time of the birth (Kiernan, 2004b). Very little is known about this group, and the data collected in the MCS are among the first that allow us to examine this group of parents.

Present at birth and name on birth certificate

Although about 14% of Millennium babies were not living with their father at 9 months, in around half of these families the baby's birth was registered by both parents (56%) and the father was present at the baby's birth (44%).[2]

Since July 2001 in Northern Ireland and from December 2003 in England and Wales, fathers who jointly registered the birth of their baby have had equal parental responsibility akin to married parents. Parental responsibility provides important legal rights such as the ability to be involved in decisions pertaining to the child's residence, education, religion and medical treatment. Unmarried fathers in Scotland (at the time of writing) do not have this right. The great majority of the unmarried fathers in the MCS study do not have this automatic right as only 3% of the babies were born in Northern Ireland. Thus, the majority of unmarried fathers of the MCS children can only acquire parental responsibility either by marrying the child's mother, or by obtaining a Parental Responsibility Agreement (PRA) signed by the mother. If the mother disagrees to a PRA, the father can apply to the courts for a Parental Responsibility Order. Facts such as being on the birth certificate or being present at the birth of the child tend to count favourably in such a submission (Families Need Fathers, www.fnf.org.uk).

We can examine fathers' closeness and involvement at around the time of the birth using two concrete indicators – namely, whether absent fathers were present at the birth of the child and whether the father's name was included on the birth certificate. As might be expected, there was a high degree of overlap between the groups of fathers present at the birth and included on the birth certificate, but they were not coterminous. Seventy-one per cent of the non-married fathers were present at the birth and on the birth certificate, 12% were neither, 13% were registered as the father on the birth certificate but were not present at the birth, and a tiny minority of these fathers, 3%, were present at the birth but not included on the birth certificate. Whether or not the father was present at the birth of the child is an indicator of the degree of closeness of the father to the mother and child at birth. This is likely to be a very important determinant of future contact and involvement based on the assumption that fathers who were present at the birth of their child are more likely to bond with that child. Moreover, presence at the birth is a more meaningful variable for the married fathers given their automatic placing on the birth certificate. Whether the father was present at the birth of his child was strongly correlated with the partnership status of the parents. The vast majority of married and cohabiting fathers were present at the birth, 93 and 92% respectively, whereas under half (45%) of the fathers not in a co-residential partnership with the mother were at the birth of their child.

Regular contact

Many non-resident fathers continued to be involved in their baby's lives at nine months, according to the reports of lone mothers. About half saw their child at least once a week and almost a third saw their child even more often – 17% of fathers saw the child three to six times a week and 14% of fathers saw the child every day. Among non-resident fathers who were in contact at nine months, about 85% were reported to be 'interested' in their baby's lives and nearly 75% were on friendly terms with the baby's mother – although only about half (48%) contributed any money to the baby's maintenance.

Another 15% of all 'non-resident' fathers were reported to be in contact with the child but either never saw them or saw them once a month or less often. However, a substantial proportion (36%) of non-resident fathers was reported to have no contact at all with their baby at nine months (according to the mother).

Only about 10% of lone parents had previously been married to the baby's father, but a substantial proportion had lived together previously (34% of lone parents). It seems likely that in these families there has been some kind of breakdown in the relationship between the parents as they were no longer living together at nine months. About another third of lone parents (35%) had never lived with the baby's father but were in some kind of relationship with him – either 'closely involved' or 'just friends' – at the time of the baby's birth. The remainder of lone parents (21%) had never lived with the baby's father and were not in any relationship with him at the time of the baby's birth. Most of these mothers either may never have had a relationship with the baby's father – or had a non-cohabiting relationship which broke down during pregnancy.

The nature of the prior relationship between the baby's parents varied with mothers' age. Only 3 in 10 teenage lone mothers had experienced a breakdown in a cohabiting relationship with the baby's father compared with nearly half of older lone mothers.

Contact arrangements for absent fathers at nine months were highly related to the prior nature of the relationship between the parents (Figure 7.7). Non-resident fathers who had never lived with the baby's mother but were in a relationship with her at the time of the baby's birth were the most likely to see their baby at least once a week (63%) and nearly a quarter saw their baby every day. A similar proportion of fathers who had previously lived with the baby's mother without being married saw their baby at least once a week (59%) although a lower proportion (15%) saw their baby every day. Non-resident fathers who had previously been married to the baby's mother were less likely to see their baby at least once a week (36%) and were also less likely to be in any kind of contact with them (33%) than non-resident fathers who had either been cohabiting or in a relationship (25%). The vast majority (77%) of non-resident fathers who had never lived with the baby's mother and were not in a relationship with her at the time of the baby's birth were not in any contact at nine months.

The 'in a relationship' group were found not to be significantly different from the 'married' group. The 'cohabiting' group were found to be significantly different from the 'married' group.

Of course, there are many other factors that affect how often non-resident parents see their children, such as how far away they live, whether or not they have other families and their own employment patterns as well as those of the mother. Some of these factors may also

Figure 7.7: Non-resident fathers' contact with baby by parents' prior relationship

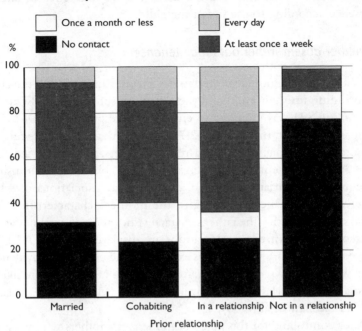

Base: All UK MCS mothers' reports on natural fathers who were not resident in the household of the cohort baby when it was 9-10 months old. Weighted percentages.
The 'in a relationship' group were found not to be significantly different from the 'married' group.
The 'cohabiting' group were found to be significantly different from the 'married' group.

be related to the relationship between the parents prior to the cohort baby's birth.

Characteristics of non-resident fathers

Resident fathers compared with non-resident fathers were more likely to have been present at the birth; if unmarried, they were more likely to be on the child's birth certificate; and the parents were more likely to have been married or cohabiting when the child was born. With reference to the age of the parents, the younger the mother the more likely the father was to be non-resident, and young fathers under age 25 were also more likely to be non-resident fathers. There is only information on educational attainment for the resident fathers in the study, but there is information for all the mothers. More of the mothers where the father was absent had low-level qualifications: 42% had less than NVQ level 2 qualifications as compared with 17% of the mothers where the father was present. Turning to the characteristics of the children, relatively more of the first-born children had resident fathers than did later born children, but there was no difference in father presence according to the sex of the child.

Whether absent father pays maintenance

Absent fathers are now expected to pay maintenance towards the cost of bringing up their child and the setting up of the Child Support Agency (CSA) was intended to enforce this responsibility. Of MCS lone mothers at interview, 32.7% reported that they received maintenance payments from non-resident fathers, although in the case of 9.9% the payments were irregular. We were able to examine, using a logistic multivariate regression, the statistical associations of who received maintenance according to the mother's characteristics, the child's characteristics, the father's characteristics and partnership status. The odds ratios of these associations are displayed in Table A7.1. A range of explanatory variables was examined. There is research evidence that, where a new partner has arrived, the child's father is more likely to lose contact and less likely to pay maintenance (Maclean and Eekelaar, 1997; Bradshaw et al, 1999).

After controlling for this range of influences, mothers who were in work or had qualifications were more likely to be in receipt of maintenance from the father, findings which are in accord with those of Bradshaw et al (1999) and Ford et al (1995). The group of mothers substantially less likely to be in receipt of maintenance were, as might be expected, those who were neither living with the baby's father at the time of the birth of their child nor had the father present at the birth. There was little suggestion that non-resident fathers from different ethnic groups, such as fathers whose origins were the Indian subcontinent or black fathers, were any less likely than white fathers to be paying maintenance to the mother. The only group that differed significantly from the set of white fathers were the fathers classified as being of mixed origin who were more likely than white fathers to be paying maintenance to the mother. The introduction of whether the father was in contact or not, although very important as a correlate of maintenance payments, did not alter the picture with respect to the other independent variables. With regard to the mother's emotional well-being, we see that the mothers who were in receipt of some money from the father of their child were less likely to report that they had low self esteem than their counterparts not in receipt of maintenance. However, mothers in receipt of maintenance were also more likely to report symptoms of depression. We were not able to disentangle this seeming paradox at this juncture, as we have no information on whether the mothers exhibited these symptoms prior to or subsequent to the birth or both. Possible, albeit speculative, explanations are that fathers take more interest in their children where the mother is unwell, or that such mothers are more likely to request help, or that father involvement is associated with more depressive symptoms among the mothers. The self-esteem findings are opposite to those relating to depression and are broadly speaking in the same direction as those relating to work and education. Mothers who were employed were more likely to receive maintenance after controlling for other factors.

Parenting beliefs and attitudes

Both mothers and fathers were asked about their parenting beliefs and some general attitudes in a self-completion section of the questionnaire which enabled them to answer in private without knowing what the other one had replied. They were allowed one of five answers ranging from 'strongly agree' to 'strongly disagree', with 'neither agree nor disagree' in the middle between 'agree' and 'disagree'. In the findings we describe below, 'agreement' includes both 'strongly agree' and 'agree' responses.

On parenting beliefs, approximately one third of mothers and fathers agreed that babies should be picked up whenever they cried. Nine in 10 felt that it was important for babies to develop a regular pattern of sleeping and feeding, almost all (95% or more) parents felt that babies need to be stimulated if they are to develop well (Figure 7.8) and that talking to and cuddling a baby are important (Figure 7.9). Most of these did not vary with age of parents but there were some notable exceptions. Older parents were more likely than younger ones to strongly agree with the statement that stimulation was important for development and that cuddling a baby was important. Less than half (48.8%) of teenage mothers strongly agreed that stimulation was important for development compared with nearly three quarters (72.7%) of mothers aged 40 or more (Figure 7.8). Similar proportions were found for fathers. In relation to the importance of cuddling, not only was there a gradient associated with age but for all age groups mothers were more likely to strongly agree than fathers (Figure 7.9).

Parents' education was related to the importance placed on stimulation for development. Approximately one half of mothers and 6 in 10 fathers with the lowest educational level (NVQ Level 1) strongly agreed that stimulation was important for a baby's development,

Figure 7.8: Proportion of parents strongly agreeing that stimulation is important for development

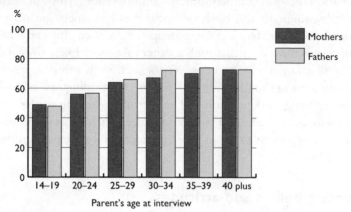

Base: All UK MCS natural mothers and natural fathers when cohort baby was 9-10 months old. Weighted percentages.

Figure 7.9: Proportion of parents strongly agreeing that cuddling is important

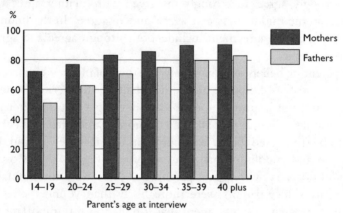

Base: All UK MCS natural mothers and natural fathers when cohort baby was 9-10 months old. Weighted percentages.

compared with three quarters of mothers and over 8 in 10 fathers with the highest educational level (equivalent to NVQ Level 5). Parents with professional and managerial occupations were the most likely to place strong emphasis on the importance of stimulation for development. A quarter of mothers with the lowest educational level agreed that babies should be picked up whenever they cried, compared with over 4 in 10 mothers with the highest educational level. Chapter 6 analyses the role of parents' beliefs in child development.

Parenting attitudes

Parents were also asked a range of attitudinal questions relating to different aspects of parenting, such as work, the roles of fathers and the importance of education. Attitudes about work and family varied according to whether the mother was in paid work or not. Both parents were asked whether a child is likely to suffer if the mother works before they start school. Mothers who were not in paid work were much more likely to agree with this statement than mothers who were in paid work, regardless of whether this was part- or full-time hours (Figure 7.10). Four in 10 mothers not in paid work agreed with the statement compared with only around 1 in 10 of mothers in paid work.

Fathers were more likely to agree than mothers that children were likely to suffer if mothers worked before they went to school (Figure 7.10). More than half of fathers whose partners were not in paid work agreed that children were likely to suffer if a mother worked before they started school, compared with more than 1 in 5 fathers whose partners worked part time and only 1 in 6 whose partners worked full time.

Parents were also asked whether they felt family life suffers when a woman has a full-time job. Once again, the proportions agreeing or disagreeing varied with mothers' paid work status, although part-time

Figure 7.10: Proportion of parents agreeing or strongly agreeing that a child is likely to suffer if the mother works before they start school

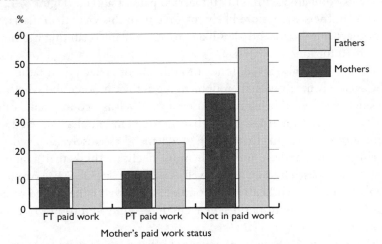

Base: All UK MCS natural mothers and natural fathers when cohort baby was 9-10 months old. Weighted percentages.

Figure 7.11: Proportion of parents agreeing or strongly agreeing that family life suffers if the mother has a full-time job

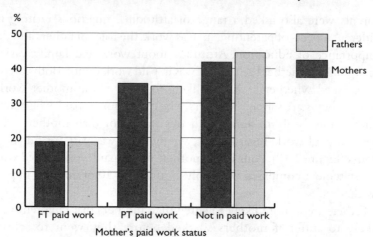

Base: All UK MCS natural mothers and natural fathers when cohort baby was 9-10 moths old. Weighted percentages.

working mothers' views were more similar to mothers not in paid work than to mothers in full-time paid work (Figure 7.11). More than 4 in 10 mothers not in paid work and over a third of mothers in part-time paid work assented to this view, compared with fewer than 1 in 5 mothers working full time. Fathers showed almost exactly the same variation in views (Figure 7.11).

Parents were also asked whether they thought that it was all right to have children without being married. More than 9 in 10 cohabiting parents compared with 6 in 10 married parents agreed (Figure 7.12). Lone mothers were more likely to agree with this view than married mothers, but significantly less likely to agree than cohabiting mothers (8 in 10 for lone mothers).

Parents were also asked if they thought children need their father to be as closely involved in their upbringing as their mother, and whether a single parent can bring up children just as well as a couple can. Lone mothers were much less likely than mothers in couples (married or cohabiting) to think that fathers need to be as closely involved in bringing up children and much more likely to think that a single parent can raise children just as well as a couple (Figure 7.13). Around 9 in 10 mothers and fathers in couples agreed that fathers need to be just as involved with raising their children, compared to just 6 in 10 lone mothers (Figure 7.13).

Nearly 9 in 10 lone mothers agreed that a single parent can raise children just as well as a couple, compared with just over two thirds of cohabiting mothers and under a half of married mothers. Fathers were much less likely to agree with this view than mothers – only 4 in 10 cohabiting fathers and just over a quarter of married fathers agreed or strongly agreed with this.

Figure 7.12: Proportion of parents agreeing or strongly agreeing that it is all right to have children without being married

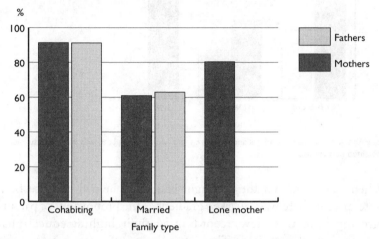

Base: All UK MCS natural mothers and natural fathers when cohort baby was 9-10 months old. Weighted percentages.

Figure 7.13: Proportion of parents agreeing or strongly agreeing that children need their father to be as closely involved in their upbringing as their mother

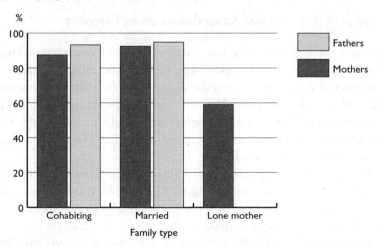

Base: All UK MCS natural mothers and natural fathers when cohort baby was 9-10 months old. Weighted percentages.

Figure 7.14: Proportion of parents agreeing or strongly agreeing that a single parent can bring up a child just as well as a couple can

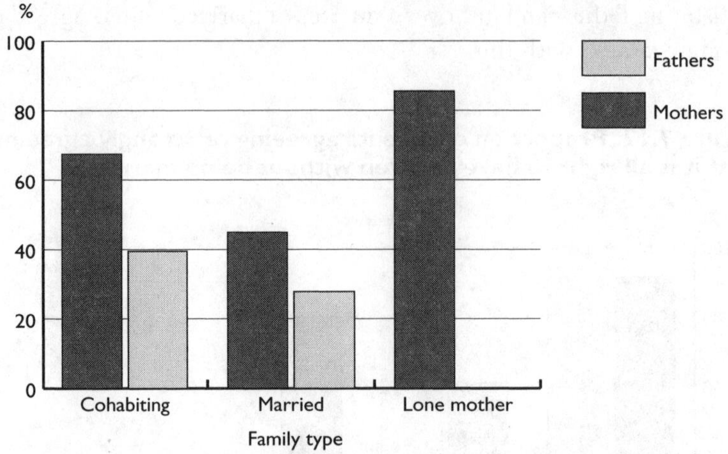

Base: All UK MCS natural mothers and natural fathers when cohort baby was 9-10 months old. Weighted percentages.

When asked whether they thought education helped them to be a better parent, there was a marked gradient of the proportions of parents agreeing with this view according to their highest educational qualification (Figure 7.15). There was also a difference between the views of mothers and fathers about education helping parenting. Fathers were more likely to agree than mothers across all qualification groups, but the gap between parents' views was largest for those with lower qualifications (NVQ 1) (Figure 7.15).

Mothers' compared with fathers' views about parenting

Mothers and fathers may not always hold the same views about parenting. Rarely is this explored in surveys. The effects of parents' disagreeing about how to treat the children can be a source of marital discord which may have outcomes in the future on their own relationship and on the child's development. In the first sweep of MCS data, we are able to document the extent of overlap and difference on a selected set of parents' views.

Couple parents reported unanimity about the baby's need for cuddling, stimulation and talking to (Table 7.2). They also mainly agreed that fathers needed to be involved in the baby's upbringing (86.4%) and that the baby needed a regular feeding pattern (86.6%). Most inconsistency (16.8% of couples) was evident on whether the baby should be picked up whenever it cried, with slightly more fathers

Figure 7.15: Proportion of parents agreeing or strongly agreeing that education helps you to be a better parent

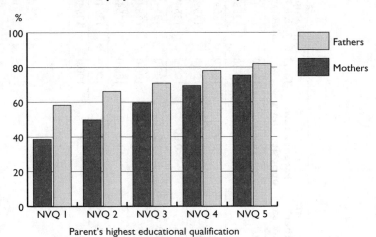

Parent's highest educational qualification

Base: All UK MCS natural mothers and natural fathers when cohort baby was 9-10 months old. Weighted percentages.

thinking it should when the mother thought it should not than vice versa.

On more general attitudes, outright disagreement was relatively uncommon. Approximately 1 in 6 or fewer couples disagreed about whether it was good for mothers to work and whether couples should not separate if they had children.

Overall, on this small set of indicators, couples mostly see eye-to-eye on parenting and gender roles, with outright and clear differences of view being restricted to a small minority of couples. This is consistent with the mainly harmonious responses on the quality of couples' relationships.

Mothers' thoughts/feelings about their baby

Mothers indicated they had a variety of feelings about their babies (Table 7.3). The majority of mothers admitted to getting annoyed with the baby occasionally (69.3%) or impatient (49.6%), although frequent annoyance was very rare (3.1%) as was being 'very impatient' (3.5%). Feelings of frequent annoyance and impatience were higher among those who had never had a job: 7.7% of those who had never worked were annoyed with the baby compared with 3.3% of the total sample, and 7% were very impatient compared with 3.5% of the total sample. However, a higher percentage of those who had never worked had also never been annoyed with the baby (37.3% compared with

Table 7.2: Extent of overlap in parenting views of parents

	Both parents agree	Both parents disagree	One parent 'neither' or can't say	Parents have opposite views	Total %	Sample size N unweighted
Should pick up baby whenever they cry	16.7	17.6	49.0	16.8	100.0	13547
Important to develop regular feeding pattern	86.6	>0.00	10.3	3.0	100.0	13551
Baby needs stimulation to develop well	93.2	0.0	6.7	0.01	100.0	13542
Talking to baby is important	99.0	0.0	0.9	<0.00	100.0	13551
Cuddling baby is important	97.6	<0.00	2.3	<0.00	100.0	13549
Child suffers if mother works	14.5	23.2	50.8	11.5	100.0	13545
Family life suffers if woman has full-time job	17.3	15.7	51.9	15.1	100.0	13545
Couples should not separate if they have kids	13.5	9.0	63.0	14.5	100.0	13546
It's OK to have kids if not married	56.8	5.1	31.4	6.7	100.0	13546
Fathers need to be closely involved in child's upbringing	86.4	<0.00	10.9	2.7	100.0	13548

Base: All UK MCS mothers and fathers when cohort baby was 9-10 months old. Weighted percentages.

27.5% in the total sample). Those in semi-routine or low supervisory and technical socioeconomic categories were more likely than mothers from managerial and professional or intermediate occupations to be never annoyed with their baby, although the extent of impatience did not vary systematically by NS-SEC groups. Mothers who were frequently annoyed had considerably higher malaise depression scores than mothers in general.

The majority of mothers also thought about the baby when they were away from them (96.6%) and felt some sadness at being apart (96.8%) (Table 7.3). Rates of thinking about the baby when apart and often feeling sad were higher among those who were not employed at the time. This is probably because mothers who were employed had become used to the separation from their baby, whereas those who were not employed had not been parted to the same extent. There was still a high level of sadness about being parted from the baby among employed mothers, 65.6% of whom frequently thought about the baby and 46.6% of whom often or always felt sad about being separated. Rates of thinking about the baby all the time when apart were also higher among mothers from semi-routine or low supervisory and technical occupations, compared with mothers from managerial, professional and intermediate occupations. However, the extent of feeling sad about being apart from the baby displayed little variation by NS-SEC.

Feelings of resentment about giving things up for the baby were relatively rare: 80.2% never resented this (Table 7.3). Mothers who had never worked were slightly more likely to feel this resentment

Table 7.3: Mothers' feelings about the baby

	Frequently	Occasionally	Never or cannot say	Very impatient	A bit impatient/can't say	Extremely patient	Resent it a lot	Resent it a bit/can't say	Don't resent at all	Total %	Unweighted sample size
Feelings of annoyance	3.1	69.3	27.5							100	17752
Think about baby when apart	88.3	8.4	1.4							100	17757
Feeling sad when leave baby*	45.0	51.8	3.2							100	17745
Extent of impatience with baby				3.5	49.6	46.9				100	17753
Resent giving up things because of baby							0.9	19.0	80.2	100	17754

Base: All UK MCS mothers when cohort baby was 9-10 months old. Weighted percentages.

* Categories vary.

(3.7%, compared with 0.9% in the total sample). There was little variation in the extent of resentment by NS-SEC group. Mothers who felt a lot of resentment about the baby also had higher malaise depression scores than mothers in general.

Conclusions

Parenting is clearly an essential activity for new babies and also for older children. Most Millennium parents gave very positive reports about their experiences of the new baby joining their family. They also expressed views that showed they understood, placed a high value on and appreciated the importance of the parental role in child development – one of stimulation, cuddling, warmth and communication for language development. Furthermore, most mothers and fathers were agreed in their views about their own importance to the baby. However, there were more disagreements when it came to their attitudes to the place of women's employment, to marriage and separation and about the best context in which to bring up children.

Not everything was so rosy. There were small minorities where one partner thought their relationship had suffered since the new baby arrived. A minority of lone parents expressed negative views about the absent father. A few mothers (3-4%) admitted they had frequent feelings of annoyance and resentment towards the new baby. These mothers were more likely to be depressed. While all very small scale, these are worrying signs for the welfare of these babies. Neither are they necessarily the total expression of such feelings, since recognition of social disapproval would probably lead many parents to hide such feelings from interviewers.

Within families, the domestic division of labour bore all the hallmarks of earlier studies. Mothers still reported doing a greater share of the domestic work and childcare than fathers. Clearly mothers reported variations in the extent of fathers' involvement in domestic work, according to fathers' socioeconomic status, ethnic origin and the combination of fathers' and mothers' hours of paid work. It is not a picture of New Men, even though some men in lower status occupations, whose hours of work were not prohibitively long and who had full-time working wives, were doing more domestic work than other men. There are some other notable inroads to the traditional division of labour. This can be seen in nappy-changing – an exercise of physical and psychological intimacy. Nearly all fathers, Pakistani and Bangladeshi fathers excepted, take a turn at nappy-changing for babies, albeit to differing degrees, related to jobs, hours and cultural traditions and roles.

This area of family life raises a number of policy issues. The first is the discussion about where the limits of government intervention in family life should be drawn. On the whole, governments have tended to treat the within-family behaviour as outside its remit. Clearly, there has always been a concern for vulnerable children and child protection issues. It is also clear that identifying genuine cases where children are at serous risk is a tricky area, as high profile child abuse and murder cases regularly show. This is largely because it occurs within this accepted area of private family life. The post-1997 Labour government have started to make further incursions across the 'private' boundary by drawing up legislation about violent behaviour between spouses, largely in order to offer more protection to women who suffer from this.

The sphere of domestic division of labour, while part of this private sphere, has long been recognised as of central importance to gender inequality in the labour market. Where one partner, the woman, takes on most responsibility for domestic work and does less paid work than her male partner, it is not surprising that market wage rates favour men over women. Feminists have seen this as arising from and reinforcing a power imbalance. They have tended to assume women, the less powerful, are pressured into taking this private domestic role at the expense of their current and future earning power and pensions by more powerful men. The power imbalance can arise merely through a difference in wage rates at the start of the process, since this will lead to a division of labour within households that reinforces the existing wage differential. In earlier generations, wives and husbands probably thought of themselves more as a cooperative unit, sharing any resources that came into the household. In the days of high divorce and separation rates, a division of labour that makes one partner focus on market work and the other on domestic work leaves the latter vulnerable in the event of a partnership breakdown. This may be one of a large number of reasons why women are now more interested in participating in the market sector to do paid work, in order to diversify and shield themselves against risks of marital breakdown. But, as the results of this chapter show, women still think they do a larger share of certain domestic jobs in the home. This is despite their increased paid workload, and increased share in contribution to family earnings.

One might argue that government should intervene to address this inequality, but it is not clear how they could do so, even were they to want to. Indeed, some of the qualitative studies of the domestic division of labour have shown women liking their managerial and gatekeeper roles in the home and being unwilling to give them up to men (Warin et al, 1999; Hochschild, 1990).

An alternative approach has been discussed at various points in time, but never taken up as a serious policy option. It is the idea of paying wages for housework. A weaker alternative of the same idea is to improve the credits for caring which translate into social security and pension entitlements rather than move the social security system towards rights based solely on individuals as paid workers (Joshi and Davies, 1994; Lewis, 2004). This would recognise the value and necessity of such work in the home. It could also offer a route to address the pension inequality that results for women as a result of taking time out of the labour force to look after a family and their vulnerability to marital breakdown if they have not kept a foot in the labour market. Although the mothers of the Millennium babies were on average more attached to the labour market than ever before, their contributions to raising the next generation involve the foregoing of considerable earnings to their families, even if they had paid jobs. The contribution of parenting time and attention to the welfare of the children, by fathers as well as mothers, is not normally quantified, but the follow-up of the children in this survey should, in due course, provide rare evidence on the benefits children derive.

Notes

[1] We cannot be sure of this interpretation since fewer of the 1958 birth cohort couples interviewed in 1991 had children at the time.

[2] All the information on non-resident fathers including that on whether the father was present at the birth and whether they were included on the child's birth certificate comes from the mothers' reports. See Chapter 4 for further discussion of who was present at the birth by ethnic group.

Table A7.1: Odds ratios for associations of whether non-resident fathers are in contact with the mother or whether they pay maintenance with parent and child characteristics

	Father pays maintenance		
	Bivariate analysis	Multivariate analysis	Multivariate analysis and including whether father is in contact
Child characteristics			
Firstborn	1.10	1.00	1.05
Male	1.01	0.98	0.99
Parents' characteristics			
Mother's qualifications			
Some	1.91***	1.47**	1.40*
Mother's age at birth			
Under age 20	1.00	1.00	1.00
20-24 years	1.03	1.04	1.10
25-29 years	1.14	1.06	1.03
30 or older	1.09	0.98	0.95
Father's age at birth			
Under age 24	1.00	1.00	1.00
25-34 years	1.21	1.09	1.16
35-44 years	1.21	1.09	1.07
45 and older	1.06	1.04	0.98
Father's ethnic origin			
White	1.00	1.00	1.00
Mixed	1.59	2.36*	1.79
Indian	0.73	1.24	1.00
Pakistani/Bangladeshi	0.87	0.94	0.93
Black	0.93	1.09	1.01
Other	0.59	0.83	0.92
Mum in work	2.14***	1.96***	1.87**
On a low income	0.60***	0.82	0.79
On means tested benefits*	0.52***	0.89	0.88
Mother depressed**	0.99	1.51**	1.48*
Mother has low self esteem***	0.79**	0.71*	0.70*
Mother has a low level of life satisfaction****	0.80**	0.84	0.81
Living arrangements			
On own	1.00	1.00	1.00
Partner in household	0.59	0.67	0.65
Grandparent in household	0.99	1.12	1.25
Partnership status and father present at birth			
Married and present at birth	1.00	1.00	1.00
Married and not present	0.23***	0.52	0.57
Cohabiting and present	0.68	0.99	0.89
Cohabiting and not present	0.61	0.94	0.91
Not in partnership and present	0.65*	0.95	0.89
Not in partnership and not present	0.17***	0.22***	0.40**
In contact	—	—	9.97***
Number in sample, unweighted	3566	2755	2755

Base: All UK MCS mothers where the father was non-resident at the time of interview. (NB: Some mothers may have re-partnered after interview, they will still be included in analysis).

***p< 0.001, **p<0.01, *p<0.05, ˙p<0.10.

*In receipt of Jobseeker's Allowance, Income Support, Working Families Tax Credit or Disabled Person's Tax Credit.
**The depression indicator was derived from the abbreviated 9-item Rutter Malaise Inventory with a score of four or more items being taken as an indicator of depression.
*** The self-esteem variable was derived from responses to six items on how the mother felt about herself.
**** A score of 6 or less was used to indicate low levels of life satisfaction.

Standard errors adjusted for cluster sample design and weighted.

EIGHT

Parents' employment and childcare

Shirley Dex, Denise Hawkes, Heather Joshi and Kelly Ward

Since 1980, there have been very large increases in labour force participation among mothers with pre-school children, doubling over 20 years. In 1980, 27% of mothers with a child under 5 were employed (Martin and Roberts, 1984, Table 2.6, p 13), compared with 54% in 2001 (Labour Market Trends, 2003, p 505). Many mothers work part time when children are young, but there have also been more mothers working full time at this stage. There has not been a corresponding decrease in fathers' participation rates or hours of work. Fathers' contributions to childcare have increased a little, but are still far outweighed by mothers' contributions. Increased paid work among mothers has also necessitated increased childcare outside the immediate family. These have all raised issues for families. How do mothers manage the double burden of employment, childcare and domestic work? This also involves the responsibility for arranging childcare, often outside the home, and the logistics of getting children to childcare providers, getting to and from work and collecting children on time (Skinner, 2003). Chapter 7 considered how childcare in the home was shared between mothers and fathers. In this chapter we consider childcare while parents are doing their paid jobs.

Some of this discussion has revolved around whether parents, and especially mothers, have 'work–life balance', whether they have sufficient flexibility at the workplace to cope with these new demands. There is concern that increasing hours and intensity at work faced by dual-earner families are putting pressure on family life, as reviewed in Dex (2003). At the same time, companies are under pressure from global competition to intensify demands on their workforce. These pressures can result in increasing levels of sickness, turnover, stress and absence from work (DTI, 2000). In order to help achieve greater work–life balance and help parents combine work and family life, employers are being called on to provide more family-friendly policies within workplaces. There are also issues and questions surrounding the quality of childcare providers and the effects of non-parental care on young children.

Public policy stepped into this arena around the turn of the century as described in Chapter 1, especially as the employment of parents is seen as a major route to combat child poverty (see Chapters 1 and 3). As well as encouraging employers to offer more flexibility to parents, the government has introduced improvements to statutory entitlements for parents and increased formal childcare provision over the 1990s. The question is 'Are these changes making a significant impact in helping families combine paid work and caring?' Data from the Millennium Cohort Study (MCS) (2001) show how parents entering the new millennium are managing to combine employment, domestic work and family life. This examination of their experiences gives us an opportunity to see how the new family policy environment is affecting their lives.

Plan of this chapter

This chapter focuses on paid work and childcare while mothers are employed, as elements of family life, at the dawn of the 21st century. The chapter describes first the employment status of parents at the point where their baby was aged 9-10 months, and then the childcare they arranged while they were employed. Finally, we examine indicators of mothers' and fathers' work–life balance.

Parental employment

Almost one half of mothers (48.7%) and 90.9% of fathers, where families had two parents, were employed at the interview when the baby was 9-10 months old (Table 8.1). While the vast majority of the employed were employees, a sizeable minority of fathers were self employed – 15.7% across the UK, but varying substantially by country. The employment rates for mothers were higher than average in Northern Ireland (54.9%) and Scotland (53.9%). Employment rates for fathers were highest in England (91.3%). Fathers in Northern Ireland had a higher rate of self employment than other countries (21.0%) but a corresponding lower rate of employee employment (68.7% compared with the 75.2% UK average).

Mothers' and fathers' rates of employment and hours worked varied considerably by minority ethnic identity (Figure 8.1). Among mothers, those of white or Black Caribbean identity had the highest rates of employment followed by Indian and Black African mothers. However,

Table 8.1: Millennium Cohort Study mothers' and fathers' employment at interview, by country

| | Country | | | | | | | | | |
| | % England | | % Wales | | % Scotland | | % N Ireland | | % All UK total | |
Employment at interview	Mothers	Fathers	Mothers	Fathers	Mothers	Fathers	Mothers	Fathers	Mothers	Fathers
In paid work – employees	43.8	75.3	46.5	76.3	50.8	76.0	51.4	68.7	44.9	75.2
In paid work – self employed	3.9	16.0	3.9	12.0	3.1	13.4	3.5	21.0	3.8	15.7
Has a paid job, but on leave	2.5	–	2.5	–	2.1	–	2.8	–	2.5	–
No current paid work	42.5	8.1	40.6	11.0	40.7	10.4	37.6	9.2	42.1	8.5
Has never had a paid job	7.3	0.6	6.6	0.7	3.3	0.3	4.6	1.2	6.8	0.6
Total	100.0	100.0	100.0	100.0	100.0	100.0	100.0	100.0	100.0	100.0
N unweighted	11499	8317	2754	1905	2327	1706	1914	1269	18494	13197
Mean age of baby at interview, months	9.2		9.2		9.1		9.3		9.2	
Employed full time at interview (% of all respondents)	12.4	85.6	14.5	83.0	16.1	84.7	23.9	83.7	13.3	85.3
Unweighted sample size of all employed at interview	4797	7262	1253	1619	1218	1475	996	1098	8264	11454

Base All Millennium Cohort Study main respondent mothers or partner fathers (natural, foster, adoptive, step).

Percentage weighted.

A Chi square test on mothers by country rejected the null hypothesis that mothers' behaviour was the same in all countries (p = 0.00)

A Chi square test on fathers by country rejected the null hypothesis that fathers' behaviour was the same in all countries (p = 0.00); the possibility that higher employment rates in Scotland and Northern Ireland might be accounted for by variation in the age of the child at interview has been investigated and rejected.

Figure 8.1: Economic activity rates of mothers/fathers by minority ethnic identity

(a) Mothers

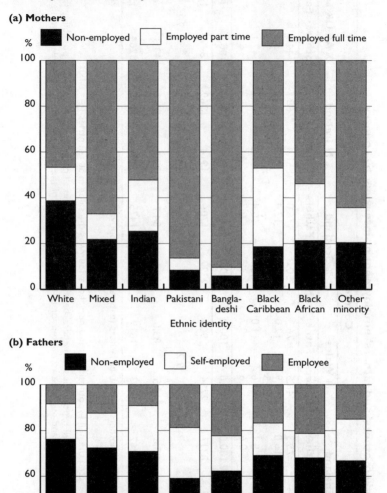

(b) Fathers

Base: Main respondent mothers and partner respondent fathers by own ethnic identity. Figures weighted by UK weight.
On leave group are classified as 'non-employed' group in these graphs.

there were considerable differences in the breakdown of hours. Only a minority of employed mothers, around one third, were working full time when their cohort baby was 9-10 months old, and this proportion varied considerably by ethnic identity. White mothers had the highest proportion of employed mothers working full time (38.7%), with Indian (25.4%), mixed origin (21.8%) and Black African mothers (21.3%) following on. Black Caribbean (34.3%) and Black African (24.8%) employed mothers had the highest proportion of mothers working part time. Mothers of Bangladeshi or Pakistani origin were much less likely to be employed either full or part time than mothers in other groups; 86.4% of Pakistani and 90.4% of Bangladeshi mothers were not employed.

The majority of fathers were employees although with variations by ethnic identity in the extent of overall employment and self employment. Pakistani (81.2%), Bangladeshi (77.7%) and Black African (78.7%) fathers had the lowest rates of employment, and white (91.6%) and Indian (90.8%) fathers the highest rates. Self-employment rates were highest among Indian (20.0% of all fathers) and Pakistani (22.2% of all fathers) fathers.

The distribution of employment varied across families with 51.8% of the couples having two earners; 41.3% had one earner, usually the man, and 6.9% had no earner because neither partner was currently employed. Many mothers appeared to emulate their partner's labour market participation. When fathers were employed, 59.9% of mothers were also employed, against 26.4% of the mothers where the father was not employed. Couples' joint worklessness may in part reflect the rules of the benefit system or the conditions in the local labour market in which they live (Dex et al, 1995). Lone mothers were also often 'workless'. They were far less likely to be in employment (22.1%) than mothers living in couples (54.1%), and they were also more likely to be younger, even teenagers, many of whom had never worked. As noted in Chapter 3, poverty was linked to having no partner, as well as being out of employment.

We first look at two-parent families according to the father's age in Table 8.2, which tends to be correlated with the age of his partner. The small percentage of fathers who were under 20 (1.3%) were more likely than others not to be the child's natural father (2.2%) and also had the lowest employment rates (some were still in college/school). Considering employment rates by types of fathers, 73.3% of non-natural fathers were employed compared to 90.9% of natural fathers. Teenage fathers were also much more likely to be attached to a mother who was not active in the labour market. In part, this was because

Table 8.2: Age of father, employment and other characteristics

	Under 20	20- 29	30- 39	40- 49	50+	Total
	Father's age at birth of cohort baby					
1) % of non-natural fathers	2.2	0.7	0.1	0.3	1.0	0.4
2) % fathers employed	67.6	87.0	93.6	90.9	75.4	90.9
3) % mothers employed	27.2	49.5	59.0	56.0	50.1	55.3
4) % families living on less than £10400 a year	52.4	18.6	7.3	9.3	11.7	11.6
5) % families on benefits*	76.4	40.7	19.6	19.6	24.0	26.8
6) % families on WFTC	30.7	27.2	14.0	11.8	13.0	18.0
7) % families on CTC	9.3	20.1	20.3	17.1	12.0	19.7
8) % families on HB	39.5	9.9	3.7	5.0	9.2	6.2
9) % fathers with post compulsory education **	39.3	46.8	55.7	68.3	68.2	54.1
10) % mothers with post compulsory education **	27.2	47.9	61.9	63.5	60.4	57.4
11) % fathers married	9.1	56.2	80.8	76.4	78.0	72.2
12) % couples living in an advantaged area	42.4	53.0	70.2	68.9	64.6	64.5
Unweighted sample sizes	245	5127	8372	1412	140	15296

Base: All UK MCS male partner fathers (natural, adoptive, step, foster). Includes those who are single or part time resident fathers: All of the characteristics are significantly associated with age. Percentages weighted.

* Defined as those reporting being in receipt of Income Support, Jobseekers' Allowance, Working Families Tax Credit or Disabled Person's Tax Credit.

** 16 for those born after 1958, 15 otherwise.

many young fathers were living with young mothers (74.4% of fathers under 20 had teenage partners).

Given the employment patterns described, it is no surprise that families who had a teenage father were much more likely to be living in a household receiving less than £10,400 a year in joint income (Table 8.2) and to be claiming Working Families Tax Credit (WFTC). Teenage fathers were also four times more likely to be receiving housing benefit than any other age group. In summary, babies living in families with young fathers were much more likely to be starting life in poverty than those with older fathers.

Fathers in their 40s and 50s at the baby's birth were more likely to have stayed in education beyond compulsory school-leaving age. Of those fathers with post-compulsory education, 94.4% were employed compared to 87.5% of those without post-compulsory education. Of those fathers who were married, 93.6% were employed compared to 84.1% of natural cohabiting fathers who were interviewed.

The relationship of mother's age to employment is particularly striking if we consider her age when she first became a mother rather than her age at the interview. Although a large minority had their first child in the survey, and hence a mother's current age and her age at first birth are identical, among those with more than one child, current age may mask an early age at which some had their first child. As we have seen in Chapter 4, this tends to be associated with disadvantaged antecedents and circumstances. These earlier circumstances tended to persist up to the time of the survey (Joshi and Wright, 2005). Lone mothers were more likely to have embarked on parenthood early: 39% of those who became mothers at or under 18 had no partner at the time of the survey, in contrast to 4.3% of those having their first child at 31 or over (Table 8.3).

Employment rates were also strongly positively related to age at motherhood – 20.7% among the youngest group rising to 63.3% among the oldest entrants. The proportion of mothers working part time rose across those having their first child in their teens and early 20s to reach a plateau at just over 41.4% for women who had their first child at or after age 25. The minority of mothers working full time rose steadily to 21.9% with the later births. As motherhood is delayed, there would have been more time to get established in careers to which they are likely to have returned.

Workless couples were younger, when measured by the woman's age at first birth as well as the father's current age (Table 8.3). There is also an age-at-motherhood gradient in the chances of a lone mother having paid work. This age pattern in employment is reflected in the current financial circumstances of these families. There is more than a six-fold difference in the chances of early mothers' families claiming means-tested benefits over mothers in their 30s (75.9% compared

Table 8.3: Employment and financial circumstances of MCS families by mother's age at first live birth

	Mother's age at first live birth						
	Under 18	19-21	22-24	25-27	28-30	31+	Total
Lone mother (%)	39.0	25.5	13.6	6.9	4.8	4.3	13.8
Employment							
Mother employed full time (%)	4.0	6.1	10.2	12.9	18.3	21.9	13.3
Mother employed part time (%)	16.7	24.7	35.4	41.5	43.4	41.4	35.2
Any job (%)	20.7	30.8	45.6	54.4	61.7	63.3	48.5
Workless couple families (%)	26.0	15.1	7.7	3.5	2.2	2.4	7.1
Financial circumstances							
Receives one or more means-tested benefits (%)*	75.9	62.9	43.2	24.2	15.7	12.3	35.3
Experiencing financial difficulties (%)	51.8	49.3	41.2	33.2	28.1	25.5	36.6
Maximum unweighted sample size	2544	3712	2944	3026	3038	3253	18517

Base: All UK MCS natural mothers only. Weighted percentages.

*Receiving one or more of the following: Jobseekers' Allowance, Income Support, Working Families Tax Credit or Disabled Persons Tax Credit.

with 12.3%). Possibly because these benefits help to redress the lack of earnings, the contrast between early and late mothers on their subjective rating of financial difficulties is not so dramatic, although there is still a contrast: 51.8% of the mothers who had started childbirth earliest said they were experiencing financial difficulties, compared with 25.5% of the women who had waited until they were 31 or older to give birth.

The higher rates of employment of the later mothers, illustrated again in the far right-hand block of Figure 8.2, are partly the result of their being better qualified. As qualifications rose, so too did the chances of employment. Two thirds of those with qualifications equivalent to a degree or postgraduate qualification (NVQ 4 or 5) were employed compared with one in 7 (14.5%) of those with no qualifications. However, the differences in timing of motherhood were not entirely accounted for by education, as there was an upward slope within each set of bars by education level (Figure 8.2). Multivariate analysis of the predictors of mothers' employment found education and age at motherhood among the significantly positive correlates, along with Black Caribbean ethnic identity and living with a partner. Factors which were negatively associated with being employed, other things being equal, included longstanding illness, divorce or separation of the woman's parents, being of Pakistani, Bangladeshi, mixed or other

Figure 8.2: Employment of mothers by highest qualification and age at first child

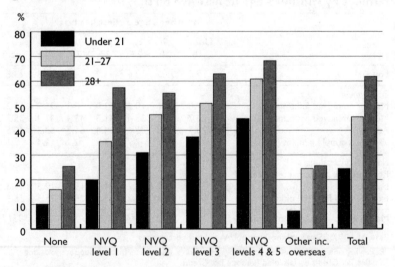

Base: All UK MCS natural mothers. Weighted percentages.

minority ethnic identity and living in England, particularly in an area of high minority ethnic population (Hawkes et al, 2004).

Being employed 9-10 months after the birth of the cohort child was also very closely associated with being employed in pregnancy. Eighty four per cent of mothers with a first birth were employed in pregnancy, and 69% of them returned to work after the pregnancy.

Maternity and parental leave

Over half of the mothers (55%) had taken maternity leave from work to have their baby. Out of the whole sample of mothers, half had received some maternity pay, although varying slightly by UK country, and more substantially by type of area families lived in (58% in non-disadvantaged areas, 43% in other disadvantaged and 21% in wards with high minority ethnic populations).

Seventy-eight per cent of UK-employed fathers took some leave when the cohort baby was born. Approximately two thirds of all employed fathers took leave that involved getting paid, although not necessarily paid paternity leave or parental leave. In some cases, it was annual leave or sick leave that enabled them to be paid. Parental or paternity leave was taken by 46% of fathers (who were employed and had taken any leave).[1] There was slight variation in the extent of employed fathers taking leave across the UK countries, the lowest levels being in Northern Ireland (71% compared to 80% in England).

The break in mothers' employment

The period between the birth of a baby and a mother's first return to the labour market has been the major change in women's participation over time. The gap has been getting progressively shorter over time and is evident in the experiences of successive cohorts of mothers.

In the MCS, roughly half of all mothers were in paid work two to three months before their baby's first birthday. Another way to put this is that half the mothers had an employment gap of less than one year, 30 years earlier. It took the mothers of the 1970 birth cohort nearly five years before half of them had ever worked since a birth (Joshi and Verropoulou, 2000). This in turn was a shorter gap in employment than followed births among mothers born in 1958. The NCDS children born in 1958 were aged 7 by the time that half their mothers had ever been employed since the survey birth. The gap was still longer after births in the 1946 cohort study. Joshi and Hinde (1993) reported an eight-year median time to first employment after a *last* child in 1946. In the

1950s and 1960s, it was working–class and less educated mothers who took up work sooner after childbirth than others. But, by the last decades of the 20th century, the relative position had reversed, with highly educated mothers being in the vanguard of those returning earlier and sustaining near continuous careers (Macran et al, 1996).

Highly educated mothers are higher earners and suffer greater loss of earnings when they stop work. They would forfeit more career advancement if they stayed away for long. Their opportunity cost of being out of work is therefore greater and they have a stronger incentive to keep the gap short. They also have the means to pay for childcare. Statutory maternity leave, introduced after 1973, and giving eligible mothers a right to return to work, has contributed to many more mothers shortening the gap to fit into the entitlement period to paid leave.

Unsocial hours

Parents working early mornings, evenings and at weekends has become increasingly common (La Valle et al, 2002). This proliferation of working-time arrangements has resulted from the same pressures operating in different product market environments. Many parents have been caught up in these trends.

Fathers have two main reasons for working long hours. One is linked to financial necessity and job insecurity (La Valle et al, 2002). This is clearly the driver for lower income families. Another driver is that working long hours, unpaid and beyond contracted hours, has been a growing expectation in higher qualified occupations for both men and women (Hogarth et al, 2000). Mothers' reasons for working at atypical times are linked to the desire to balance work and family life and were seen, therefore, as part of the solution to combining work and family for mothers.

Clearly, the increases in long hours of work, particularly among the more highly qualified, run counter to the development of work–balance policies in the workplace.

In the MCS, parents had high rates of working at atypical times of day (Table 8.4). Evenings were the most common outside the usual working day, with one third of mothers and 42.3% of fathers working every week between 6 and 10pm. Weekend work was the next most common pattern with 22.8% of mothers and 27.7% of fathers working at weekends. Calculating the percentages of parents who worked at any of the times indicated showed very high levels of working at atypical times of day: 42.2% of mothers and 53.7% of fathers (Table 8.4). Among lone mothers who were employed, 35.2% were working

Table 8.4: Percentage of employed mothers/fathers who, every week, worked at time indicated, by country

Time worked	Country									
	% England		% Wales		% Scotland		% N Ireland		% All UK total	
	Mothers	Fathers	Mothers	Fathers	Mothers	Fathers	Mothers	Fathers	Mothers	Fathers
6pm-10pm	34.2	42.4	33.5	44.3	31.4	41.1	27.9	40.8	33.6	42.3
10pm-7am	10.4	15.7	10.3	19.4	9.0	15.0	8.3	15.1	10.2 #	15.8
Weekends	22.7	27.4	24.2	33.8	24.5	25.2	17.4	29.4	22.8	27.7
Away overnight	2.2	6.2	2.3	6.4	3.2	6.8	3.8	5.9	2.4	6.2 #
Any of above	42.8	53.9	42.0	56.5	40.9	50.9	33.8	50.9	42.2	53.7
% working more than 48 hours per week	2.2	39.4	2.6	36.9	1.7	38.1	1.9	29.5	2.2#	38.9
N unweighted	4809	7296	1255	1633	1222	1506	996	1106	8282	11540

Base: UK MCS employed mothers/fathers (natural, foster, adoptive, step). Weighted percentages

A one way ANOVA was produced for each flexible working arrangement offered by country. Majority of values are less than or equal to p = 0.01, suggesting systematic differences in the extent of working arrangements offered to both employee mums and dads by country.

These relationships are not significantly varying by country at p = 0.05.

between 6pm and 10pm and 12.3% working from 10pm to 7am; 30.2% of these mothers reported working weekends, and 2.9% reported that they worked away overnight.

Childcare while at work

Childcare, as mentioned in Chapter 1, has been the subject of considerable government spending through the National Childcare Strategy and also through the Sure Start programme. Whereas Britain in the 1970s had relatively few childcare places in formal providers, the numbers of places has increased markedly, especially for 3-4 year olds. However, balanced against the growth in childcare, some research has sent out warning signals. A number of studies suggest that full-time maternal employment during the early stages of a child's life can have some small negative effects on the child's development (Ermisch and Francesconi, 2001). Because of the lack of data on day care settings, let alone their quality, British longitudinal studies have not been able to examine the quality of care children receive. Concern about childcare for babies under 1 year has been channelled into arguments for extending maternity and parental leave entitlement to be available in the UK until the baby is 1 year or more, to match arrangements that are offered in Scandinavia.

Childcare arrangements for the 49% of Millennium babies whose mothers were employed were predominantly informal.[2] Formal arrangements were in the minority for babies still under 1 year old, despite the enormous increase in such mother's employment. A very small proportion of employed MCS mothers (4.8%) managed to work and look after their own cohort babies either by taking them to work, or by working at home. This type of arrangement was highest among employed Pakistani mothers (9.5%, Figure 8.4) and mothers in the small employer and self-employed group (40.9%, Figure 8.3). Another larger group of employed mothers had partners as childcarers while they were at work (31.2%), in some cases by organising their hours of work to fit around their partner's availability. Provision of care by partners was much less frequent among Black Caribbean mothers (18.4%, Figure 8.4). The source of care used most by employed mothers was grandparents (44.9%). This type was highest among Indian (56.1%) and Pakistani (55.1%) and lower among Black Caribbean (34.5%) and Black African employed mothers (18.1%). Childminders were being used to care for 13.8% of cohort babies while mothers were employed. Formal providers as a whole were used by 37.1% of employed mothers. Informal types of childcare were still the most

Figure 8.3: Type of childcare used by employed mothers while they are at work by mothers' NS-SEC (5)

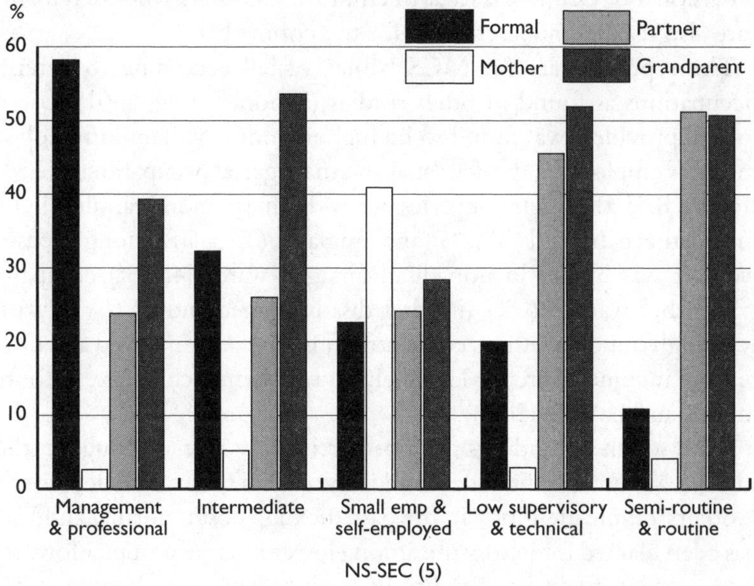

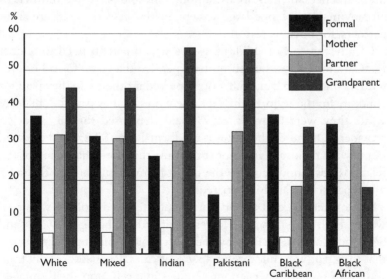

Base: All UK MCS employed mothers who use childcare while at work. Weighted percentages.

Figure 8.4: Type of childcare used by employed mothers while they are at work by mothers' ethnic identity

Base: All UK MCS employed mothers who use childcare while at work. Weighted percentages.

common forms of care, therefore, for young babies. Even where mothers used formal childcare, they still had to rely on supplementary informal provision. For example, 21.8% of employed mothers who used formal care also used grandparent care for the cohort baby.

The types of care for MCS babies varied according to parents' occupations as found in other studies (Mooney et al, 2001). Use of formal providers was found to be higher among Millennium Cohort mothers employed in professional and managerial occupations (72.5%) (Figure 8.3). Between countries, it was highest among families living in Northern Ireland (37.2%) and England (37.5%). Among types of ward, it was higher in non-disadvantaged wards (42.1%) compared with other wards, 26.3% in other disadvantaged and 24.6% in wards with high minority ethnic concentrations. The self employed and those on low incomes were far less likely to use formal childcare, as found in Bell and LaValle (2003).

Many of these findings are not particularly new although earlier studies have not specifically examined the care of babies, or differences by mothers' ethnic identities. In the past, the high cost of formal childcare has been blamed for its low use among lower income groups. However, more recent qualitative studies of parents have found some strong preferences among lower income groups for informal care (Dex, 2003).

Among MCS mothers, those who were employed lone mothers were slightly less likely to use formal childcare (Figure 8.5) and more likely to use grandparent care than mothers in couple families. However, the differences in childcare use among lone and partnered mothers in employment were not large except in the case of childcare from partners, for obvious reasons.

Clearly, the cost of childcare is one which parents need to budget for. Care for babies is often more expensive than care for other pre-school children. In fact, 45.8% of employed mothers said they paid for childcare for the cohort baby. Of those who said they paid for childcare while they were at work, 82.7% said they used formal childcare providers. Of those who did not use formal care, 87.2% said they did not pay for childcare. It is not surprising, therefore, that many of the relationships found between the use of formal childcare are the same when paid childcare is compared.

In Northern Ireland, the proportion of employed mothers who paid was as high as 55.1%, the lowest proportions being in Wales and Scotland each at 42%. Employed cohort mothers in England reported that they paid for childcare in 45.7% of cases. Payment for childcare was again much higher among families living in non-disadvantaged wards (50.5%) compared to those living in wards with high minority

Figure 8.5: Childcare usage of employed lone and partnered MCS mothers

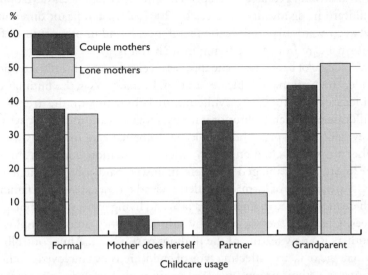

Base: All UK MCS mothers who are employed regardless of employment status of partner (if applicable) and who use childcare while at work. Weighted percentages.

ethnic populations (31.5%) and other disadvantaged wards (34.8%). For mothers employed in higher managerial and professional occupations, it was the norm to pay for care (79.1% of mothers in this group paid and 60.8% in lower managerial or professional occupations). Of mothers in routine jobs, only 13.2% and in semi-routine 18.2% paid for childcare There was also considerable variation in payment for childcare by the ethnic identity of the mother. Compared with the 45.9% of employed white mothers, 54.9% of mixed, 32.9% of Indian, 25.4% of Pakistani, 54.7% of Black Caribbean and 41.9% of Black African employed mothers paid for childcare. None of the Bangladeshi mothers paid for childcare, but only a very small number of them were employed or using paid childcare.

Variations by ethnic identity of whether mothers either paid for childcare or used formal care were found to be significant in comparison with white mothers for Indian and Pakistani employed mothers after controlling for a range of other differences between ethnic groups (NS-SEC groups, working hours, country, ward and partnership status). This suggests there are cultural differences between some ethnic groups in their childcare preferences when they are employed. Use of formal care was less in wards with high minority ethnic populations and other disadvantaged wards than in non-disadvantaged wards, after controlling for other factors (Table A8.1).

This could reflect formal childcare places being more available in non-disadvantaged areas, except that Sure Start had been developing childcare in disadvantaged areas by 2001. This significant difference between wards may reflect the preference, found in other studies, for informal care from those living in such wards.

Childcare of babies is a topic that has received relatively little attention under the National Childcare Strategy. In many ways, the findings on childcare used for these Millennium babies mirror the trends in childcare and relationships of who uses formal care and who pays for it evident for all pre-school children. Informal care for babies, as for other pre-school children, is very extensive and more common among the more disadvantaged mothers in lower paid jobs. Payment for childcare and use of formal providers is clearly most extensive in families where mothers are in higher paid jobs and living in non-disadvantaged areas. Charting the variation by ethnic identity among employed mothers is a new feature of the findings of this book. After controlling for a range of factors affecting type of childcare, only employed mothers from Asian ethnic groups appeared significantly less likely to use formal types of childcare in comparison with white, mixed, Black Caribbean and Black African mothers. The initial differences between white and other mothers were largely explainable by differences in their occupations, hours, partnerships status, and in the UK country and area of residence. If, in due course, studies confirm Gregg and Washbrook's (2003) findings that there are disadvantaging effects on children from being away from their parents full time with a childcare provider in the first year of life, some Millennium babies will be at risk of such effects.

The work–life balance of mothers and fathers

Juggling work and family can be stressful and challenging. It is not surprising that discussions about work–life balance emerged in the late 1980s and 1990s among female workers, as more mothers were working full time and when their children were at younger ages than in the past. The MCS data from parents gave us an opportunity to measure some of the impact on parents using a number of approximate measures of work–life balance (see Box 8.1). These measures focus more on the 'life' side of work–life and do not fully capture the relationship between individuals' work and their life.

Box 8.1 Proxy work–life measures

- **Life control.** This measure (based on 3 questions) captures the extent to which parents felt in control of their lives (increases in the 15 point scale indicate a greater degree of feeling in control);
- **Life satisfaction.** This second measure (based on one question) captures the extent to which they were satisfied with their lives (10 point scale);
- **Malaise depression.** This third measure (based on 9 questions) captures the extent of feeling depressed (increases in the 10-point scale indicate higher levels of feeling depressed)

When their new baby was 9-10 months old, feelings of satisfaction and control were slightly higher among mothers than among fathers in the same circumstances (Table 8.5). The self employed tended to display the highest levels of life satisfaction and control and the lowest levels of depression. Those who had never had paid work had the lowest levels of life balance.

Those who were out of work (but not on leave) had levels of satisfaction and control, or feelings of depression, somewhere between the better life balance of the employed and the worse life balance of

Table 8.5: Mean scores on work–life measures by economic activity status of mothers and fathers

| | Life balance measures | | | | | |
| | Mothers (%) | | | Fathers (%) | | |
Employment at interview	Life control	Life satisfaction	Malaise	Life control	Life satisfaction	Malaise
Employee	8.27	7.81	1.59	8.14	7.76	2.44
Self employed	8.48	7.90	1.46	8.32	7.83	1.34
Has a paid job, but on leave	8.36	7.98	1.46	–	–	–
No current paid work	8.01	7.65	1.71	7.43	7.04	2.01
Has never had a paid job	7.27	7.56	2.05	7.18	6.70	2.44
Unweighted sample size	17820	17810	17840	12584	12584	12595

Base: All UK MCS mothers/fathers when cohort baby was 9-10 months old. Weighted percentages.

*One-way ANOVA tests of difference between means by economic activity status all rejected the null hypothesis of same means at 0.05 level of significance.

those who had never been employed. Mothers who were on leave felt better about their life than those who were back at work. The extent of life balance varied by the ethnic identity of the parents. White mothers were the group who felt the most in control of their lives and had the highest levels of satisfaction and lowest levels of depression. Mothers of mixed ethnic identity had the next highest levels of feeling in control, but they had the lowest levels of satisfaction across these ethnic identity groups. Black African and mothers in other ethnic groups also had low group levels of depression. Those with the lowest levels of feeling in control were Bangladeshi mothers, and the lowest group levels of life satisfaction were seen among the mixed and Black Caribbean mothers. Highest group levels of depression were seen among Pakistani followed by Indian mothers.

White fathers, closely followed by mixed and Black African fathers felt most in control of their lives, although life satisfaction was highest among Bangladeshi fathers followed by white and Black African fathers. Depression was lowest among Black African and Black Caribbean fathers. Lowest average levels of being in control of life were expressed by Bangladeshi and Pakistani fathers, and lowest levels of life satisfaction by mixed and Black Caribbean fathers. Highest levels of depression were found among fathers of Indian and mixed identity.

Extent of flexible working for employees

Flexible working has been heralded as a way of improving the work–life balance of parents. For this to work, employee parents first need to be offered flexible working and then to take up the offer.

The extent to which British and UK employees are able to benefit from flexible working arrangements is visible in the official large-scale surveys of employees that have been generated to monitor the government's new family policies. In 2000, 50% of employees (of all ages, both sexes and all family states) claimed to have the possibility of part-time work. This figure had risen to 67% in 2003. This and the other comparisons in Table 8.6 indicate a general increase in access to flexible working arrangements in Britain by 2003. Comparisons with earlier surveys, while not possible with strict precision, do suggest there is a longer increasing trend in all forms of employers' provisions. The frequency of working at or from home on a regular basis is the exception, since it has remained stable at one fifth of employees being able to do this. It is likely that there are limits to the types of jobs where working at or from home is realistic.

Among employee mothers in the MCS, access to part-time working

Table 8.6: Prevalence of flexible working patterns among British employees by source and date

	Per cents of employees in sample offered arrangement		
	WERS GB survey of employees, 1998*	**DfEE first work–life balance baseline survey 2000** GB**	**DTI second work–life balance study 2003** GB**
Part time		50	67
Flexitime	34	42	48
Term time only		25	32
Job share	18	32	41
Working from or at home on regular basis	11	20	20
Parental leave	28		
Annualised hours		13	20
Compressed working week		23	30

* Employees in workplaces with 10+ employees in Workplace Employee Relations Survey.

** Employees in workplaces with 5+ employees. Results quoted for first and second survey are those published in the second 2004 publication (Stevens et al, 2004) adjusted to be as comparable as possible for definition and sample population changes based on populations of all employees and including those who said they worked using this arrangement as well as those who did not use the arrangement but said it was available.

was the most common type of arrangement offered at their workplaces (Table 8.7); 86.1% of mothers but only 47.0% of fathers thought part-time working was available. Flexible working (42.0%) and jobshare schemes (available to 36.2%) were the next most likely arrangements available to these mothers; for fathers, 35.1% had access to flexible working, 28.8% had access to working at home occasionally, and 19.8% to jobshare or special shifts. Special shifts were available to 28.9% of mothers, working at or from home occasionally to 20.9% of mothers and a higher proportion of fathers. School term-time contracts were available to 15.4% of mothers and 6.1% of fathers. Access to the various arrangements varied slightly by country, with Northern Ireland mothers and fathers having less access than parents in other UK countries to flexible arrangements (Table 8.7).

Access to part-time work was generally high for mothers across all occupations although, for fathers, part-time work was almost twice as likely to be available in the management/professional and intermediate categories than in the lower supervisory or semi-routine types of occupations. Access to most other types of flexibility at work was considerably higher in the management/professional and intermediate categories than in the lower supervisory and semi-routine types of occupations for both mothers and fathers, with the exception of special shifts for mothers. There were relatively small differences in access to

Table 8.7: Percentages of employed MCS mothers/fathers with access to flexible working arrangements, by country

Flexible working arrangements	Country									
	% England		% Wales		% Scotland		% N Ireland		% All UK total	
	Mothers	Fathers	Mothers	Fathers	Mothers	Fathers	Mothers	Fathers	Mothers	Fathers
Part time working	86.9	47.8	83.5	42.2	85.0	44.6	76.2	39.1	86.1	47.0
Job-sharing	35.8	19.6	34.4	19.6	40.7	21.9	35.8	19.2	36.2#	19.8#
Flexible working hours	43.0	36.0	42.1	30.6	37.3	31.8	35.2	29.4	42.0	35.1
Working at or from home, occasionally	22.3	30.2	16.8	20.3	16.6	25.6	10.8	17.1	20.9	28.8
Working at or from home, all the time	6.0	8.1	3.8	6.1	4.8	7.3	1.5	3.9	5.5	7.7
Special shifts (i.e. evenings)	30.1	20.3	28.0	18.1	23.9	18.3	20.1	14.0	28.9	19.8
9-day fortnights/4½-day working week	5.6	6.7	3.7	6.4	3.6	5.9	5.0	6.3	5.3#	6.6#
School term-time contracts	15.7	6.2	12.6	6.4	13.4	5.0	17.9	7.6	15.4	6.1#
None of these	6.8	35.0	8.4	41.8	6.8	38.8	12.1	42.9	7.1	35.9
Maximum (N) unweighted	4439	6054	1168	1421	1153	1285	940	850	7700	9610

Base: All UK MCS main respondent mothers and partner respondent fathers (natural, foster, adoptive, step) who are in paid work when cohort baby 9-10 months old.

A one way ANOVA for each flexible working arrangement offered by country, the majority of values are less than or equal to p = 0.01 suggesting systematic differences in the extent of working arrangements offered to both employee mums and dads by country.

These values are not significant at p = 0.05 suggesting that there are no significant differences in the extent of working arrangements offered to employee mothers and fathers by country. Weighted percentages.

flexible arrangements for mothers according to whether they worked full or part-time hours. However, it is important to remember that other detailed workplace case studies have found that it is the professional and managerial grade workers who, while allowed to work flexibly, often fail to take advantage of this. This is particularly the case for managers who, while often saying that work–life policies and flexibility get the best out of the workforce, feel it is not appropriate for them to take advantage of such arrangements. It is also the case that access to workplace flexibility has been found to be lower in workplaces with a predominantly male workforce even though within any one workplace it was rare to find work–life policies being offered to women but not to men (Dex, 2003). This would lead to the expectation that fathers would have less access than mothers, as the MCS data confirm.

Thinking you have access to flexible working arrangements has also been found to rest on whether employees are first aware of their employers' policies (Dex, 2003). Detailed workplace studies have found that levels of awareness were generally low and varied across different workplaces and types of employee. Awareness has been found to be higher among those likely to benefit; where leave was paid; in unionised workplaces where communication is often better; where employers put more effort into communication; in small businesses; where employees were involved in the implementation of the policies; where line managers were offered training; and in favourable workplace cultures.

Take up of family friendly arrangements

Employees' access to flexible working arrangements is not the same as their take up of the provisions. When flexibility is offered but only with loss of pay, it is beyond the reach of many families. The 1998 Workplace Employee Relations Survey (WERS) data found that, in 25% of British establishments with some family-friendly practices, no employees had taken them up (Cully et al, 1999). For establishments where there had been some take up, in two thirds of these cases it was a small proportion of the workforce only who had used the provisions (Dex and Smith, 2002). Case study research projects that have surveyed their organisations' employees about take up also found very low levels of take up when measured across the workforce (Phillips et al, 2002; Yeandle et al, 2002).

The Millennium Cohort Study findings

In the MCS, the greatest usage, given that a flexible arrangement was available, was use of part-time hours for mothers (Table 8.8). Approximately three quarters of employed mothers with access had worked part time with their current employer. Mothers' next highest usage was for flexible working hours (56.2%) followed by working at home occasionally (51.5%). For fathers, they were most likely to take up working at home occasionally (61.5%) when it was on offer, followed by flexible working (55.1%) and the nine-day fortnight (31.4%). Other working arrangements were far less used by fathers, where offered. This picture may suggest a higher level of take up of these arrangements among parents than has been thought to be the case more generally. One also needs to remember that there was low availability to employees for some of these arrangements. Factors found in other studies to limit take up of employers' flexible provisions included:

- low awareness of the provisions, especially where policies were new;
- unpaid provisions;
- the inability of employees to stand loss of income;
- lean staffing practices made it less likely;
- workplace cultures where long hours of work were the norm; and
- less take up at particular stages of the life course – for example, being young and single.

These types of barriers are the reasons why take up has often been found to be low in other surveys of workplaces. The fact that it is higher among MCS parents may be because they are, as noted earlier, at this point in their life course likely to be particularly aware of the policies and interested in accessing them. It will be interesting, therefore, to examine in the next section whether the availability and use of these policies makes a difference to employees' work–life balance.

What determines parents' work–life balance?

We might expect parents' feelings about their lives to vary according to a range of circumstances they find themselves in. Here, we are particularly interested in the effects of factors that are the subject of government policy. Childcare provision and flexible working arrangements are two important sets of factors. But, to be sure that we are not identifying spurious effects on parents, we need to consider

Table 8.8: Percentages of employed mothers and fathers who had used their employers' flexible working arrangements, by country (unweighted sample sizes in parentheses)

Flexible working arrangements	Country									
	% England		% Wales		% Scotland		% N Ireland		% All UK total	
	Mothers	Fathers	Mothers	Fathers	Mothers	Fathers	Mothers	Fathers	Mothers	Fathers
Part time working	77.4 (3946)	8.0 (2727)	75.5 (1016)	7.4 (636)	71.4 (1001)	8.0 (586)	64.8 (735)	9.7 (361)	76.2 (6698)	8.0# (4138)
Job-sharing	21.5 (1543)	3.1 (1116)	19.3 (385)	3.1 (295)	23.8 (468)	1.7 (287)	14.8 (327)	0.6 (177)	21.4 (2723)	2.9# (1748)
Flexible working hours	55.8 (1963)	54.4 (3050)	59.9 (504)	54.1 (462)	57.2 (433)	60.7 (418)	57.2 (336)	58.8 (372)	56.2# (3236)	55.1# (3083)
Working at or from home, occasionally	52.1 (919)	62.1 (1719)	45.6 (180)	62.4 (306)	51.0 (180)	56.0 (336)	45.4 (95)	60.1 (158)	51.5# (1374)	61.5# (2221)
Working at or from home, all the time	40.4 (261)	20.3 (459)	35.4 (39)	37.0 (92)	28.6 (50)	25.0 (96)	**	36.1 (36)	39.1# (363)	21.7 (597)
Special shifts (i.e. evenings)	37.0 (1338)	20.0 (1159)	38.6 (342)	26.4 (273)	37.3 (280)	24.5 (240)	32.9 (202)	26.4 (120)	37.0# (2162)	20.8# (1763)
9-day fortnights/4½-day working week	8.3 (238)	31.3 (351)	**	26.8 (97)	19.0 (41)	29.5 (79)	19.6 (49)	37.9 (58)	9.7# (369)	31.4# (585)
School term-time contracts	21.3 (687)	8.8 (351)	25.0 (149)	9.2 (97)	20.0 (156)	11.8 (671)	21.5 (164)	5.8 (70)	21.3# (754)	9.0 # (546)

Base: All MCS main respondent mothers/partner respondent fathers (natural, foster, adoptive, step) who are in paid work or on leave and were offered flexible working arrangement in question. Weighted percentages.

In a one-way ANOVA these values are not significant at p = 0.05 and therefore suggests that there are no significant differences in the extent of working arrangements offered to employee mums and dads by country.

and control for the whole range of potential effects on their feelings about life and work.

Multivariate models were used to unravel some of the factors that were associated with mothers' feelings when the baby was 9-10 months. The factors associated with mothers' feelings about life at this time were summarised in Table 8.9; the precise results are in Table A8.2. A wide range of circumstances were found to be associated with having better life balance; these included age, religion, health, ethnic identity, family size, baby's sleeping patterns, NS-SEC and qualification levels, partnership status and area of residence and, in very few cases, country of residence.

Before allowing for the wide range of explanatory variables together, mothers felt more in control, more satisfied with life and less depressed where they used formal childcare, if they had access to and used employers' help with childcare or flexible working arrangements, where they used two or more types of childcare, and where they were self employed. Childcare usage was clearly related to working patterns and working at atypical times of day, and these characteristics interacted with each other. Mothers with jobs at atypical times tended to feel less in control, less satisfied and more depressed than other mothers. Working atypical hours was also linked to fathers providing the childcare while mothers were at work, and this also was associated with lower feelings of being in control among mothers. After adjustment, use of employers' help with childcare or flexible working arrangements, or the use of formal childcare, were the only significant factors in helping mothers to feel in control. Feeling more depressed was likely at very high weekly hours. Self employment remained important, in the adjusted (multivariate) model, in promoting mothers to feel in control and more satisfied with life.

Of course, these findings are only based on data at one point in time. We cannot claim to have found causal relationships, and it is quite possible that mothers' feeling dissatisfied, depressed or less in control provoked changes in either their own or their partner's behaviour. The relationship between mothers working at atypical times of day and fathers providing the childcare was noted in an earlier survey by La Valle et al (2002). There, as here, it was fathers in manual or semi-skilled occupations who were more likely to be providing the childcare.

Table 8.9: Summary of factors associated with all mothers' life balance when cohort baby was 9-10 months old

Life control	Life satisfaction	Malaise depression
Better feelings associated with:		
Age groups 30-39 best then 20-29	age groups 30-39 best then 20-29	age groups 30-39 best then 20-29
Belonging to a religion	Belonging to a religion	
No limiting ill health	No limiting ill health	No limiting ill health
Low and high grade qualifications		Low and high qualifications
Best for whites and Black Caribbean followed by Mixed, Pakistani, Black African, Bangladeshi, Indian	Worst for mixed compared with all other groups	Worst for Indian and Pakistani compared with all other groups
Baby no sleep problems	Baby no sleep problems	Baby no sleep problems
Smaller family size	Smaller family size	Smaller family size
Lone parent	Lone parent	Lone parent
NS-SEC 1 and 2	NS-SEC 1 and 2	
Dad employed	Dad employed	Dad employed
Living in non-disadvantaged ward compared with minority ethnic and other disadvantaged ward	Living in advantaged or ethnic compared with disadvantaged	Living in advantaged or ethnic compared with disadvantaged
	Living in Wales compared to England, Scotland & Northern Ireland	Living in England, Scotland or Northern Ireland compared to Wales
After allowing for the above: better feelings associated with:		
Using formal childcare	Not using formal childcare	Not using formal childcare
	Not using dad for child care	Not using dad for child care
Using 2 or more types of care	Using 2 or more types of care	Using 2 or more types of care
Using employer help with childcare		
		Working 1-13 hours compared to zero hours
Working 30-38 hours		Not working above 39 hours
Using employer flexibility		
Self-employed	Self-employed	

Analysis adjusted standard errors for cluster sample design.

Conclusions

Whereas in previous generations mothers generally stayed away from paid work while they had young children, it is now equally common for mothers of babies as young as 9 months to have a paid job as not. The implications of mothers' employment and earnings for families should not be underestimated. The idea that mothers contribute pin money is a thing of the past. As well as playing an important part in the family budget, mothers' earnings, as demonstrated in Chapter 3, are instrumental in keeping many families out of poverty. At the same time, it tends to be in families which are least advantaged in other respects where the mother does not have a job. As discussed further in Chapter 3, families where the mother does not earn, and especially those where no-one earns, are at high risk of poverty.

Lone mothers, a target group for much of the government's employment and childcare initiatives, have increased their labour force participation in official statistics over the period since the initiatives were introduced. However, when they have young babies, as in the MCS sample, they are still highly unlikely to be employed. This is due to a number of reasons: their lack of qualifications, low levels of work experience, living in disadvantaged areas which may have fewer job opportunities and, in this case of course, having a small baby. Some would consider it a good thing to be at home with babies under 1 year old. As mentioned in Chapter 3, there is also the attraction of the risk-free, if low, level of Income Support plus Housing Benefit to compare with the prospect of risky, vulnerable and low-paid employment opportunities identified in other studies.

Increases in formal provision of childcare are showing themselves in the practices and arrangements of couple families, and mainly those with higher paid jobs. The extent to which they have induced mothers back to work when they otherwise might have stayed at home is unclear, since for many it is a part of facilitating their desire and financial need to have a paid job. The lack of popularity of formal as compared with informal arrangements seen in this (and other) studies, and among lone parents, may partly be a result here of notions of ideal forms of care for young babies. The high cost of formal care for young babies may also be a factor alongside the greater flexibility offered by informal arrangements, the constraints of working hours and the location of formal and informal childcare establishments.

This chapter investigated how far new working arrangements and the provisions of government policy are helping parents to combine work and care and to feel they have a better quality of life. Flexible working arrangements appear to be on the increase both because employers are making them more available and because employees are taking them up. This increase is highly visible in the practice of the parents of MCS babies at the turn of the 21st century. The very fact that so many parents are taking up these provisions when they are offered shows their popularity.

Work–life balance for parents has been receiving considerable attention in the media and through government initiatives to help working parents and encourage employers to be more flexible. Our analysis of parents' work–life satisfaction identified some of the factors that are associated with better as well as with worse work–life balance for parents with a new baby. Negative effects on parents' feelings about life were found when they worked longer hours. Positive effects on parents' feelings came from using employers' flexible working arrangements or help with childcare. However, some of these benefits were accounted for by a range of other associated characteristics of parents and the baby's sleep patterns. Formal childcare and employers' flexibility and help with childcare continued to help mothers feel more in control of life, after other controls were made, but their satisfaction and feelings of depression were not always improved by these arrangements. Fathers' involvement in childcare was also not associated with mothers' higher satisfaction or lower depression scores; in fact, quite the reverse. The fact that this form of shared labour is not associated with happy mothers may be because fathers are getting involved to help unhappy mothers, or because shift parenting arrangements put too much pressure on families leaving no time for parents to be together. The downgrading of the partner relationship in order to juggle demands of work and caring for children has been noted in other studies (Reynolds et al, 2003).

These findings suggest that government policy to encourage greater flexibility at work for parents and increases in formal childcare is bringing some benefits for parents, but that there is still scope for improvement. Tackling the long hours culture of many workplaces is something that still needs attention and to be on the government's, employers' and unions' agendas.

Table A8.1: Log odds results of whether mother reports a) paying for childcare or b) using formal childcare

Variable	Whether pays for childcare	Whether uses formal childcare
Ethnic group		
White	1	1
Mixed	1.84	1.08
Indian	0.45**	0.53**
Pakistani	0.22**	0.21**
Bangladeshi	0.05**	0.09**
Black Caribbean	1.03	0.83
Black African	0.68	0.67
Other	0.57*	0.75
NS-SEC		
Professional/managerial	5.68**	7.14**
Intermediate	2.78**	3.19**
Small employer and self employed	1.58	1.65*
Low supervisory and technical	1.45**	1.49**
Semi routine and routine	1	1
Country		
England	1	1
Wales	0.81*	0.89
Scotland	0.76*	0.81
Northern Ireland	1.34*	0.84
Type of ward		
Non-disadvantaged	1	1
Other disadvantaged	0.63**	0.58**
Minority ethnic	0.71*	0.66**
Partner		
Has a partner	0.69**	0.61**
Employment		
Self employed	1.37	1.08
Hours worked		
20-29 hours per week	2.02**	2.02**
30-39 hours per week	2.29**	2.11**
40+ hours per week	4.12**	3.24**
Unweighted sample size	7541	7613

Base: All UK MCS mothers (natural, step, adoptive, foster) who are employed.

* significant at $p = 0.05$ **significant at $p = 0.01$.
Standard errors adjusted for cluster sample design.

Key: Formal childcare includes the use of a nanny/au pair, childminder (registered or unregistered) or nurseries/crèche (which may be workplace, college, local authority or private).

Table A8.2: Results of ordered logit model coefficient estimates on mothers' life balance scales

Variables	Life control		Life satisfaction		Malaise depression	
	Coeff.	Std. error	Coeff.	Std. Error	Coeff.	Std. Error
Mother characteristics						
Age Under 19	−0.206	0.059**	−0.047	0.058	0.170	0.076**
Age 30-39	0.156	0.034**	0.056	0.028**	−0.160	0.038**
Age 40+	−0.089	0.086	0.030	0.071	−0.082	0.082
No Religion	−0.149	0.036**	−0.119	0.030**	0.043	0.038
Limiting Illness	−0.714	0.049**	−0.649	0.048**	1.138	0.056**
NVQ 1 or 2	0.389	0.039**	−0.059	0.037	−0.080	0.046*
NVQ 4 or 5	0.673	0.050**	−0.051	0.045	−0.110	0.052**
Ethnic - Mixed	−0.248	0.113**	−0.279	0.139**	0.108	0.176
Indian	−0.844	0.103**	−0.136	0.103	0.461	0.154**
Pakistani	−0.485	0.108**	0.073	0.097	0.424	0.098**
Bangladeshi	−0.564	0.155**	0.279	0.184	−0.158	0.173
Black Caribbean	−0.216	0.166	−0.102	0.122	0.102	0.126
Black African	−0.490	0.081**	−0.041	0.111	−0.148	0.124
Ethnic - other	−0.664	0.098**	−0.063	0.122	−0.041	0.121
Number of children	−0.109	0.016**	−0.092	0.016**	0.084	0.017**
Baby has sleep problems	−0.091	0.031**	−0.137	0.029**	0.410	0.032**
Lone parent	−0.619	0.044**	−0.945	0.044**	0.275	0.052**
Dad not employed	−0.440	0.053**	−0.341	0.057**	0.372	0.064**
Wales	0.010	0.047	0.136	0.041**	0.101	0.040**
Scotland	−0.041	0.046	0.001	0.035	0.037	0.043
Northern Ireland	0.068	0.055	0.050	0.056	−0.042	0.062
High minority ethnic ward	−0.212	0.061**	−0.179	0.064	0.042	0.088
Other disadvantaged ward	−0.148	0.040**	−0.079	0.030**	0.142	0.039**
F Prob >F	96.1**		53.4**		40.85**	
*Additional variables**						
Works under 13 hours	0.016	0.080	0.078	0.077	−0.145	0.076*
Works 13-20 hours	−0.083	0.074	0.009	0.065	−0.081	0.062
Works 21-30 hours	0.012	0.078	0.008	0.063	0.005	0.068
Works 31-38 hours	0.182	0.071**	0.013	0.057	−0.016	0.058
Works 39+ hours	0.074	0.077	0.000	0.058	0.221	0.061**
Uses employer flexibility	0.190	0.062**	0.024	0.050	0.009	0.052
Works atypical time	−0.014	0.025	−0.034	0.019	0.030	0.019
Self employed	0.681	0.105**	0.155	0.082**	−0.002	0.085
Uses formal childcare	0.128	0.057**	−0.133	0.033**	0.133	0.039**
Uses 2 or more childcarers	0.160	0.060**	0.126	0.037**	−0.104	0.040**
Dad does childcare while employed	−0.049	0.051	−0.072	0.039*	0.094	0.042**
Uses employer help for childcare	0.073	0.041*	−0.010	0.029	−0.013	0.035
Unweighted sample size	17834		17824		17866	

Base: All UK MCS mothers who completed self completion section and relevant questions.

* Results from the entry of additional variables alter the size of coefficients in the set of mother characteristics displayed above, but did not alter their levels of significance. Standard errors adjusted for cluster sample design.

*/** Significant at 0.1/0.05 level of confidence

Notes

[1] Of the 78% who took leave.

[2] Informal arrangements include parents/partners, grandparents, other relatives, friends and neighbours; formal arrangements include nanny/au pair, childminder (registered or unregistered), nurseries or crèche (which may be workplace, college, local authority or private).

NINE

Conclusion

Shirley Dex and Heather Joshi

In what has been an unprecedented time in the UK for family policy initiatives and developments, it has been useful, and perhaps not entirely coincidental, that a new large-scale longitudinal survey of babies was launched. In starting the Millennium Cohort Study (MCS) of 18,819 babies, we were following in well-worn footsteps of earlier generations, this being the fourth nation-wide birth cohort study launched in the UK. However, in other ways, new pathways were being charted in this survey that were very clearly in tune with and driven by millennium policy issues on families and children. This volume has given us the chance to start to dip into the richness of this new survey, explore its potential, compare with earlier generations and provide some benchmarks for the future with this new generation of children who have started out life in this era of new UK family policy.

The policy context into which this new birth cohort arrived had many dimensions. Clearly, there was and is concern about the sizeable numbers of children growing up in poverty. Concern has grown alongside mounting evidence, not least from the earlier birth cohorts, that this leads to poorer outcomes for these children when they become adults. The devolved UK administrations, with their potential to have differing health and education policies, are another strong policy interest. It is important to know whether children's and families' experiences will start to diverge more within the UK than in the past. The role of fathers has become a concern in this era of increasing lone-parent families and reductions in men's labour force participation rates. Minority ethnic communities are a growing component of the UK population partly because some have higher fertility rates, and yet, in many cases, live in disadvantaged conditions and areas. In this era of concern about equality of opportunity, how are minority ethnic children faring? Finally, in an era of low fertility and increasing childlessness, looking after this generation of children becomes a more pressing societal issue. We will be relying on these Millennium children more in the future, given the demographics of ageing, to look after us all over our increasing life spans. These are some of the main broad policy concerns of the new millennium which helped to persuade the Economic and Social Research Council and governments to initiate and fund this new large-scale study.

Longitudinal surveys have to take the long view. It is a long way ahead before we will be able to see the effects of early experiences on this cohort's adult lives. The potential for such quasi-causal analyses is of course one of the main strengths of longitudinal data. These over-time relationships of experiences and the durations of time spent in different circumstances can be examined. Cohort studies are not suited to investigating the short-term effects of the latest government intervention (for example, changes in Income Support level). This is especially true if the intervention is focused on a particular subgroup of the population who, even in a large-scale survey, will have relatively few who have experienced the policy change. Deciding on the questions to put in longitudinal as opposed to cross-sectional surveys is consequently more demanding, given they have to be there for the long term and not for short-term policy interests. We cannot foresee 25 years ahead exactly what will be in policy concerns about young adults, or the next generation of babies.

Nonetheless, the start of a new cohort study does offer a unique opportunity, at its first contact, to view the experiences, in this case, of a large-scale representative survey of families and babies. This volume is unique in this cohort study's life, therefore, as well as being the starting point for a hugely valuable future dataset. However, since there are elements of recalled information in the first sweep of the MCS dataset, there was also some potential for limited longitudinal analyses.

What we have here is a new cohort of babies starting out in life in an era of unprecedented initiatives on family policy. The policy and economic environment is very distinguishable from the times the earlier studies of birth cohorts started. In the jargon, this may be a 'period effect' if the policy climate does not persist. If it does, it may form a long-term 'cohort effect' distinguishing this generation of babies from their predecessors. In due course, it will be possible to analyse these and future period effects on Millennium babies' later life outcomes, and by comparing cohorts, disentangle period from age effects. It will also be possible to look at differences in development within the cohort for different outcomes from different beginnings.

To put this study in its historical context, it may be interesting to contrast the concerns of the Millennium survey with the first investigation of the 1946 cohort, *Maternity in Great Britain* (RCOG, 1948). At the dawn of the Welfare State, childbirth was a dangerous experience for both mother and child. It frequently took place without analgesia, often at home and usually had to be paid for. The evidence collected in the 1946 and subsequent birth surveys of 1958 and 1970 has helped build the services used by the Millennium mothers before and during their almost universal short-stay hospital deliveries, controlled pain and very much more frequent caesareans. The authors of the 1946 maternity survey were concerned about the mother's health after 'confinement', which usually lasted two weeks, and her return to housework. In those days, before central heating and washing machines (almost universal in the new survey), housework was heavy – carrying coal, laundry by hand, making beds – and the authors of the survey recommended help for the new mother. By contrast, among the themes which emerge from the study of parenthood at the dawn of the 21st century is a concern for work–life balance, the division of domestic and parenting work between mothers and fathers, and the provision of childcare services, still in their own infancy.

It was not possible to include birth out of wedlock in the 1946 survey, due to the stigma of illegitimacy and the high rate of adoption, but there were not many of them. By contrast, lone and cohabiting mothers are sizeable groups in the MCS with important differences in their circumstances from married couples. A final contrast between the surveys is that the 1946 survey, in its follow-up, over-represents 'white collar' classes, as there were then relatively few fathers in these occupations. The MCS over-represents the other end of the social spectrum: people living in areas of high child poverty as well as minority ethnic groups, who were not a feature of the post-war population. The change in weighting represents less a change of focus towards under-privileged people than a change in the underlying abundance of reasonably advantaged people. This itself is a credit to the economic and social policy of the last half-century.

Policy questions

We started out this volume with a list of more specific policy questions that the Millennium Cohort data had the potential to answer. It is to these we now return.

How are babies developing under different family structures and parenting regimes?

The odds of conventionally defined low birthweight were somewhat higher for lone than married mothers (by a factor of 1.36) and for mothers who were poor (according to the indicator constructed in Chapter 3) by a factor of 1.49. Analyses reported in Chapter 5 show that a number of socioeconomic factors and mothers' smoking, associated with lone parenthood, contributed to variations in birthweight. So, the children are starting out with an unequal physical endowment reflecting the disadvantages that precede and follow lone motherhood.

The vast majority of babies were developing at the normal rate for a 9-10-month-old child, and it is very early to start ranking children by their achievements. The MCS data allowed us to investigate their gross motor, fine motor and communicative gesture development as well as their birthweight and growth. There were social as well as biological factors associated with the ethnic minorities' display of delays in development on the motor skills and gestures. However, having a lone parent or being overcrowded were not significantly related to achievement of development milestones, after controlling for other characteristics. These other characteristics included those of the child, the mother and the socioemotional environment. However, some of the characteristics that were significantly associated with some development delays were also those that lone parents were likely to have – namely, lower or no educational qualifications and being teenage mothers. In this sense, there were some relationships between development delays and different household structures. In terms of the policy implications, one emphasis needs to be on addressing mothers' educational standards in order to avoid development delays in children. The results also suggest that children will benefit, in this and other ways, if women can be persuaded or helped to avoid becoming teenage mothers and waiting instead until they are older to give birth.

Our analysis of family poverty showed that the lack of employment, dramatically more pronounced among lone parents, was a major factor associated with the family being in poverty. It is too early, with the Millennium Cohort babies, to show effects on children (or adults) of growing up in poverty beyond the first milestones. However, previous studies have already pointed to a range of poorer outcomes from the lack of household resources. Clearly, being in the state of poverty is related to certain family structures, albeit also mediated by employment status.

However, being of Bangladeshi or Pakistani origin in the case of all three developmental skills, and mixed origin in the case of gestures, were also associated with delays in development. Growing up in a Bangladeshi or Pakistani family meant having two natural married parents. Ethnic origin here was also an indicator of household structure, with more traditional family structures in this case being associated with development delays. Being of Bangladeshi or Pakistani ethnic origin also became less significant when elements of the socioemotional environment like mother's depression and the physical environment of overcrowded housing were controlled. The focus of policy to safeguard against child development delays, therefore, may need to be more on addressing the issues of mothers' depression (which affects one fifth to one quarter of mothers) and improving overcrowded housing conditions (affecting 8%).

How do babies develop when their father is involved with them, whether present or absent from the household, compared with babies whose fathers are not involved?

There is no evidence yet, from the MCS survey, on whether and how children benefit from father involvement, but there is plenty of new evidence that many non-resident fathers take an interest in their child both at birth and into the first year. Also, approximately one third of the non-resident fathers contributed to the mother's cash resources, although not all did so regularly. There is also enough variation in the range of practices and attitudes on the part of the fathers in two-parent families for future research to look for related outcomes in child development as well as family stability.

Are new century babies growing up in more insular privatised family units with less contact with other generations?

Millennium babies are growing up, in the vast majority of cases, with their grandparents thoroughly involved with them and their families. The relationships, as far as we can tell, appear to be in good shape and working in both directions. Cohort parents are keeping in touch with their own parents, although cohort mothers more so than fathers, and grandparents are keeping in touch and offering childcare and other financial and non-financial help for their children and grandchildren. It is not a picture of atomised and isolated nuclear families, sometimes shrunken to one parent. Rather, there are some very extensive contributions being given from grandparents to the families of their children in many cases. However, marital breakdown in the grandparent generation was associated with lower levels of contact between cohort parents, cohort children and their grandparents.

It may be that we are witnessing, in the case of some of these families, what others have called 'the pivot generation' (see Mooney et al, 2002). Pivot generation mothers are those who delayed childbearing well into their 30s who still have substantial caring responsibilities for children. At the same time, they are starting to have caring responsibilities for their older parents and relatives. Earlier generations had largely completed the childcaring responsibilities before the parental caring responsibilities crept up on them.

Cultural patterns of relating to wider families and caring were evident in the findings about different minority ethnic households. Given the higher frequency of grandmothers living with their children, especially in Asian families, compared to other ethnic groups, we expected that this might lead to a greater degree of involvement of grandparents overall for these minority ethnic families. Our results suggest this was not necessarily the case. Some minority ethnic families had lower levels of contact with grandparents, partly because their parents were not alive, and partly, we suspected but will not confirm until the next survey, because they were not living in the country. These differences acted to equalise the contact with grandparents for most ethnic groups. However, it still left Black African families in the survey substantially less supported by grandparents than other families. In this sense, the extent to which families are recent immigrants was found to be the main indicator of how isolated they were from older generations and wider family, rather than a preference for an isolated lifestyle.

As found in other studies, the extent of grandparent involvement with childcare for their grandchildren was a very significant cementing element in these intergenerational relationships. When governments consider the expansion of formal childcare, they also need to take account of the value to families and communities of these informal childcare networks and of the social capital they generate. These reach beyond intergenerational relationships with grandparents into reciprocal relationships with neighbours and friends. It is also clear that, even with the expansion of formal childcare places, many families where the mother is in paid work cannot manage without the assistance of informal childcare arrangements.

What proportion and which babies start out in poverty in the four countries at the turn of the 21st century?

Our analysis of poverty, as far as this was possible with the data, suggested that as many as 23.7% of babies were starting out their life in a family facing poverty. This proportion was broadly consistent with official estimates. However, different measures of poverty were used and the percentages of families in poverty were found to be very sensitive to the measure of poverty used (19.8% of families on means-tested benefits, or 27.5% with household income less than 60% of the median). That a sizeable proportion of Millennium babies are growing up in poverty, along with other analyses of perceived changes in families' financial circumstances around the birth, suggest that the point of arrival of a baby in the family is one which often makes family finances particularly vulnerable. More attention may need to be paid to this point in the life course by policy provisions.

When we compared, using our own measure, the extent of poverty in Millennium Cohort families across UK countries, we found that families living in Wales had a significantly higher chance of living in poverty. However, after controlling for a range of other characteristics which might explain the extent of a mother living in poverty, living in Wales was not significantly different from living in England. Country differences turned out to be sensitive to the measure of poverty used. When using a low income measure of poverty, families in all the other UK countries had higher odds of being poor than families living in England, with those in Northern Ireland having the highest chance.

Country differences, however, were very small in comparison with the largest contributors to the odds of mothers living in poverty which were being a lone parent and having no earner in the family. This endorses the thrust of anti-poverty policy being aimed at getting families some employment and, if it were possible, more than one parent. Analysis also draws attention to the characteristics of families without jobs; they were un-partnered, young mothers with little education, poor health, living in areas with poorer job prospects and, for some, belonging to some of the minority ethnic groups. Effective policy should be aware of their specific needs.

How soon do mothers return to work after childbirth compared with earlier generations?

Comparison of the mothers in the Millennium Cohort with the mothers of earlier cohort studies shows an increasingly fast rate of returning to work after childbirth. In the 1946 and 1958 generations, it was common for women to have all their children before considering a return to work, whereas by the millennium the norm is for mothers to return to work after each child, bearing in mind there are fewer children, and to have very short gaps from employment. This implies not only shorter time out of paid work for childbirth in this millennium generation of mothers, but also a change in the patterns of being in and out of paid work. This more continuous pattern of labour market participation now accounts for approximately one half of these mothers.

Millennium mothers are the generation of major beneficiaries of the earlier introduction of statutory maternity leave, made increasingly generous in leave entitlement and payments over the 1980s and 1990s. Millennium mothers are roughly the same generation as birth cohort members born in 1970 (likely to be mothers around the millennium). Mothers born in the 1958 cohort started to benefit from these statutory arrangements where they entered childbearing relatively late (in their 30s at the start of the 1990s), but those who gave birth in their 20s would have seen less benefit than Millennium mothers from these entitlements. By the millennium, maternity rights had been extended to cover the majority of mothers rather than the minority previously eligible. Also, a cultural change had established maternity and other parental leave as the normal expectation in all workplaces by the turn of the millennium.

The original introduction of statutory maternity leave in the 1970s, and the successive enhancement to the entitlements, were accompanied by arguments in favour of giving mothers rights to longer periods of leave and more financial support while they were off work for the benefit of the mother and her child. Mothers' successive shortening of the period away from work has run in the opposite direction. To some extent, statutory entitlements have focused behaviour on the end of the period of paid leave (18 weeks) rather than on the end of the period of leave (29 weeks), which was longer but not all paid. But this and other survey evidence suggests that many mothers are returning before their leave entitlement runs out. It is somewhat ironic, therefore, to see the changes in mothers' behaviour patterns, with their successively shorter periods spent away from paid work for childbirth, against the pressure to continue to lengthen the statutory leave entitlement period.

On the other hand, polarisation between mothers, as detected in the early 1990s by Dex and Joshi (1996), may be increasing. Set against the pattern of continuous labour force participation has been a growing group of mothers without any labour force experience or involvement. This group of low-qualified, younger, often teenagers and lone mothers, with larger families, living in disadvantaged areas, on benefit and often in poverty, seem to have little chance of markedly improving their circumstances. These are, of course, the mothers whom the government seeks to move into employment in order, primarily to raise their children's standard of living.

Just before the millennium (1999), statutory entitlements to parental leave were introduced for UK parents. Again, some cohort fathers benefited from this new provision, although others may have benefited if their employer already offered such a provision. Parental leave is now offered to fathers in the form it was eventually adopted in Sweden on a non-transferable basis. If fathers do not take up their leave, they cannot transfer it to mothers. The change from being a transferable to a non-transferable entitlement in Sweden saw a marked increase in the take up of leave by men. It will be interesting to see how take up develops in the UK. Statutory entitlements to paid paternity leave became available in the UK in 2003 and were too late to have affected fathers for the birth of this cohort child, though some had employers who already offered a non-statutory paternity leave scheme.

How many employed fathers and mothers have access to flexible working arrangements, and does taking them up make a difference to their childcare choices or to their feelings of work-life balance?

In the lead up to the new millennium, government was considering how to help working parents. Various consultations showed that one of the things parents wanted most was greater flexibility in the workplace. Surveys also charted the extent of that flexibility among employers and employees.

We were able to compare MCS findings with turn of the millennium large-scale representative sources on the extent of employee access to flexible working arrangements. MCS survey findings suggested that this set of parents, with a young baby, had more access than employees in general. This could be either because parents with a young baby have far more access to flexible working arrangements than the population in general, the other sources are underestimating, or the MCS is overestimating the extent of flexible working arrangements offered to employees. The same higher rates were true of MCS parents' uses and take up of these arrangements which, again, appeared more extensive among MCS parents than other surveys might lead us to expect.

Mothers' use of flexible working arrangements, where they were offered, varied from the high of 76% in the case of using part-time hours, 56% for flexible working hours and 21% for jobshare or term-time only work. Fathers' use of flexible working arrangements was generally lower than mothers' use, ranging from 62% use in the case of working at home occasionally, 55% using flexible working hours and 8-9% in the use of part-time work or term-time only work.

Our analysis showed that using an employer's flexible working arrangements, although not merely having access to them, did make a small but significant improvement to mothers' feelings of control over their lives, as did using formal childcare and two or more types of childcare. However, using formal childcare was associated with a decline in mothers' satisfaction with life and an increase in their depression scores. However, other correlates of feeling more in control of life and depression were more important than flexible working or childcare arrangements. Factors which were associated with lower levels of satisfaction and feeling in control of life included the ethnic origin of mothers, with some Asian groups often being less satisfied or feeling less in control than other groups; being a younger mother; having a large family; being a lone parent; having a non-employed partner, baby not sleeping; and living in areas of high minority ethnic population or other disadvantaged areas.

Since this first sweep of MCS data was collected, the government has introduced more rights for parents. Since 2003, parents with a child under 6 years have the right to request flexible working arrangements of their choice from their employer. Their employer has a duty to give this request serious consideration. It will be interesting to see in future MCS sweeps whether cohort parents extend their use of flexible working arrangements under this new statutory right, in comparison with their use at this first sweep in 2001.

What proportion and which babies start out with good health across our four countries?

Health is measured in different ways. When babies are first-born, prematurity and birthweight can be indicators of normal or poor health. Using these indicators, approximately 7% of singleton babies were preterm (gestation of 28-36 weeks) and 8% of singleton babies were of low birthweight and subject, therefore, to greater health risks. There were only small variations across countries in the extent of these health risks. But there were more substantial variations according to socioeconomic status and area of residence. Risks also increased for babies whose parents were in routine occupations or had never been employed, and for families living in areas of high minority ethnic population or other disadvantaged areas.

Risks of delays in babies' motor skill and gesture development were extremely small, ranging from a maximum of 7% of babies with delay on one of the gross motor skills, 5% delayed on one of the fine motor skills and only a maximum of 0.5% of babies delayed on any of the communicative gestures. Country differences were unimportant.

The extent of breastfeeding, a factor known to improve children's health status, varied to some extent by country as did the extent of mothers' smoking while pregnant, known to put children's health at risk. Breastfeeding was highest in England and lowest in Northern Ireland, and lower among lone mothers. Smoking in pregnancy was highest in Wales, followed by Northern Ireland, and lowest in England and Scotland. The extent to which babies were completely immunised was lower in England than in the other UK countries.

When a measure of positive health status was constructed from a number of health indicators, there was considerable variation across the UK countries, with the lowest rate of positive health for babies in Northern Ireland, the next lowest in Wales, and the highest in England. This was one health indicator where it was beneficial rather than a disadvantage to be living in an area of high minority ethnic population. This was largely because many mothers from minority ethnic groups living in such areas, and predominantly in England, breastfed their babies and did not smoke during pregnancy.

Access to health services was very much more differentiated in this sample varying typically across socioeconomic categories and for some minority ethnic groups, although less so by country. Pakistani and Bangladeshi mothers did not receive antenatal care, attend antenatal classes and were late in having their first antenatal visit and their pregnancy confirmed by a doctor or midwife to a greater extent than mothers of other ethnic identities. The language difficulties of immigrant groups are thought to contribute to this shortfall in access to services.

In summary, while there were some country differences between Millennium babies in their health at birth and over the first year, these were mostly fairly small relative to other differences by socioeconomic circumstances and lone-parent status. Devolved administrations might want to follow up on some of the larger differences, but greater effect would probably result where policy interventions can target lower social class groups and lone parents with health-improving measures or parental education.

Are parents' health and circumstances related to the baby's health and development?

Mothers' mental health status has been found in earlier studies to be a risk factor for their children's health, development and well-being.

The analysis of development delays of babies in this volume supported these earlier findings that mothers who showed signs of being depressed at the interview were more likely to have babies with motor and gesture development delays. Mothers' depression was also a feature of the small group of mothers who often felt annoyed or resentful towards the baby. Identifying and assisting depressed mothers should be an important policy target.

How does mothers' smoking affect birthweight and baby growth?

The analysis of the baby's birthweight, after controlling for a range of other factors including minority ethnic group, confirmed the results of other studies that mothers who smoked while pregnant had lower birthweight babies. Mothers' smoking during pregnancy was also associated with other poor health indicators for babies – namely, incomplete immunisation, admission to hospital, and wheezing and asthma in the child. Mothers' smoking itself was strongly related to low occupational status and its associated stresses.

Is it an additional disadvantage to live in a poor neighbourhood?

The type of neighbourhood families live in was part of the design of the MCS sample, and this offers the opportunity to consider the role played, after controlling for other factors, by the neighbourhood in explaining differences between cohort families and cohort children. Neighbourhoods in themselves may not be the explanation for differences found, since an area is defined by other sets of characteristics and it can be these that are the explanation of neighbourhood differences or similarities. However, it can also be the case that there are unmeasured or unobserved effects indicated by a neighbourhood indicator. Insofar as certain areas are associated with certain ethnic groups, there can be ethnic cultural influences reflected in neighbourhood measures. There could also be work–culture differences if there is high unemployment in an area or large amounts of ill health. Boundary drawing, even at a ward level, can sometimes be arbitrary and cut across sub-areas with homogeneous characteristics, or put together, within one boundary, areas with heterogeneous characteristics. Nonetheless, this is a topic of interest since government policy provision is often delivered based on spatial areas using official boundaries. These areas are also the level at which the success of any policy interventions is evaluated.

We are only at the beginning of analysing the effect of

neighbourhoods through the MCS data. On the whole, these early analyses have been done through linear rather than hierarchical models and, as such, need to be tested further to be sure that the neighbourhood influence is robust. However, what these early analyses suggest is that living in a disadvantaged neighbourhood (defined by having a high amount of child poverty) or an area of high minority ethnic population do signify additional disadvantage in most of the topics covered. So, for example, parents' health is worse in such disadvantaged areas and, not unexpectedly, so is child poverty, and measures of child health. However, areas of high minority ethnic population were not found to be always and unequivocally disadvantaged. In particular, families living in these areas were not particularly disadvantaged on measures of child health. However, in access to services they did not score so highly, but possibly due to choice or ignorance rather than the lack of available services.

We examined the availability of health and social services aimed at young families in the different study localities by asking health visitors about services offered in or adjacent to study wards (Brassett-Grundy et al, 2004). The 'law of inverse care' led us to believe that the disadvantaged areas might be worst served. However, as far as we can tell from the health visitors' replies to a postal questionnaire, National Health Service facilities were fairly evenly and universally spread, once one allowed for access to adjacent areas, particularly for rural wards. Despite being under different jurisdictions, the services available in Wales, Scotland and Northern Ireland were also fairly uniform.

Social capital

We introduced, at the start of this book, a framework of social capital and capabilities as both a context and starting point in life for these new Millennium babies and as a dynamic developmental framework. A large number of elements of social, cultural, human and financial resources and relationship capital and their variations have been charted in this volume. It is a picture of substantial inequalities between families and, by extension, between the cohort babies. Many of the lines of division between advantaged and disadvantaged family circumstances correspond with ward boundaries, the areas built into the design of this survey, but not all. There are also many overlaps of advantage and disadvantage with socioeconomic classifications based on occupations. However, minority ethnic status, especially in the case of South Asian ethnic minorities, does not run along all the same lines of disadvantage. Although the Bangladeshi and Pakistani families were financially disadvantaged, the South Asian communities were found to be richer in relationship capital due to the greater stability of their marriages in the parents' and grandparents' generations, and higher in the baby's although not in the parents' health capital. Also, what appears associated with many disadvantages in white and black families – having a child during the teenage years, usually outside marriage or even partnership – was less disadvantaging in Asian families where it was largely within the context of marriage.

Respondents to the MCS revealed their capabilities to parent. The vast majority of mothers and fathers showed they understood, valued and appreciated the importance of the parental role in child development – one of stimulation, cuddling, warmth and communication for language development. Furthermore, most mothers and fathers were agreed in their views about their importance to the baby. Although many found there were considerable changes in adjusting to a new baby, more so when it was a first baby, the majority of parents were enjoying the adjustment. While all very small scale, there were worrying signs for the welfare of some babies where mothers admitted to feelings of annoyance and resentment towards the cohort baby. These were linked to mothers feeling depressed. A surprisingly small proportion also reported that the baby's arrival had led to a deterioration in their relationship with their partner, possibly also eroding capability. Future sweeps will show whether these negative feelings and effects are reinforced into lower levels of capability and future capital, and the positive feelings into higher levels.

Many of the dimensions of inequality noted in the MCS findings coincided with a divide between young teenage and older mothers. This increasing polarisation was noted earlier. This could be thought of as a divide in capital. Many younger mothers and fathers, because of their age and lack of experience in life, were low on human, relationship, financial and even social capital. Older mothers, in contrast, had more abundant supplies of these capitals. Where young mothers were embedded within Asian ethnic communities, this was serving to compensate, to some extent, for their low levels of capital. Outside this environment, the lack of capital was being felt more acutely and its effects on the cohort baby may be greater therefore.

A new era of family policy

After decades lagging behind an agenda set in other European countries, the new century has ushered in an era of unprecedented development of family policy in the UK. All political parties are competing to be the friendliest. The signs are that many of the government initiatives are in tune with parents' needs and preferences about family life and their children's well-being. The MCS may yet be able to demonstrate that the new century, despite its legacy of inequalities, was a good time to have been born.

References

Acheson, D. (1998) *Independent inquiry into inequalities in health report*, London: The Stationery Office.

Allen, I. and Bourke-Dowling, S. (1998) *Teenage mothers: Decisions and outcomes*, London: Policy Studies Institute.

Amato, P.R. and Sobolewski, J.M. (2001) 'The effects of divorce and marital discord on adult children's psychological well-being', *American Sociological Review*, vol 66, no 6, December, pp 900-21.

Aveyard, P., Cheng, K.K., Manaseki, S. and Gardosi, J. (2002) 'The risk of preterm delivery in women from different ethnic groups', *British Journal of Obstetrics and Gynaecology*, vol 109, no 8, pp 894-9.

Bach, J.F. (2002) 'The effect of infections on susceptibility to autoimmune and allergic diseases', *New England Journal of Medicine*, vol 347, pp 911-20.

Baines, S., Wheelock, J. and Gelder, U. (2003) *Riding the rollercoaster: Family life and self employment*, Bristol: The Policy Press.

Bartington, S.E., Foster, L.J., Tate, A.R., Dezateux, C. and the Millennium Cohort Child Study Group (2005) (submitted for publication) 'Evaluation of the UNICEF UK Baby Friendly Initiative for promotion of breastfeeding: findings from the Millennium Cohort Study'.

Bates, E., O'Connell, B. and Shore, C. (1987) 'Language and communication in infancy', in J.D. Osofsky (ed.) *Handbook of infant development*, 2nd edn, New York: Wiley.

Baxter Jones, A.D.G., Cardy, A.H., Helms, P.J., Phillips, D.O. and Smith W.C.S. (1999) 'Influence of socioeconomic conditions on growth in infancy: the 1921 Aberdeen birth cohort', *Archives of Diseases of Children*, vol 81, no 1, pp 5-9.

Becker, G.S. (1975) *Human capital*, Washington DC: National Bureau of Economic Research.

Bee, H. (1994) *Lifespan development*, Boston: Allyn & Bacon.

Bell, A. and LaValle, I. (2003) *Combining self-employment and family life*, Bristol: The Policy Press.

Beresford, B. (2002) 'Children's health', in J. Bradshaw (ed.) *The well-being of children in the UK*, London: Save the Children.

Berrington, A. (2004) 'Perpetual postponers? Women's, men's and couple's fertility intentions and subsequent fertility behaviour', *Population Trends*, vol 117, pp 9-19.

Berthoud, R. (2001a) 'Teenage births to ethnic minority women', *Population Trends*, vol 104, pp 12-17.

Berthoud, R. (2001b) *Family formation in multi-cultural Britain: Three patterns of diversity*, University of Essex, Institute for Social and Economic Research.

Berthoud, R. (2003) 'Ethnic minority children and their grandparents', paper given at a meeting *Kinship and relationships beyond the household*, London: Royal Statistical Society, 4 February.

Blair, P.S., Fleming, P.J., Bensley, D., Smith, I., Bacon, C., Taylor, E., Berry, J., Golding, J. and Tripp, J. (1996) 'Smoking and the sudden infant death syndrome: Results from 1993-95 case-control study for confidential inquiry into stillbirths and deaths in infancy', *British Medical Journal*, vol 313, pp 195-8.

Bourdieu, P. and Passeron, J-C. (1977) *La reproduction*, Paris: Les èditions de minuit.

Bowling, A. (1995) 'The most important things in life: comparisons between older and younger population age groups by gender', *International Journal of Health Sciences*, vol 6, pp 169-75.

Bradshaw, J. (ed.) (2001) *Poverty: The outcomes for children*, London: FPSC/ESRC.

Bradshaw, J. and Finch, N. (2003) 'Overlaps in dimensions of poverty', *Journal of Social Policy*, vol 32, issue 4, pp 513-25.

Bradshaw, J., Stimson, C., Skinner, C. and Williams, J. (1999) *Absent fathers?*, London: Routledge.

Brannen, J., Moss, P. and Mooney, A. (2003) 'Care-giving and independence in four-generation families', in J. Brannen and P. Moss *Re-thinking children's care*, Buckingham: Open University Press.

Brassett-Grundy, A., Butler, N.R. and Joshi, H. (2004) *Millennium Cohort Study Health Visitor Survey: Interim report*, London: Centre for Longitudinal Studies, Institute of Education (http://www.cls.ioe.ac.uk/studies.asp?section=00010002000100140003).

Braun, D. (2001) 'Perspectives on parenting', in P. Foley., J. Roche and S. Tucker (eds) *Children in society: Contemporary theory, policy and practice*, Hampshire: Palgrave.

British Medical Association (2004) *Smoking and reproductive life: The impact of smoking on sexual, reproductive and child health*, London: British Medical Association, Board of Science and Education and Tobacco Control Resource Centre.

Bronfenbrenner, U. (1979) *The ecology of human development: Experiments by nature and design*, Cambridge, MA: Harvard University Press.

Brown, J.C. and Small, S. (1985) *Family income support, part 9: Maternity benefits*, London: Policy Studies Institute.

Burghes, L., Clarke, L. and Cronin, N. (1997) *Fathers and fatherhood in Britain*, Occasional paper no 23, London: Family Policy Studies Centre.

Bushnell, E. and Boudreau, J. (1993) 'Motor development and the mind: the potential role of motor abilities as a determinant of aspects of perceptual development', *Child Development*, vol 64, pp 1005-21.

Butler, N.R. and Bonham, D.G. (1963) *Perinatal mortality: The first report of the 1958 British Perinatal Mortality Survey*, Edinburgh and London: E & S Livingstone.

Cabinet Office Social Exclusion Unit (1999) *Teenage pregnancy*, Cm 4342 (http://www.socialexclusionunit.gov.uk).

Campbell, D., Hall, M., Barker, D., Cross, J., Shiell, A. and Godfrey, K. (1996) 'Diet in pregnancy and the offspring's blood pressure 40 years later', *British Journal of Obstetrics and Gynaecology*, vol 103, pp 273-80.

Campbell, R. and Macfarlane, A. (1994) *Where to be born? The debate and the evidence*, 2nd edn, Oxford: National Perinatal Epidemiology Unit.

Carnegie (1994) *Starting points: Meeting the needs of our youngest children: Report of the Carnegie Task Force on meeting the needs of young children*, New York: Carnegie Corporation.

Chahal, K. (2000) *Ethnic diversity, neighbourhoods and housing*, York: Joseph Rowntree Foundation (www.jrf.org.uk/knowledge/findings/foundations/110.asp).

Chalmers, I. (1978) 'The implications of the current debate on obstetric practice', in S. Kitzinger and J.A. Davis (eds) *The place of birth*, Oxford: Oxford University Press.

Chamberlain, R., Chamberlain, G., Howlett, B. and Claireaux, A. (1975) *British births 1970, vol 1: The first week of life*, London: William Heinemann.

Chamberlain, G., Philipp, E., Howlett, B. and Masters, K. (1978) *British births 1970, vol 2: Obstetric care*, London: William Heinemann.

Cochrane, A.L. (1972) *Effectiveness and efficiency: Random reflections on the health service*, London: Nuffield Provincial Hospitals Trust.

Coleman, J.S. (1988) 'Social capital in the creation of human capital', *American Journal of Sociology*, vol 94 (suppl), pp 95-120.

Confidential Enquiry into Maternal and Child Health (2004) *Why mothers die 2000-02. The sixth report of the confidential enquiries into maternal deaths in the United Kingdom*, London, RCOG Press.

Conger, R.D., Conger, K.J., Elder, G.H., Lorenz, F.O., Simons, R.L. and Whitbeck, L.B. (1993) 'Family economic stress and adjustment of early adolescent girls', *Developmental Psychology*, vol 29, pp 206-19.

Cook, D.G. and Strachan, D.P. (1999) 'Health effects of passive smoking: summary of effects of parental smoking on the respiratory health of children and implications for research', *Thorax*, vol 54, pp 357-66.

Corcoran, M. (1995) 'Rags to rags: poverty and mobility in the United States', *Annual Review of Sociology*, vol 21, pp 237-67.

Cossette, L., Malcuit, G. and Pomerleau, A. (1991) 'Sex differences in motor activity during early infancy', *Infant behavior and development*, vol 14, pp 175-86.

Cully, M., Woodland, S., O'Reilly, A. and Dix, G. (1999) *Britain at work: As depicted by the 1998 Workplace Employee Relations Survey*, London: Routledge.

Dale, A. and Egerton, M. (1997) *Highly educated women: Evidence from the National Child Development Study*, Research Studies RS25, Department for Education and Employment, London: The Stationery Office.

DEFRA (Department for Environment Food and Rural Affairs) (2002) National Food Survey 2000, DEFRA, National Statistics.

Den Ouden, L., Rijken, M., Brand, R., Verloove-Vanhorick, S.P. and Ruys, J.H. (1991) 'Is it correct to correct: developmental milestones in 555 "normal" preterm infants compared with term infants', *Journal of Paediatrics*, vol 118, pp 399-404.

Dench, G. and Ogg, J. (2002) *Grandparenting in Britain*, London: Institute of Community Studies.

Dex, S. (ed) (1999) *Families and the labour market*, London: Family Policy Studies Centre and Joseph Rowntree Foundation.

Dex, S. (2003) *Families and work in the twenty-first century*, York: Joseph Rowntree Foundation.

Dex, S. and Joshi, H. (1996) 'A widening gulf among Britain's mothers', *Oxford Review of Economic Policy*, vol 12, no 1, pp 65-75.

Dex, S. and Joshi, H. (eds) (2004) *Millennium Cohort Study First Survey: A user's guide to initial findings*, London: Centre for Longitudinal Studies, Institute of Education.

Dex, S. and Smith, C. (2002) *The nature and patterns of family-friendly employment policies in Britain*, Bristol: The Policy Press for the Joseph Rowntree Foundation.

Dex, S., Gustafsson, S., Callan, T. and Smith, N. (1995) 'Cross-national comparisons of the labour force participation of women married to unemployed men', *Oxford Economic Papers*, vol 47, pp 611-35.

DfES and DH (Department for Education and Skills and Department of Health) (2004) *National service framework for children, young people and maternity, standard 11, maternity*, London: Department of Health.

DH (Department of Health) (1993) *Changing childbirth. Report of the Expert Maternity Group*, London: The Stationery Office.

DH (1998) *Saving lives: Our healthier nation*, London: The Stationery Office.

DH (1999) *Reducing health inequalities: An action report. Our Healthier Nation*, London: The Stationery Office.

DH (2002a) *Improvement, expansion and reform the next 3 years. Priorities and planning framework 2003-06*, London: Department of Health.

DH (2002b) *NHS maternity statistics, England, 1998-99 to 2000-01, Statistical Bulletin 2002/11*, London: Department of Health.

DH (2003) *NHS maternity statistics, England 2001-02*, Bulletin 2003/09, London: Department of Health.

DH (2004) *Choosing health: Making healthier choices easier*, London: The Stationery Office.

DH and UNICEF (United Nations Children Fund) (1993) *Memorandum of understanding between the National Breastfeeding Working Group and the UNICEF UK Baby Friendly Initiative*, London: Department of Health and UNICEF UK Baby Friendly Initiative.

DHSS (Department of Health and Social Services) (1996) *Health and wellbeing: Into the next millennium. Regional strategy for health and social wellbeing, 1997-2002*, Belfast: Department of Health and Social Services.

Diekmann, A. and Engelhardt, H. (1999) 'The social inheritance of divorce: effects of parent's family type in post war Germany', *American Sociological Review*, vol 64, no 6, December, pp 783-93.

Dobson, B., Beardsworth, A., Keil, T. and Walker, R. (1994) *Diet, choice and poverty: social, cultural and nutritional aspects of food consumption among low income families*, Loughborough: Loughborough University of Technology, Centre for Research in Social Policy.

Dowler, E. and Calvert, C. (1995) *Nutrition and diet in lone-parent families in London*, London: Family Policy Studies Centre.

D'Souza, L., Turner, A. and Garcia, J. (2002) *Access to care for very disadvantaged childbearing women: Report of a descriptive survey of services for women from non-English speaking backgrounds, asylum seekers and women at risk from domestic violence*, Oxford: National Perinatal Epidemiology Unit (www.npeu.ox.ac.uk/inequalities).

DTI (Department of Trade and Industry) (2000) *Work and parents: Competitiveness and choice: A research review*, London: DTI.

DTI (2003) *24th annual report of the Home and Leisure Accident Surveillance System (HASS) 2000-02*, London: Department of Trade and Industry.

Duncan, G.D. and Brooks-Gunn, J. (eds) (1997) *Consequences of growing up poor*, New York: Russell Sage Foundation.

Dunscombe, J. and Marsden, D. (1993) 'Love and intimacy: the gender division of emotion and "emotion work"', in *Sociology*, vol 27, no 2, pp 221-42.

DWP (Department for Work and Pensions) (2000/01) *Households below average income, an analysis of the income distribution from 1994/95-2000/01*, Leeds: Department for Work and Pensions.

DWP (2003a) *Opportunity for all: Fifth annual report*, Cm 5956, London: Department for Work and Pensions.

DWP (2003b) *Households below average income 1994/95-2001/02*, Leeds, Corporate Document Services (www.dwp.gov.uk/asd/hbai/hbai2002/pdfs/Chapter_4.pdf).

Elder, G. (1978) 'Family history and the life course', in T. Hareven (ed.) *Transitions: The family and the life course in historical perspective*, New York: Academic Press.

Eriksson, J.G., Forsen, T., Tuomilehto, J., Winter, P.D., Osmond, C. and Barker, D.J. (1999) 'Catch-up growth in childhood and death from coronary heart disease: longitudinal study', *British Medical Journal*, vol 318 (7181), pp 427-31.

Ermisch, J.F. (1991) *Lone parenthood: An economic analysis*, Cambridge: Cambridge University Press.

Ermisch, J.F. (2004) *Parent and adult-child interactions empirical evidence from Britain*, Working paper no 2, University of Essex, Institute for Social and Economic Research.

Ermisch, J. and Franscesconi, M. (2001) *The effects of parents' employment on children's lives*, London: Family Policy Studies Centre and Joseph Rowntree Foundation.

Families Need Fathers (www.fnf.org.uk).

Fedrick, J. and Butler, N.R. (1978) 'Intended place of delivery and perinatal outcome', *British Medical Journal*, vol I, pp 763-5.

Fenson, L., Dale, P.S., Resnick, J.S., Thal, D., Bates, E., Hartung, J.P., Pethick, D. and Reily, J.S. (1993) *MacArthur communicative development inventories (CDI)*, San Diego, CA: Singular Publishing Group.

Ferri, E. and Smith, K. (1996) *Parenting in the 1990s*, London: Family Policy Studies Centre.

Ferri, E., Bynner, J. and Wadsworth, M. (2003) *Changing Britain, changing lives*, London: Institute of Education.

Ford, R., Marsh, A. and McKay, S. (1995) *Changes in lone parenthood*, Department of Social Security research report no 40, London: HMSO.

Frankenburg, W.K., Dodds, J. and Archer, P. (1967) 'The Denver Developmental Screening Test', *Journal of Paediatrics*, vol 71, pp 181-97.

Frankenburg, W.K., Dodds, J. and Archer, P. (1990) *Denver II: Screening manual*, Denver, CO: Denver Developmental Materials, Inc.

Frankenburg, W.K., Dodds, J., Archer, P., Shapira, H. and Bresnick, B. (1992) 'The Denver II: A major revision and restandardisation of the Denver Developmental Screening Test', *Paediatrics*, vol 89, pp 91-7.

Furedi, F. (2001) *Paranoid parenting: Abandon your anxieties and be a good parent*, London: Allen Lane.

Gent, A.E., Hellier, M.D., Grace, R.H., Swarbrick, E.T. and Coggon, D. (1994) 'Inflammatory bowel disease and domestic hygiene in infancy', *Lancet*, vol 343, pp 766-7.

Gershuny, J. (2000) *Changing times: Work and leisure in post industrial society*, Oxford: Oxford University Press.

Gesell, A. (1973) *The first five years of life: A guide to the study of the preschool child*, New York: Harper & Row.

Gordon, D., Shaw, M., Dorling, D. and Davey Smith, G. (eds) (1999) *Inequalities in health, the evidence presented to the independent inquiry into inequalities in health, chaired by Sir Donald Acheson*, University of Bristol: The Policy Press.

Gornick, J.C. and Meyers, M.K. (2003) *Families that work: Policies for reconciling parenthood and employment*, New York: Russell Sage Foundation.

Graham, E. and Boyle, P. (2003) 'Low fertility in Scotland: A wider perspective', in *Registrar General's review of demographic trends*, Edinburgh: General Register Office for Scotland, pp 40-52.

Gregg, P. and Washbrook, L. (2003) *The effects of early maternal employment on child development in the UK*, Working paper no 03/070, University of Bristol (www.bris.ac.uk).

Gregg, P., Harness, S. and Machin, S. (1999) *Child development and family income*, York: Joseph Rowntree Foundation.

Grundy, E., Murphy, M. and Shelton, N. (1999) 'Looking beyond the household: intergenerational perspectives on living kin and contact with kin in Great Britain', *Population Trends*, vol 97, pp 19-27.

Gunnell, D.J., Frankel, S., Nanchahal, K., Braddon, F.E.M. and Smith, G.D. (1996) 'Lifecourse exposure and later disease: a follow-up study based on a survey of family diet and health in pre-war Britain (1937-39)', *Public Health*, vol 110, no 2, pp 85-94.

Gunnell, D., Smith, G.D., McConnachie, A., Greenwood, R., Upton, M. and Frankel, S. (1999) 'Separating in-utero and postnatal influences on later disease [letter]', *Lancet*, vol 354 (9189), pp 1526-7.

Hadler, S.C., Cochi, S.L., Bilous, J. and Cutts, F.T. (2004) 'Vaccination programs in developing countries', in S.A. Plotkin and W.A. Orenstein (eds) *Vaccines*, 4th edn, Pennsylvania, Saunders (Elsevier inc.), pp 1407-41.

Hall, D and Elliman, D. (eds) (2003) *Health for all children*, 4th edn, Oxford: Oxford University Press.

Hamlyn, B., Brooker, S., Oleinikova, K. and Wands, S. (2002) *Infant feeding 2000. A survey conducted on behalf of the Department of Health, the Scottish Executive, the National Assembly of Wales and the Department of Health, Social Services and Public Safety in Northern Ireland*, London: The Stationery Office.

Hareven, T. (ed.) (1978) *Transitions: The family and the life course in historical perspective*, New York: Academic Press.

Harker, L. and Kendall, L. (2003) *An equal start: Improving support during pregnancy and the first 12 months*, London: IPPR.

Harkness, S. (2003) 'The household division of labour: changes in families' allocation of paid and unpaid work, 1992-2002', in R. Dickens, P. Gregg and J. Wadsworth (eds) *The labour market under New Labour: The state of working Britain 2003*, Basingstoke: Palgrave Macmillan.

Hatter, W., Vinter, L. and Williams, R. (2002) *Dads on dads: Needs and expectations at home and work*, Research discussion series, Manchester: Equal Opportunities Commission.

Hawkes, D., Joshi, H. and Ward, K. (2004) *Unequal entry to motherhood and unequal starts in life: Evidence from the first survey of the UK Millennium Cohort*, CLS Cohort Studies Working Paper no 6 (www.cls.ioe.ac.uk/core/documents download.asp?id=299&log_stat=1).

Hay, D.F., Pawlby, S., Shark, D., Asten, P., Mills, A. and Kumar, R. (2001) 'Intellectual problems shown by 11-year-old children whose mother had postnatal depression', *Journal of Child Psychology and Psychiatry*, vol 42, pp 871-89.

Health Education Authority (1999) *Black and minority ethnic groups and tobacco use in England*, London: Health Education Authority.

Health Protection Agency (2004) *Quarterly communicable disease reports on the COVER programme for childhood immunisation*, London: Health Protection Agency.

Hemingway, H., Saunders, D. and Parsons, L. (1997) 'Social class, spoken language and pattern of care as determinants of continuity of carer in maternity services in East London', *Journal of Public Health Medicine*, vol 19, no 2, pp 156-61.

Henderson, J. and Garcia, J. (2000) *Knowledge and uptake of benefits and the financial impact of childbearing*, Oxford: National Perinatal Epidemiology Unit (www.npeu.ox.ac.uk/inequalities).

HM Treasury (2004) *Child poverty review* (www.hm-treasury.gov.uk./spending_review/spend_sr04/associated_documents/spending_sr04_childpoverty.cfm).

Hobcraft, J. (1998) *Intergenerational and life-course transmission of social exclusion: influences of childhood poverty, family disruption, and contact with the police*, CASE paper CASE/15, London: London School of Economics, Centre for Analysis of Social Exclusion.

Hochschild, A. (1990) *The second shift: The revolution at home*, London: Piatkus.

Hochschild, A. (1997) *The time bind when work becomes home and home becomes work*, New York: Henry Holt and Company.

Hogarth, T., Hasluck, C., Pierre, G., Winterbotham, M. and Vivian, D. (2000) *Work-life balance 2000: Baseline study of work-life balance practices in Great Britain*, Warwick: Institute for Employment Research, Warwick University.

Howie, P.W., Forsyth, J.S., Ogston, S.A., Clarke, A. and du V Florey, C. (1990) 'Protective effect of breastfeeding against infection', *British Medical Journal*, vol 300, pp 6-11.

HSQ (Health Services Quarterly) (2003) 'Report infant and perinatal mortality by social and biological factors, 2002', winter, no 20, pp 61-5.

Illingworth, R.S. (1975) *The development of the infant and young child: Normal and abnormal*, Edinburgh: Livingstone.

ISD Scotland (2004a) *Teenage pregnancies* (www.isdscotland.org/isd/files/mat_tp_table1b.xls. Accessed 20 December 2004).

ISD Scotland (2004b) *Scottish health statistics. Births and babies. Table 5* (www.isdscotland.org/isd/files/mat_bb_table5.xls. Accessed 7 January 2005).

ISD Scotland and Scottish Programme for Clinical Effectiveness in Reproductive Health (1998) *Small babies in Scotland: A ten-year overview, 1987-96*. Edinburgh: ISD Scotland and Scottish Programme for Clinical Effectiveness in Reproductive Health.

Jackson, A.A., Langley Evans, S.C. and McCarthy, H.D. (1996) 'Nutritional influences in early life upon obesity and body proportions', *Ciba Foundation Symposium*, vol 201, pp 118-29.

Jarvis, M.J., Goddard, E., Higgins, V., Feyerabend, C., Bryant, A. and Cook, D.G. (2000) 'Children's exposure to passive smoking in England since the 1980s: continuing evidence from population surveys', *British Medical Journal*, vol 321, pp 343-5.

Jayaweera, H. (2003) 'Mother and baby outreach study', Presentation to the Institute of Health Sciences seminar, June, Oxford: University of Oxford.

Jayaweera, H. and Garcia, J. (2000) *Living on a low income: A structured review of women's views of poverty and childbearing*, Oxford: National Perinatal Epidemiology Unit (www.npeu.ox.ac.uk/inequalities).

Jenkins, S. and Rigg, J. (2001) *The Dynamics of Poverty in Britain*, DWP Research Report No 157, Leeds: Corporate Document Services.

Joshi, H. (2002) 'Production, reproduction and education: women, children and work in contemporary Britain', *Population and Development Review*, vol 28, no 3, pp 445-74.

Joshi, H.E. and Davies, H.B. (1994) 'The paid and unpaid roles of women: how should social security adapt?', in S. Baldwin and J. Falkingham (eds) *Social security: New challenges to the Beveridge model*, Hemel Hempstead: Harvester Wheatsheaf, pp 234-54.

Joshi, H.E. and Hinde, P.R.A. (1993) 'Employment after childbearing: cohort study evidence', *European Sociological Review*, vol 9, pp 203-27.

Joshi, H. and Verropoulou, G. (2000) *Maternal employment and child outcomes*, Occasional paper, London: The Smith Institute, pp 1-41.

Joshi, H. and Wright, R.E. (2005) 'Starting life in Scotland', in D. Coyle and W. Alexander (eds) *Committing to growth in European regions The Scottish experience*, Princeton, NJ: Princeton University Press.

Joshi, H., Layard, R. and Owen, S. (1985) 'Why are more women working in Britain?', *Journal of Labor Economics*, vol 3, no 1, pp S147-76.

Katbamna, S. (2000) *'Race' and childbirth*, Buckingham: Open University Press.

Kempson, E. (1996) *Life on a low income*, York: Joseph Rowntree Foundation.

Kiernan, K. (1997) *The legacy of parental divorce: Social, economic and demographic experiences in adulthood*, CASE paper CASE/1, London: London School of Economics, Centre for Analysis of Social Exclusion.

Kiernan, K. (2004a) 'Cohabitation and divorce across nations and generations', in P.L. Chase-Lansdale, K. Kiernan and R. Friedman (eds) *Human development across lives and generations: The potential for change*, New York: Cambridge University Press, pp 139-70.

Kiernan, K. (2004b) 'Unmarried cohabitation and parenthood in Britain and Europe', *Journal of Law and Policy*, vol 26, no 1, pp 33-55.

Kiernan, K. and Friedman, R. (eds) *Human development across lives and generations The potential for change*, New York: Cambridge University Press, pp 139-70.

Laming, Lord (2003) *The Victoria Climbié Inquiry report of an inquiry by Lord Laming*, London: The Stationery Office.

Laurie, H. and Gershuny, J. (2000) 'Couples, work and money', in R. Berthoud and J. Gershuny (eds) *Seven years in the lives of British families: Evidence on the dynamics of social change from the British Household Panel Survey*, Bristol: The Policy Press.

La Valle, I., Arthur, S., Millward, C., Scott, J. and Claydon, M. (2002) *Happy families? Atypical work and its influence on family life*, Bristol: The Policy Press.

Law, C.M. (1996) 'Foetal and infant influences on non-insulin-dependent diabetes mellitus (NIDDM)', *Diabetes & Medicine*, vol 13 (suppl 6), pp 49-52.

Lewis, G. and Drife, J. (2004) *Why mothers die 2000-02: Report on confidential enquiries into maternal deaths in the United Kingdom*, London: RCOG Press (www.cemach.org.uk/publications.htm).

Lewis, J. (2001) *The end of marriage?*, Cheltenham: Edward Elgar.

Lewis, J. (2004) 'Individualisation and the need for new forms of family solidarity', in T. Knijn and A. Komter (eds) *Solidarity between the sexes and the generations*, London: Edward Elgar.

Lindley, J., Dale, A. and Dex, S. (2004) 'Ethnic differences in women's demographic, family characteristics and economic activity profiles 1992 to 2002', *Labour Market Trends*, April, vol 112, no. 4, pp 153-165.

Lobstein, T. (1991) *The nutrition of women on low income*, London: Food Commission.

Lobstein, T., Baur, L. and IASO International Obesity Task Force (2004) 'Obesity in children and young people: a crisis in public health', *Obesity Review*, vol 5, pp 4-104.

Maccoby, E.E. (1990) 'Gender and relationships: a developmental account', *American Psychologist*, vol 45, pp 513-20.

Macfarlane, A. and Mugford, M. (2000) *Birth counts: Statistics of pregnancy and childbirth, vol I*, London: The Stationery Office.

Macfarlane, A., Mugford, M., Henderson, J., Furtado, A., Stevens, J. and Dunn, A. (2000) *Birth counts: Statistics of pregnancy and childbirth, vol 2,* London: The Stationery Office.

Macfarlane, A., Grant, J., Hancock, J., Hilder, L., Lyne, M., Costeloe, K. and Hird, M. (2004) *Early life mortality in East London: A feasibility study. Summary report on foetal and infant death in East London*, London: City University.

MacGillivray, I., Campbell, D.M. and Thompson, B. (1988) *Twinning and twins*, Chichester: John Wiley.

Maclean, M and Eekelaar, J. (1997) *The parental obligation*, Oxford: Hart Publishing.

Macran, S., Joshi, H. and Dex, S. (1996) 'Employment after childbearing: A survival analysis', *Work Employment and Society*, vol 10, no 2, pp 273-96.

Maher, J. and Macfarlane, A. (2004a) 'Trends in live births and birth weight by social class, marital status and mother's age, 1976 to 2000', *Health Statistics Quarterly*, vol 23, pp 34-42.

Maher, J. and Macfarlane, A. (2004b) 'Trends in infant mortality and birth weight by social class and mother's age, 1976 to 2000', *Health Statistics Quarterly*, vol 24, pp 14-22.

Management Executive Letter (1994) *Local breastfeeding targets*, MEL 110, Edinburgh: Scottish Office.

Martin, J. and Roberts, C. (1984) *Women and employment: A life time perspective*, Department of Employment and Office of Population Censuses and Surveys, London: HMSO.

Maternity Alliance (2002) (www.maternityalliance.org.uk/).

McIlwaine, G., Boulton-Jones, C., Cole, S. and Wilkinson, C. (1998) *Caesarean section in Scotland 1994/95: A national audit*, Edinburgh: Scottish Programme for Clinical Effectiveness in Reproductive Health.

McLanahan, S. and Sandefur, G. (1994) *Growing up with a single parent: What hurts, what helps*, Cambridge, MA: Harvard University Press.

Melhuish, E., Sylva, K., Sammons, P., Siraj-Blatchford, I. and Taggart, B. (2001) *Social/behavioural and cognitive development at 3-4 years in relation to family background*, Eppe technical paper no 7, London: Institute of Education.

Millar, J. and Ridge, T. (2001) *Families, poverty, work and care: A review of the literature on lone parents and low-income couple families with children*, research report no 153, London: Department for Work and Pensions.

Modood, T., Berthoud, R., Lakey, J.J., Nazroo, J., Smith, P., Virdee, S. and Beishon, S. (1997) *Ethnic minorities in Britain: Diversity and disadvantage*, London: Policy Studies Institute.

Montgomery, S.M., Bartley, M.J. and Wilkinson, R.G. (1997) 'Family conflict and slow growth', *Archives of Diseases in Children*, vol 77, pp 326-30.

Mooney, A. and Statham, J. with Simon, A. (2002) *The pivot generation: Informal care and work after 50*, Bristol: The Policy Press.

Mooney, A., Knight, A., Moss, P. and Owen, C. (2001) *Who cares? Childminding in the 1990s*, London: Family Policy Studies Centre and Joseph Rowntree Foundation.

Murray, L., Cooper, P.J., Wilson, A. and Romaniuk, H. (2003) 'Controlled trial of the short- and long-term effect of psychological treatment of post-partum depression. Impact on the mother-child relationship and child outcome', *British Journal of Psychiatry*, vol 182, pp 420-7.

Natcen (2004) *Millennium Cohort Study first survey: Technical report on instrumental development and fieldwork* (www.cls.ioe.ac.uk/core/documents/download.asp?id=265&log_stat=1).

National Assembly for Wales (2002) *Maternity statistics, Wales: Method of delivery, 1995-2000*, SDR49/2002, Cardiff: National Assembly for Wales.

National Sentinel Caesarean Section Audit Report (2001) London: RCOG Clinical Effectiveness Support Unit.

NCCWCH (National Collaborating Centre for Women's and Children's Health) (2003) *Antenatal care: Routine care for the healthy pregnant woman, a clinical guideline*, London: RCOG Press (www.rcog.org.uk/resources/public/Antenatal_care.pdf).

Neill, S.J. (2000) 'Acute childhood illness at home: The parents' perspective', *Journal of Advanced Nursing*, vol 31, pp 821-32.

NICE (National Institute for Clinical Excellence) (2004) *Caesarean Section. Clinical Guideline 13*, London: NICE.

Northern Ireland Perinatal Information Project. (2001) *Year 2000 report*. Belfast: Eastern Health and Social Services Boards.

O'Brien, M. and Shemilt, I. (2003) *Working fathers earning and caring*, Research discussion series, Manchester: Equal Opportunities Commission.

Ong, K.K.L., Preece, M.A., Emmett, P.M., Ahmed, M.L. and Dunger, D.B. (2002) 'Size at birth and early childhood growth in relation to maternal smoking, parity and infant breastfeeding: longitudinal birth cohort study and analysis', *Paediatric Research*, vol 52, pp 863-7.

ONS (1999) *Poverty and Social Exclusion Survey*, ONS, funded by Joseph Rowntree Foundation.

ONS (2003) *Health Statistics Quarterly*, vol 20, winter, London: The Stationery Office.

ONS (2004a) *Birth statistics. Review of the Registrar General on birth and patterns of family building, 2003*, Series FM1 No 30 (revised), London: Office for National Statistics.

ONS (2004b) *Social Trends No 34, 2004 edition*, London: The Stationery Office.

O'Sullivan, J.J., Pearce, M.S. and Parker, L. (2000) 'Parental recall of birth weight: how accurate is it?', *Archives of Disease in Childhood*, vol 82, pp 202-3.

Parsons, L., Macfarlane, A. and Golding, J. (1993) 'Pregnancy, birth and maternity care', in W.Ahmad (ed.) *'Race' and health in contemporary Britain*, Buckingham: Open University Press.

Peach, C. (ed.) (1996) *Ethnicity in the 1991 Census*, vol 2, London: HMSO.

Peckham, C.S. (1998) 'Child health and development', in M. Marinker and M. Peckham (eds) *Clinical futures*, London: British Medical Journal Publications.

Phillips, J., Bernard, M. and Chittenden, M. (2002) *Juggling work and care: The experiences of working carers of older adults*, Bristol: The Policy Press.

Plewis, I. (2003) 'Multilevel models', in R.L. Miller and J.D. Brewer (eds) *The A-Z of social research*, London: Sage.

Plewis, I., Calderwood, L., Hawkes, D., Hughes, G. and Joshi, H. (2004) *The Millennium Cohort Study: Technical report on sampling*, 3rd edn, London: Institute of Education.

Putnam, R. (1999) *Bowling alone: The collapse and revival of American community*, New York: Simon and Schuster.

Radford, A. (2001) 'Unicef is crucial in promoting and supporting breast feeding', *British Medical Journal*, vol 322, p 555.

RCOG (Royal College of Obstetricians and Gynaecologists) (1948) *Maternity in Great Britain*, Oxford: Oxford University Press.

Rendall, M.S. and Smallwood, S. (2003) 'Higher qualifications, first-birth timing and further childbearing in England and Wales', *Population Trends*, vol 111, pp 18-26.

Reynolds, T., Callendar, C. and Edwards, R. (2003) *Caring and counting: The impact of mothers' employment on family relationships*, Bristol: The Policy Press.

Rigby, M. and Kohler, L. (2004) *Child health indicators of life and development (CHILD): Report to the European Commission*, European Union Community Health Monitoring Programme.

Rutter, M. (1990) 'Psychosocial resilience and protective mechanisms', in J. Rolf, A.S. Masten, D. Chichetti, K.H. Nuechterlin and S. Weintraub (eds) *Risk and protective factors in the development of psychopathology*, New York: Cambridge University Press, pp 181-214.

Rutter, M. and Madge, N. (1976) *Cycles of disadvantage: A review of research*, London: Heinemann Educational Books.

Sameroff, A.J. (1983) 'Developmental systems: contexts and evolution', in W. Kessen (ed.) and P.H. Mussen (series ed.) *Handbook of child psychology, vol 1: History, theory and methods*, New York: Wiley, pp 237-94.

Sandall, J., Grellier, R., Ahmed, S. and Savage, W. (2001) *Women's access, knowledge and beliefs around prenatal screening in East London*, London: St Bartholomew School of Nursing and Midwifery, City University, Nightingale School of Nursing and Midwifery, and King's College.

Schoon, I., Bynner, J., Joshi, H., Parsons, S., Wiggins, R.D. and Sacker, A. (2002) 'The influence of context, timing and duration of risk experiences for the passage from childhood to early adulthood', *Child Development*, vol 73, pp 1486-504.

Schuller, T., Bynner, J. and Feinstein, L. (2004) *Capitals and capabilities*, London: Centre for Research on the Wider Benefits of Learning, seminar paper.

Schultz, T.W. (1961) 'Investment in human capital', *American Economic Review*, vol LI, pp 1-17.

Scott, J. (1997) 'Changing households in Britain: do families still matter?', *Sociological Review*, vol 45, no. 4, pp 591-620.

Searle, B. (2002) 'Diet and nutrition', in J. Bradshaw (ed.) *The well-being of children in the UK*, London: Save the Children.

Sen, A. (1992) *Inequality re-examined*, Cambridge, MA: Harvard University Press.

Shepherd, P., Smith, K., Joshi, H. and Dex, S. (2004) *Millennium Cohort Study first survey: A guide to the SPSS dataset*, 3rd edn (www.cls.ioe.ac.uk/core/documents/download.asp?id=263&log_stat=1).

Shouls, S., Whitehead, M., Burstrom, B. and Diderichsen, F. (1999) 'The health and socioeconomic circumstances of British lone mothers over the last two decades', *Population Trends*, vol 95, pp 41-46.

Singhal, A. and Lucas, A. (2004) 'Early origins of cardiovascular disease: is there a unifying hypothesis?', *Lancet*, vol 363, pp 1642-5.

Skinner, C. (2003) *Running around in circles: Coordinating childcare education and work*, Bristol: The Policy Press.

Skuse, D., Reilly, S. and Wolke, D. (1994) 'Psychosocial adversity and growth during infancy', *European Journal of Clinical Nutrition*, vol 48 (suppl 1), pp S113-30.

Smallwood, S. and Jefferies, J. (2003) 'Family building intentions in England and Wales: trends, outcomes and interpretations', *Population Trends*, vol 112, pp 15-28.

Smith, G., Hart, C., Upton, M., Hole, D., Gillis, C., Watt, G. and Hawthorne, V. (2000) 'Height and risk of death among men and women: aetiological implications of associations with cardio respiratory disease and cancer mortality', *Journal of Epidemiology and Community Health*, vol 53, no 10, pp 97-103.

Stevens, J., Brown, J. and Lee, C. (2004) *The second work-life balance study: Results from the employees' survey*, DTI, Employment Relations Research Series no 27.

Tallman, I., Rotolo, T. and Gray, L.N. (2001) 'Continuity or change? The impact of parents' divorce on newly married couples', *Social Psychology Quarterly*, vol 64, no 4, pp 333-46.

Tanner, J. (1990) *Foetus into men: Physical growth from conception to maturity*, Cambridge, MA: Harvard University.

Tappin, D.M., Mackenzie, J.M., Brown, A.J., Girdwood, R.W.A., Britten, J. and Broadfoot, M. (2001) 'Breastfeeding rates are increasing in Scotland', *Health Bulletin*, vol 59, pp 102-7.

Tate, A.R., Dezateux, C., Cole, T.J., Davidson, L. and the Millennium Cohort Study Child Health Group (2005) 'Factors affecting a mother's recall of her baby's birth weight', *International Journal of Epidemiology*, vol 34, no. 3, pp 688-695.

Thomas, M. and Avery, V. (1997) *Infant feeding in Asian families*, London: The Stationery Office.

UNICEF (United Nations Children Fund) (1999) *The Baby Friendly Initiative in the community: An implementation guide*, London: UNICEF UK Baby Friendly Initiative.

Walton, K.A., Murray, L.J., Gallagher, A.M., Cran, G.W., Savage, M.J. and Boreham, C. (2000) 'Parental recall of birth weight: a good proxy for recorded birth weight?', *European Journal of Epidemiology*, vol 16, pp 793-6.

Walton, S., Bedford, H., Dezateux, C. and the Millennium Cohort Study Child Health Group (2005) (submitted for publication) 'Use of Personal Child Health Records in the UK: findings from the Millennium Cohort Study.

Warin, J., Solomon, Y., Lewis, C. and Langford, W. (1999) *Fathers, work and family life*, London and York: Family Policy Studies Centre and Joseph Rowntree Foundation.

Werner, E.E. and Smith, R.S. (1992) *Overcoming the odds: High risk children from birth to adulthood*, Ithaca: Cornell University Press.

Williams, A.S. (1997) *Women and childbirth in the twentieth century: A history of the Nation Birthday Trust Fund 1928-93*, Sutton: Thrupp Glos.

WHO (World Health Organization) and UNICEF (1989) *Protecting promoting and supporting breastfeeding: the special role of maternity services*, Geneva: WHO.

WHO (1992a) *Baby Friendly Hospital Initiative*, Geneva, WHO.

WHO (1992b) *International statistical classification of diseases and related health problems. Tenth revision*, vol 1, Geneva, WHO.

WHO (1998) *Evidence for the 10 steps to successful breastfeeding*, Geneva: WHO.

WHO (2002) *Infant and young child nutrition; global strategy for infant and young child feeding*, Geneva: WHO.

Yeandle, S., Wigfield, A., Crompton, R. and Dennett, J. (2002) *Employed carers and family-friendly employment policies*, Bristol: The Policy Press.

Index

Note: Page numbers followed by *fig* or *tab* indicate information is to be found only in a figure or table.